Stalinist Values

STALINIST VALUES

The Cultural Norms of
Soviet Modernity, *1917–1941*

Davd L. Hoffmann

Cornell University Press

ITHACA AND LONDON

First published 2003 by Cornell University Press
First printing, Cornell Paperbacks, 2003

Printed in the United States of America

Library of Congress Cataloging-in-Publication Data
Hoffmann, David L. (David Lloyd), 1961–
    Stalinist values : the cultural norms of Soviet modernity, 1917–1941 /
David L. Hoffmann.
        p. cm.
Includes bibliographical references and index.
    ISBN 0-8014-4089-0 (cloth : alk. paper) — ISBN 0-8014-8821-4 (pbk. :
alk. paper)
    1. Communism—Soviet Union—History.   2. Social values—Soviet Union.
3. Political culture—Soviet Union.   4. Soviet Union—Social conditions.
5. Soviet Union—Politics and government—1936–1953.   I. Title.
    HX313.H58 2003
    947.084′1—dc21   2002155926

Cornell University Press strives to use environmentally responsible
suppliers and materials to the fullest extent possible in the publishing
of its books. Such materials include vegetable-based, low-VOC inks
and acid-free papers that are recycled, totally chlorine-free, or partly
composed of nonwood fibers. For further information, visit our
website at www.cornellpress.cornell.edu.

Cloth printing   10 9 8 7 6 5 4 3 2 1

Paperback printing   10 9 8 7 6 5 4 3 2 1

To Patricia

Contents

Illustrations

Acknowledgments

I express my appreciation first to the institutions that supported eight years of work on this book. I received year-long fellowships from the Hoover Institution, the Kennan Institute, and the National Council for Eurasian and East European Research. I also received travel grants from the Mershon Center, the National Endowment for the Humanities, and the Ohio State University College of the Humanities. None of these organizations is responsible for the opinions expressed in this book.

I conducted research in a substantial number of archives and libraries, and I thank their respective staffs for their help. In Russia I worked in the Center for the Preservation of Documents of Youth Organizations, the Central Municipal Archive of Moscow, the Central State Archive of the Social Movements of Moscow, the Russian State Archive of Economics, the Russian State Archive of Social and Political History, and the State Archive of the Russian Federation. I also conducted archival research in the Public Record Office of the United Kingdom and the Hoover Institution Archives. The libraries I used include the Library of Congress, the New York Public Library, the Ohio State University libraries, the Russian State Library, the Stanford University libraries, the University of Illinois Library, and the Widener Library of Harvard University.

I am especially grateful to friends and colleagues in the Russian history field who have helped me in various ways during my work on this project. While historical scholarship entails long, solitary hours of research and writing, it is nonetheless a collective venture, and the comments, suggestions, and comradeship of friends and colleagues have been invaluable to me and my work. Among those who have read and commented on parts of the manuscript, either at conferences and workshops or as a personal favor, are Robert Argenbright, Daniel Brower, Michael David-Fox, Ben Eklof, Sheila Fitzpatrick, Wendy Goldman, Dan Healey, Peter Holquist, Igal Halfin, Yanni Kotsonis, Hiroaki Kuromiya, Norman Naimark, Karen Petrone, Kenneth Pinnow, Amy Randall, David Ransel, Toivo Raun, Henry Reichman, Nicholas Riasanovsky, Kenneth Slepyan, Yuri Slezkine, Jeffrey Veidlinger, Lynne Viola, Amir Weiner, Serhy Yekelchyk, and Reginald Zelnik. The two anonymous referees for Cornell University Press also provided me with an ideal combination of enthusiastic comments and insightful criticisms.

I have discussed my research with other friends and colleagues in the field and appreciate the advice and encouragement they have given me. They include Golfo Alexopoulos, Francesco Benvenuti, Frances Bernstein, Frederick Corney, Sarah Davies, Thomas Ewing, Delia Fontana, Anne Gorsuch, Paul Hagenloh, James Harris, Jochen Hellbeck, Francine Hirsch, Oleg Kharkhordin, Oleg Khlevniuk, Nathaniel Knight, Stephen Kotkin, David McDonald, Laurie Manchester, Julie Kay Mueller, Eric Naiman, Amy Nelson, Elena Osokina, Jeffrey Rossman, Blair Ruble, David Shearer, Lewis Siegelbaum, Andrei Konstantinovich Sokolov, Charles Steinwedel, Tricia Starks, Kenneth Straus, Ronald Suny, Robert Thurston, Paul Valliere, Mark von Hagen, and Elizabeth Wood. I thank my friends Liza Tikhomirova and Sasha Meissner for their hospitality in Moscow, and my friend Iulia Trubikhina for her hospitality in both Moscow and New York. I am also grateful to friends at The Ohio State University who have not only read and discussed my work with me but provided greatly appreciated support and camaraderie. In particular I thank Nicholas Breyfogle, Angela Brintlinger, Steven Conn, Ted Hopf, Birgitte Soland, and Judy Wu.

Some of the material in Chapter 3 was published as an article, "Mothers in the Motherland: Stalinist Pronatalism in Its Pan-European Context," *Journal of Social History*, Fall 2000, and I thank the editor for permission to use that material here. I am also grateful to the staff of Cornell University Press for their highly professional and expeditious handling of my manuscript. In particular I thank director John Ackerman, manuscript editor Karen Laun, and copyeditor Barbara Salazar. My gratitude also goes to Stephanie Gilmore for preparing the index.

Finally, and most of all, I thank my family for their unfailing support, without which I would never have finished this book. My parents, George Hoffmann and Irene LaPlante Hoffmann, and my sisters, Jill Hoffmann and Karen Hoffmann, have helped and encouraged me in every way. My daughter, Sarah, has already, in her first year of life, brought me enormous joy. My greatest debt is to my wife, Patricia Weitsman. She has discussed my ideas with me, read and commented on drafts of my work, celebrated my successes, and lifted my spirits when I felt down. I am eternally grateful for her support, her encouragement, and her love. It is to her that I dedicate this book.

D. L. H.

Lancaster, Ohio

Stalinist Values

Introduction

The social meaning of the Soviet Thermidor now begins to take
form before us. The poverty and cultural backwardness of the
masses has again become incarnate in the malignant figure of
the ruler with a great club in his hand. The deposed and abused
bureaucracy, from being the servant of society, has again become
its lord.
　　　　　—LEON TROTSKY, *The Revolution Betrayed*, 1937

In 1934, the offensive broke down and a period began for which
the term "The Great Retreat" seems to fit best. This term will be
used throughout this work, though it is personal to this writer
and could not be found in any official source.
　　　　　—NICHOLAS TIMASHEFF, *The Great Retreat*, 1946

The October Revolution of 1917 marked not only a momentous political turning point for Russia but a new era in the realm of culture
and values as well. Communist Party leaders heralded the Revolution as an opportunity to remake the world by introducing a new way of
life. Cultural radicals, riding a wave of revolutionary iconoclasm, called for
the complete elimination of "bourgeois" behavioral standards, traditional
institutions such as the family, and Russian art and literary classics. Yet by
the mid-1930s, Soviet leaders endorsed conventional norms, patriarchal
families, and respect for authority. They also promoted elements of traditional culture, including folklore, Russian literary classics, and tsarist patriotic heroes. The country that had embarked on the great socialist
experiment thus embraced traditional culture and values as part of its official ideology. Did this shift in Soviet official culture signify a retreat from

1

socialism? What implications does it have for our understanding of Stalinism?

The first person to address these questions was Stalin's rival and critic Leon Trotsky. Writing in exile, Trotsky denounced these changes in official culture as the Soviet Thermidor—a betrayal of revolutionary socialist values. He blamed this Thermidor on the "triumph of the bureaucracy," of which he called Stalin the personification. According to his analysis, the bureaucracy had displaced the proletariat to become "the sole privileged and commanding stratum in the Soviet society," and the bureaucratic elite resorted to traditional institutions and notions of bourgeois respectability in order to secure its newfound power and status. Trotsky also blamed the backwardness of the population for this Thermidor. Describing Soviet family legislation as bourgeois, he concluded that "economic and cultural backwardness has produced a cruel reaction." In all realms, from the Soviet government's abandonment of world revolution to its policy of widening economic differentiation in society, Trotsky saw Stalinism as the betrayal of socialism and a return to bourgeois ways and bureaucratic despotism.[1]

From an anticommunist perspective, Nicholas Timasheff came to a similar conclusion when he labeled this shift in official Soviet culture "The Great Retreat" from socialism. According to him, Soviet leaders in 1934 recognized that socialist ideas had not taken hold among the population. Faced with the rising threat of Nazi Germany, he argued, they decided to win the population's support by restoring traditional institutions and culture. Stalin and his fellow leaders thus abandoned their goal of world revolution and resorted to patriotic appeals. Simultaneously they buttressed the family and schools as key institutions in Soviet society, replaced iconoclastic avant-garde culture with Russian classics, and discarded leather jackets and revolutionary asceticism in favor of tailored suits and material rewards.[2]

Both Trotsky and Timasheff, then, understood Stalinist culture of the mid-1930s as a return to traditional values, undertaken to buttress the power of the new Soviet elite. For them Stalinism was a retreat from socialism, and hence not a product of socialist ideology. Trotsky explained it as a consequence of the population's backwardness and the bureaucracy's conservative authoritarianism. Timasheff argued that Soviet leaders resorted to traditional appeals and institutions to win the population's support in the face of a rising threat from abroad. Trotsky and Timasheff approached the problem from opposite political points of view. Trotsky deplored Stalinist culture as a betrayal of the Revolution and its ideals, whereas Timasheff welcomed the repudiation of socialist values and emphasized the incompatibility of socialism with Russian traditions. He saw the Great Retreat as a return to Russia's natural course of development and an end to the destructive utopian experimentation of the Communists.

Many scholars have followed the lead of Trotsky and Timasheff by arguing that Stalinism was a departure from socialism. They explain Stalinist policies as the result not of socialist ideology but of authoritarian Russian political culture or the backwardness of Russian society. Robert Tucker, for example, argues that Stalinism had strong elements of archaization, and that "Stalinist revolutionism from above had a prehistory in the political culture of Russian tsarism." He draws a parallel with the Muscovite autocracy, pointing to the way Stalin bound all classes of the population in compulsory service to the state and to Stalin's conscious use of Ivan the Terrible's *oprichnina* as his model for the Great Purges.[3] Moshe Lewin writes, "The more the Stalinist system rushed ahead with its economic development and socialist transformations, the deeper it sank into the quite traditional values of authority, hierarchy, and conservatism." Lewin emphasizes the social and ideological degeneration of the Party bureaucracy and the peasantry's patriarchalism, which provided a basis for Stalin's patriarchal authoritarianism.[4]

These studies have done much to enrich our understanding of Soviet history, but interpretations that depict Stalinism as a retreat from socialism present several problems. At no time did the Stalinist leadership declare or effect a retreat from socialism. Far from being a partial retreat or a return to the prerevolutionary past, Stalinism remained, for both Party leaders and the Soviet population, a system dedicated to socialist ideology and progress toward communism.[5] Indeed, the opening of the Party archives has revealed that in private as well as in public, Stalin and his fellow leaders resolutely adhered to their version of socialism and its categories. Never did they contemplate a retreat from socialist ideology or a dismantling of the Soviet system. The fundamental elements of Soviet socialism—the planned economy, state ownership of the means of production, and the Party's vanguard role in leading the country toward communism—were all maintained or even strengthened under Stalin.

Moreover, to characterize Stalinism as a retreat from socialism and a return to prerevolutionary ways is to ignore the Stalinist leadership's continuing commitment to social transformation and the creation of the New Soviet Person. In addition to its policies of industrialization, urbanization, and modernization, Stalin's government sought to instill socialist values in all members of society and to transform human nature itself. This attempt at social and human transformation contrasts sharply with the social conservatism of tsarism; it represents a particular Soviet version of the more general Enlightenment impulse to remake and improve society. Stalinist propaganda relied on some traditional institutions and appeals, but as I will demonstrate, it did so for distinctly modern mobilizational purposes. And the state violence employed by Stalin and his fellow leaders, far from being a medieval *oprichnina,* was based on modern conceptions of the social sphere and modern technologies of social cataloguing and excision.

Stalinist culture did undergo a shift in the mid-1930s, but this shift was precipitated not by an abandonment of socialism but by its purported realization. At the Seventeenth Party Congress in 1934, Stalin declared that socialism had been built. According to him, the First Five-Year Plan and the collectivization drive had created an entirely socialist economy and had eliminated the exploiting classes and the remnants of capitalism.[6] The achievement of socialism permitted the use of traditional institutions and culture to support and further the new order. The family, previously suspected of perpetuating bourgeois beliefs, could now be trusted to promote socialism among children. Monumentalist art and architecture, formerly instruments of the old order, now helped to legitimate the new socialist order and symbolized its accomplishments. Patriotic appeals, elsewhere used to foment bourgeois nationalism, in the Soviet Union inspired defense of the socialist motherland. In all these ways, Stalinist culture of the mid-1930s reflected an attempt to consolidate Soviet socialism, not a retreat from it.

Soviet Cultural Formation

The process by which the Soviet government established the official culture and values of Soviet socialism was fairly complex. Since the Soviet Union was the first socialist state in history, its leaders had no example to follow. Marxism provided a basic outline of the socioeconomic principles that would underlie a socialist society—class warfare with the agents of capitalism, collective ownership of the means of production, and the abolition of private property. But Marxist doctrine did not provide a concrete set of cultural guidelines for life under socialism. Norms of punctuality, hygiene, sexual behavior, child raising, and consumption, as well as artistic and literary values—all these things had to be formulated after the Revolution.[7]

The Soviet system was a hyper-centralized system, with ultimate decision-making authority for all matters—including cultural issues—in the hands of the Politburo, the supreme political council of the ruling Communist Party. Yet Soviet official culture was not formed by Politburo members in isolation, nor were official norms simply the personal predilections of

Stalin and other Party leaders. While Politburo members retained absolute power within the system, they could not dictate the contents of every propaganda film, hygiene poster, and school textbook produced in the Soviet Union. Instead they set up a network of institutions and control mechanisms to oversee cultural production and the promulgation of official norms and values. Within the Party, a system of control commissions policed the behavior and values of Party members themselves. A range of Party officials and nonparty professionals established norms and routines for the rest of the population to follow. Social science institutes, medical clinics, housing inspectorates, the Commissariat of Education and its schools, all helped formulate and propagate cultural norms.[8] In the realms of journalism and high culture, a system of censorship oversaw the work of newspapers, publishing houses, and artistic organizations such as the Union of Soviet Writers.

Since all of these institutions were funded by the Soviet state and controlled by the Party, they did not constitute a pluralistic system. At the same time, Soviet cultural formation was multifaceted and involved not only directives from the top but the work of thousands of cultural producers and bureaucrats. Party leaders' pronouncements set a general course for cultural matters but provided no detailed plan; propagandists and officials had to interpret the general directives as they might apply to specific matters.[9] And Party leaders' pronouncements themselves were issued within preexisting trends and debates over the shape of Soviet culture. Thus social scientists, medical researchers, pedagogues, artists, and censors all contributed to Soviet cultural norms.

To describe the role of Party leaders in Soviet culture, Katerina Clark has introduced the metaphor of a cultural ecosystem. Like an environmental ecosystem, which comprises certain flora and fauna, the cultural ecosystem Clark describes included certain ideas and values, some complementary and others in competition with one another. Over time and through interaction with political trends and social conditions, some cultural concepts flourished, others adapted, still others withered and died. Clark points out that the changes Soviet political leaders and intellectuals pursued were delimited by existing ideological and cultural formations. Communist Party leaders were not extrasystemic figures but rather part of the Soviet cultural ecosystem. Often they enacted policies suggested in intellectuals' work or resolved ongoing debates. Clark therefore refuses to draw a sharp line between intellectuals and the Party; she rejects the notion that the Party made Stalinist culture and that the intellectuals had no say in it.[10]

The metaphor of a cultural ecosystem also helps to clarify the evolution of Soviet official culture during the 1920s and 1930s. The thesis that Stalinist culture underwent an abrupt reversal in the mid-1930s obscures the fact that many cultural values of the time had already been advanced during the 1920s. Throughout the 1920s and 1930s, the principles of iconoclasm and monumentalism coexisted and competed with each other, with iconoclasm gaining the upper hand during the Great Break period of 1928 to 1931 and monumentalism triumphing after 1934. Proponents of sexual liberation and proponents of the family and propriety also engaged in lively polemics throughout the 1920s before the latter view was endorsed by new Soviet family legislation in 1936. Since there was no blueprint for socialist culture, its features were the subject of considerable debate throughout the interwar years. Rather than a sudden retreat or reversal in the mid-1930s, we see a tilt toward certain preexisting strands within the existing cultural ecosystem.

To posit a cultural ecosystem is not to endorse a static model of Soviet culture. The ecosystem could and in fact did change in fundamental ways, particularly in relation to changes in the country's socioeconomic structure. As Marxists, Party leaders and Soviet officials believed in the primacy of economic relations, and they understood culture to be part of the superstructure and thus a reflection of the economic base. For them the elimination of capitalism (through collectivization and the creation of a planned economy) and the purported attainment of socialism fundamentally altered the world in which Soviet culture was produced. No longer was it necessary to use iconoclasm to attack bourgeois culture, now that the economic basis and social classes that had spawned that culture had been eliminated in the Soviet Union. This is why the Soviet state in the mid-1930s tilted away from iconoclasm and radicalism in a range of fields, from art and architecture to education and history writing. Party leaders did not dictate the precise changes in each field, but they did send general signals—notably their proclamation that socialism had been attained—that prompted cultural producers to shift emphases in their respective areas.

The politics of cultural production also entailed the response of the general population to official culture and values. It would be incorrect to attribute Stalinist culture to the desires of workers and peasants, for they had no direct voice in the Soviet system. At the same time, Soviet authorities sought to involve the masses, in a controlled manner, in literacy campaigns, hygiene programs, antireligious festivals, and other cultural events expressing official norms and values. Moreover, the Party and secret police gathered information on the popular reception of official policies and culture. And the ways in which people conformed to or defied official values determined the degree to which Soviet leaders succeeded or failed in their quest to create a new society and new human beings.[11]

Soviet Modernity

To argue that Soviet leaders did not abandon their version of socialism is not to say that all elements of Stalinist culture derived from socialist ideology. The Soviet Union shared numerous cultural forms and values with other modern states in the interwar period. Extending the metaphor of a cultural ecosystem, I argue that the ecosystem which generated Stalinist culture contained ideas, concerns, and debates common to modern European culture more generally. Many features of Stalinist culture reflected the ambitions of nineteenth- and twentieth-century political leaders and social reformers to manage and mobilize their populations in ways unique to the modern era. In fact, the very notion of reshaping societies was a defining feature of European modernity.

"Modernity" is a rather broad term used to describe the intellectual, political, social, and economic changes that distinguished the modern world from ancient and medieval times. Modernity is often defined as the rise of liberal democracy and industrial capitalism, but such a definition excludes the Soviet Union and other illiberal states, such as Fascist Italy and Nazi Germany.[12] I define modernity instead in terms of two features common to all modern political systems—social interventionism and mass politics. By the nineteenth century, there arose in countries throughout Europe a new ethos of social intervention by which state officials and nongovernment professionals sought to reshape their societies in accordance with scientific and aesthetic norms. A number of theorists have highlighted this ethos as a defining feature of modernity and have stressed its centrality to modern state interventionism. Anthony Giddens, for example, identifies a key aspect of modernity as trust in expert systems, which established rational procedures and norms to replace traditional ways.[13] James Scott defines high-modernist ideology as "the rational design of social order commensurate with the scientific understanding of natural laws."[14] And Zygmunt Bauman sees as a fundamental characteristic of modernity the impulse to manage society through the application of bureaucratic procedures and categories.[15]

The modern ethos of social interventionism arose from a variety of strains in early modern and modern European intellectual development—most particularly cameralist thought and Enlightenment rationalism. Seventeenth-century cameralist thinkers recognized that state power depended not only on the amount of territory ruled but on the population's productive capacity and the expansion of material wealth. This recognition prompted rulers to seek knowledge of their people and resources, and to establish administrative apparatuses that would produce this knowledge. Cameralist ideas also spurred subsequent government efforts to police societies in ways that would foster economic development and to make use of the labor and reproductive capacities of the population.[16]

Eighteenth-century Enlightenment thinkers contributed further to social interventionism with their belief that society could be reshaped through the application of science to create a rational social order. It was this new understanding of society as an object to be studied and operated upon scientifically that made possible the modern ethos of social intervention. By the nineteenth century the Enlightenment idea of social science had spawned new professional disciplines (demography, epidemiology, social hygiene, psychology) and new technologies of social intervention (censuses, medical visits, housing inspections, mass psychological testing). These technologies in turn greatly heightened the ambitions of social reformers and political leaders to eliminate social problems and refashion society. Societies were increasingly conceived of as entities that could be mapped statistically, reordered and cultivated, and administered scientifically by experts who stood above the rights of individuals or the interests of specific social groups.[17]

Social transformation, however, required not only a scientific understanding of society but a means to change people's thinking and behavior. It necessitated the inculcation of new cultural norms and values that could make everyday life orderly and productive. Norms of efficiency, hygiene, sobriety, and literacy therefore received the utmost attention from government officials and nonstate professionals alike as they sought to inculcate these values in the lower classes. Reformers all across Europe sought to "civilize" the masses through productivity campaigns, housing inspections, temperance movements, and primary education. In this light, Stalinist values of labor efficiency, hygiene, sobriety, and a more general rational and aesthetic ordering of everyday life should be seen as part of broader European trends.

The Enlightenment impulse to refashion society on the basis of reason involved the self-conscious repudiation of traditional values and culture. Indeed, scientifically determined norms, as well as economic modernization and industrialization, had done much to destroy village traditions by the twentieth century. It is therefore ironic that modern states in the interwar period began to promote traditional symbols and culture as part of official propaganda. To account for this phenomenon, we must add to our description of modernity the rise of mass politics and mass warfare. As the ideal of popular sovereignty gradually spread after the French Revolution, the involvement of the masses in politics and in warfare became essential. Once sovereignty was seen as belonging to the people, the entire population had to be involved to legitimate government policies or military campaigns. Moreover, the First World War dramatically demonstrated that military power in the modern era depended on political leaders' ability to marshal mass armies and mobilize their entire populations behind the war effort. At the very moment when modern rationalism had largely destroyed existing traditions, the demands of mass politics led to the creation of invented traditions. Governments throughout Europe and around the world used the emotional and mobilizational power of traditional appeals and symbols, themselves disembedded from their original context and recast for political purposes.[18] Fascist regimes in particular, but democratic and socialist governments as well, resorted to antimodern themes such as the folk and the purity of rural life, but did so for modern mobilizational purposes.[19]

Traditional institutions too were revived, not in their original form but rather as instruments of state intervention and mobilization. The Soviet government's campaign to bolster the family in the mid-1930s did not signal a return to the traditional family or the creation of a private sphere free from state interference. Instead, as in Nazi Germany and democratic France as well, the state championed the family in order to increase the birth rate and to produce healthy citizens. In the age of mass warfare, political leaders' need to ensure the size and health of their populations led them to intervene in reproduction and child raising, and they did so by way of the family and traditional notions of morality.

While traditional institutions and symbols served instrumental purposes of political and military mobilization, they could also be used to pursue the ideal of social unity. A range of nineteenth- and twentieth-century European thinkers abhorred the alienation of bourgeois society and the deep class divisions that characterized it. Karl Marx was just one of many who proposed ways to overcome these divisions and create a society where all were truly one.[20] In what they believed to be a step toward social unity, Soviet leaders enacted Marx's prescriptions for the violent dispossession of the exploiting classes. But expropriation and dekulakization did not end dissension in Soviet society, and the Stalinist leadership sought to eliminate all "enemies of the people" and "anti-Soviet elements" during the Great Terror of the late 1930s. Simultaneously, Party leaders employed traditional symbols to try to unify the population behind the Soviet government. Other modern states similarly relied on the emotional appeal of invented traditions to overcome social strife and promote the image of a unified and harmonious people.

At the same time, the Soviet version of modernity certainly had features distinctive to itself. The norms and values promoted by the Soviet government had a particular anticapitalist, collectivist orientation. The New Soviet Person was to be not only clean, sober, and efficient but also prepared to sacrifice his or her individual interests for the good of the collective, in sharp contrast to the ideal of liberal individualism. While the Soviet state resembled other modern European states in its use of the family to foster reproduction and proper child raising, it stressed the family's role in instilling collectivist values in children. Soviet state interventionism was also distinguished by a powerful strain of Lamarckism (an emphasis on environment over heredity), which derived not only from Marxism but from prerevolutionary Russian disciplinary culture, itself formed under the particular political and social conditions of the tsarist autocracy. The Soviet version of mass consumerism, while it stressed modern values of large-scale production and efficient distribution, occurred in a noncapitalist, state-run economy that emphasized collective material progress over individual gratification. And while all modern states invented traditions to promote social unity, the Soviet state selected traditions that could be reconciled with its revolutionary heritage and enforced social unity using massive coercion.[21]

All of these features of Stalinist culture constituted a particular version of modernity—a set of norms, values, and state practices that embodied the Soviet response to the ideas and challenges of the modern world. For this reason, it is misleading to portray Stalinism either as a return to prerevolutionary Russian ways or as the product of socialist ideology alone. While socialist values were clearly a central component of Stalinist culture, the ambition to rationalize and reorder society was shared by intellectuals and social reformers throughout Europe in the nineteenth and twentieth centuries. And the Stalinist use of traditional institutions and culture for modern mobilizational purposes similarly reflected the more general demands of mass politics after the First World War. Stalinist culture was a particular Soviet incarnation of modern mass culture.

Overview

In this book I use the term "Stalinist culture" in the broad sense of official norms and values. Culture in this anthropological sense went beyond artistic expression to include notions of how society was to function and how people were to think and act under Soviet socialism. As Boris Groys has argued, Stalinist art and literature were part of an overall aesthetic-political project—an attempt to organize society and everyday life according to aesthetic sensibilities and political principles.[22] The new Soviet order was to be progressive, rational, and beautiful, in contrast to prerevolutionary society, which was seen as not only oppressive and exploitative but tradition-bound, superstitious, and fetid. Officially sanctioned art and literature expressed official Soviet values, but Stalinist culture was also defined through the propagation of behavioral norms and enforced by an array of state institutions and practices.[23] Stalinist culture, then, entailed a wide range of norms and practices intended to transform people's behavior and create a new social order.

The first chapter examines the establishment of behavioral and cultural norms for the population as a whole. Soviet leaders and officials pursued the intelligentsia's long-standing goal of enlightening and uplifting the masses. Their efforts had much in common with those of reformers in other European countries, where hygienists, epidemiologists, and other public health specialists sought to instill values of cleanliness and neatness among the lower classes. Through such efforts authorities sought both to safeguard the labor and military capacity of the population and to improve people's lives and beautify society by eliminating dirt, disease, and suffering. While the Soviet "civilizing" process had much in common with social reform in other countries, I also discuss its distinctive characteristics—its emphasis on anticapitalism, collectivist values, and atheism.

Chapter 2 concerns the Party's establishment of values and behavioral norms for its own members. Revolutionary nihilism and the dismissal of morality as bourgeois soon gave way to a fairly strict though unwritten code of behavior for Communists. Many Party officials in fact requested a moral code to follow in both their personal and professional lives. While Party leaders declined to issue written guidelines, control commissions throughout the 1920s and 1930s did establish norms of conduct by purging those members who did not behave in a manner worthy of Party membership. Official publications also promoted "cultured" dress and decorum among Party functionaries. During the Great Purges of the late 1930s, when Stalin and his fellow leaders had thousands of Party members arrested and executed, moral conduct became highly politicized, as moral failings were linked with political unreliability and treason.

Chapter 3 discusses Soviet sexual norms, family policy, and gender roles. At the time of the Revolution, Bolshevik feminists denounced the family as a bourgeois institution and put forward an ideal of love freed from the confines of marriage and of women liberated from their domestic burdens. But with the sharp drop in the birth rate during the 1930s, the Stalinist leadership, like leaders throughout Europe, sought to strengthen the family as a means to increase the population. I argue that the Soviet government's measures to bolster the family were not a return to traditional ways. Party leaders used the family for state purposes of population growth and social discipline. I also discuss the ramifications of Stalinist family policy for women and gender roles in Soviet society.

Chapter 4 analyzes Stalinist values related to consumerism and mass consumption. In the Soviet Union as in all other modern societies, people's material desires came into conflict with state calls to sacrifice for the sake of the nation or collective. The Civil War had fostered a strong strand of asceticism within Soviet official culture, as deprivation and sacrifice were held up as virtues in the struggle to defend the Revolution. Soviet leaders revived this ascetic spirit during the First Five-Year Plan, when once again food had to be rationed and consumer goods became extremely scarce. In the mid-1930s, however, Party leaders moderated the rate of economic growth and channeled more resources into consumption. At the same time, Soviet official culture began to stress that with the attainment of socialism, life had become more joyous and prosperous. The Soviet Union thus developed a version of modern consumerism, although, as we will see, it differed in both theory and practice from mass consumption in capitalist societies.

The final chapter addresses Soviet leaders' attempts to create cultural and social unity. Soviet leaders felt that by the mid-1930s they had taken a significant step toward creating a communist utopia through their elimination of class enemies. This achievement prompted them to deemphasize class and to unveil a new constitution that granted voting rights to all citizens. Modern political leaders, and the Stalinist leadership in particular, also had more practical and immediate motivations for unifying their populations behind them and behind a common cultural heritage. The demands of mass warfare required the mobilization of millions of people to fight for a common cause, and as international relations grew tense in the 1930s, Soviet leaders increasingly turned to the Stalin cult, patriotic heroes, and folk culture to unify and mobilize the population to defend the socialist motherland. They also executed and incarcerated millions of alleged oppositionists in their quest to purify society and prepare for war.

While the organization of chapters is thematic, it is necessary to bear in mind the chronological subperiods in which Soviet official culture developed. The Revolution and Civil War period was a time of both military mobilization and cultural radicalism. It was followed in the 1920s by the New Economic Policy (NEP), which permitted limited capitalism and entailed a gradualist approach to the building of socialism. The NEP era was a time of cultural ferment during which Communist officials and nonparty professionals debated policies and norms for the new society. At the end of the 1920s, the Party leadership abandoned NEP and initiated a highly coercive campaign to collectivize agriculture and industrialize the country. The "Great Break" was also a period of militancy in the cultural sphere, as Marxist radicals attacked and removed nonparty specialists from positions of authority. Cultural radicalism once again subsided after Stalin's 1931 "New Conditions" speech, and especially after he and other Party leaders declared the attainment of socialism in 1934. This period of consolidation in the mid-1930s was interrupted by the Great Terror, 1937–38—a combination of bloody purges within the Party and mass operations directed against other members of society. The final years of the interwar period, 1938–41, were characterized by cultural values stressing militarization and the mobilization of Soviet society for war. The primary focus of this book is the mid-to-late 1930s—the period after Party leaders' declaration that they had attained socialism. But rather than limit analysis to these years, I examine the interwar period as a whole, as well as prerevolutionary antecedents, in order to gain a more comprehensive understanding of Soviet official culture and values.

Soviet leaders confronted many of the same challenges that faced other state leaders and social reformers in the modern era. In order to uplift the masses and safeguard the health and physical capacity of the population, they inculcated values of cleanliness, punctuality, and sobriety. To manage reproduction and child raising, they set norms of sexual behavior and family organization. In response to mass production and consumerism, they balanced material gratification with sacrifice for the greater good. And in their quest to fashion a unified, harmonious society, they promoted a common culture, employing traditional symbols for modern mobilizational purposes. The fact that many features of Stalinism reflected modern political practices makes it clear that Stalinism was neither a return to the Russian past nor the product of socialist ideology alone.

At the same time, the Stalinist system was distinguished from most modern states by its ambition to remake society completely and to create the New Soviet Person in accordance with the collectivist values of Marxian socialism. It was also distinguished by its virtually limitless interventionism and application of state violence. Unlike other European states that reestablished institutional constraints on state power after the First World War, the Soviet state was born at this moment of total war, and it seized every means to pursue its goals of mass mobilization and revolutionary transformation. Stalinism, then, was a particular response to more general

challenges facing modern state leaders and a particularly violent implementation of modern state practices. By examining how and why the Stalinist leadership enshrined certain values and cultural norms, I hope to
achieve a deeper understanding of both the general and particular elements of Stalinism.

CHAPTER ONE

Acculturating the Masses

To teach children and their parents to wash their hands more
frequently—that is enormous revolutionary progress.
— NADEZHDA KRUPSKAIA, 1927

We have before us a large task—to raise the material and
cultural level of the masses.
— EMEL'IAN IAROSLAVSKII, 1933

T he October Revolution seemed to offer the Bolsheviks the opportunity to remake the world—to eliminate all of the oppression and
injustice of the tsarist regime and create an entirely new, socialist
society. The Revolution sparked a surge of utopian thinking, as Party and
nonparty theorists proposed ways to transform everyday life, social interaction, and human nature itself.[1] But an enormous gulf loomed between
these utopian visions and the social reality facing the Bolsheviks. Russia was
an underdeveloped, agrarian country with an overwhelmingly peasant
population. Rates of illiteracy, poverty, disease, and infant mortality remained very high. The Civil War only worsened the situation, causing millions of casualties and widespread destruction. Far from progressing
toward a utopia, the country at the close of the Civil War was ravaged by
famines, epidemics, economic collapse, and social anarchy. While such
conditions made the propagation of new cultural and behavioral norms all
the more urgent, they required authorities to focus on the most basic values of hygiene and order. To stem the tide of epidemics and infant deaths,
public health officials and doctors preached the importance of hand washing and domestic cleanliness. And to revive industrial production, factory
managers and efficiency experts promoted work discipline and sobriety.

As we have noted, Soviet efforts to instill new cultural norms for everyday life were part of long-standing aspirations throughout Europe to solve social problems and reshape society. Since the nineteenth century European political leaders, social reformers, and industrialists had sought to instill values of cleanliness, sobriety, and discipline in the working poor. Their efforts were motivated not only by instrumental hopes of molding a healthy and productive workforce but by aesthetic and altruistic ambitions to uplift the masses, to educate them, and to better their lives. Reformers' aesthetic sensibilities fused with their Enlightenment ideas regarding the need to improve housing, eradicate disease and poverty, and humanize the suffering masses. By teaching hygiene, sobriety, thrift, and literacy, they sought to civilize the lower classes and create a more perfect society.

The prerevolutionary Russian intelligentsia had a particularly strong feeling of obligation toward the masses and a desire to enlighten and uplift them. Russian professionals were keenly aware of their country's backwardness, and they believed it was their responsibility to overcome it and to improve the wretched conditions of the lower classes. They blamed the tsarist autocracy not only for its failure to ameliorate conditions but also for excluding them from power. As a self-identified but disempowered elite, the intelligentsia developed a sense of mission to lead the people, and, in the case of Russian radicals, to overthrow the oppressive autocratic system and take power in the name of the people. The particular political and social circumstances of prerevolutionary Russia thus generated an especially strong impulse within educated society to bring culture and enlightenment to the masses.[2]

Even before the Revolution, new norms and values began to be articulated through the concept of *kul'turnost'*—translated here as "culturedness" but implying not only an appreciation of high culture but civilized behavior as well. The word *kul'turnost'* first came into widespread use in the 1880s and 1890s to describe the aspirations of workers who wished to rise above their poverty and degradation. In accordance with the teachings of the intelligentsia, these "conscious" workers sought to acquire the intellectual and moral development worthy of human dignity and the respect of others.[3] By the Soviet period, the discourse on culturedness emphasized proper conduct in everyday life, including bodily hygiene, domestic order, and labor efficiency, as well as a demonstrative appreciation of high culture.[4] While Soviet cultural education paralleled similar programs in other countries, it also stressed the elimination of egoism and the championing of collectivism over individualism. Soviet authorities believed that individuals could realize their full human potential only by joining the collective and engaging in socially useful labor. They thus espoused an illiberal subjectivity that sought to enlighten and transform individuals even as it opposed individualism.

The Civilizing Process

The eminent sociologist and historian Norbert Elias coined the term "the civilizing process" to describe the establishment of behavioral norms in early modern Europe. Elias argued that the reorganization of human relationships that took place with the transition from feudalism to absolutism "went hand in hand with corresponding changes in men's manners, in their personality structure, the provisional result of which is our form of 'civilized' conduct and sentiment." As absolutist states centralized their authority over a range of territories, Elias explained, they required more controlled and uniform norms of behavior among local elites. Manners and civility facilitated the creation of a network of interacting, reliable administrators, and this transition resulted in a more complex, less violent society.[5]

Vadim Volkov has borrowed "the civilizing process" to describe the emphasis on culturedness in official Soviet discourse.[6] The term is apt, because culturedness meant more than gaining knowledge of high culture; it implied the inculcation of civilized behavior—hygienic habits, refined manners, and proper comportment. But the parallel with the civilizing process described by Elias is imprecise, because, as Volkov notes, Elias used the term to describe standards of elite behavior in the early modern period—the turning of knights into courtiers. These elites relied on their civilized codes of conduct to distinguish themselves from the lower classes and justify their elevated status. It was only later that such behavioral norms were extended to the rest of the population. Elias links this subsequent "civilization" of the lower classes (and colonized peoples) to modern states' need for political pacification and economic integration.[7]

Soviet authorities' attempts to inculcate behavioral norms in the population are more analogous to this second stage in the spread of civilized norms. Many of their programs may be compared with similar propaganda and didactic efforts intended to civilize the lower classes in Western European countries. Some nineteenth-century political leaders and social reformers in Western Europe characterized the lower classes as savages who needed to be tamed and civilized.[8] Their concerns stemmed both from a fear of unrest and disorder among the working class and also from awareness that disease among the lower classes had to be contained to safeguard the overall health of the population. Coupled with these impulses were the more narrow economic concerns of nineteenth-century industrialists, who wished to make the emerging urban workforce more efficient by instilling the values of cleanliness, punctuality, and sobriety. Some reformers were motivated by a more altruistic desire to educate and uplift the downtrodden masses. The reform impulse, whether motivated by political and economic interests or benevolent and aesthetic sensibilities, lay behind a wide range of state and expert interventions to inculcate "civilized" behavior and values.

Soviet officials shared many of the same public health concerns and aesthetic sensibilities. Their insistence that every Soviet citizen acquire "cultured" habits of hygiene and neatness clearly demonstrates that the Stalinist civilizing process was prompted by both instrumental and aesthetic considerations. These officials needed a healthy and orderly workforce, and particularly during the industrialization drive of the 1930s they emphasized values of hygiene, order, and efficiency above all others. But they also sought to improve and uplift workers and peasants for their own sake, and because cleanliness and neatness corresponded to aesthetic ideals of what a socialist society should look like. Marxism and socialism more generally drew upon Enlightenment notions of progress, improvement, and civilization, so it was natural that the Soviet government sought to civilize its population with regard to hygienic habits and orderly living.

Personal hygiene received special emphasis in Soviet propaganda on cultured behavior. As was the case throughout Europe in the nineteenth and twentieth centuries, a central goal of hygiene efforts was to ensure the bodily health and labor capacity of the population.[9] Publications issued by the Commissariat of Health instructed Soviet citizens in minute detail how to clean various parts of their body, as well as their clothes and bed linens. The Red Army included in its regulations a statement that "each serviceman is obligated to follow stringently the rules of personal hygiene, the first and most fundamental rule of which is cleanliness of the body and clothing." The regulations also required that soldiers wash their hands before eating and brush their teeth both morning and night. Schools also provided an important vehicle by which Soviet authorities could inculcate habits of bodily cleanliness. One textbook on school hygiene pronounced that "a regimen of cleanliness" should be instilled "into the flesh and blood of every cultured person." It particularly stressed the role of the school doctor in instructing and overseeing both the children and their parents in proper bodily hygiene.[10]

Soviet health officials conducted surveys to gather data on the population's hygienic progress. A survey of workers at a Leningrad factory revealed that almost all workers had three or more sets of underwear, and that increasingly most had three changes of bedsheets as well. This survey

6. Зараза чахотки (туберкулеза) передается через посуду.
Мойте посуду горячей водой. Не ешьте из общей чашки.

"Tuberculosis contagion occurs through dishes. Wash dishes with hot water. Do not eat from a common bowl." (Poster identification number RU/SU 1198.4, Poster Collection, Hoover Institution Archives.)

led an official to conclude that "with the increase in bedsheets there has also been a rise in culturedness, in this case sanitary culturedness."[11] Health inspectors also checked to make certain workers had toothbrushes. Inspectors at one Moscow barracks found that workers shared toothbrushes or had none at all, and they launched a campaign for dental hygiene.[12] Surveys and inspections acted as didactic as well as data-gathering devices. One questionnaire asked workers dozens of questions about their "hygienic habits"—whether they had their own towel, how often they bathed and brushed their teeth, how frequently they changed their bedding, and so forth.[13] Workers who filled out these questionnaires were thereby made to reflect upon their daily routine and to compare it with implicit norms. Whether or not they replied to the questions honestly, workers who had to report on these matters learned that regular bathing, teeth brushing, and laundering of clothes and linens were expected.

Neat clothing received special emphasis in Soviet cultural work. Commissar of Health Nikolai Semashko himself wrote a pamphlet titled *The Art of Dressing*, in which he stressed that clothes must be clean and neat. He pointed out that dirty clothes infested with bacteria and parasites are harmful to the human organism, and prescribed clean clothing for health reasons. But as the title of the pamphlet indicates, Semashko was also motivated by aesthetic concerns. People who are not neatly dressed, he wrote, create "a most unpleasant impression."[14] The campaign for neat dress, then, stemmed from authorities' aesthetic sensibilities as well as from their concerns for health and hygiene. A leading Soviet pedagogue wrote, "The pleasing appearance of a person . . . is as important as beautiful behavior."[15] Clean and neat clothing corresponded to Soviet leaders' notions of propriety and sense of the proper appearance for Soviet citizens. For them, neatly dressed workers embodied the antithesis of unwashed, slovenly peasants, and as such served as a symbol of progress toward socialism.

Housing was the other principal arena where Soviet authorities imposed hygienic norms. One Party official, I. D. Kabakov, called on cultural workers "to free [the masses] from age-old backwardness and lack of culture" by improving living conditions, while another called dirty housing evidence "of our unculturedness."[16] The practical impetus for stressing hygienic housing came from epidemiological findings about the transmission of diseases. Studies had shown that rates of contagious diseases were higher in dark, unventilated dwellings (because direct sunlight was shown to kill the tuberculosis bacillus). Moreover, some researchers assumed that tuberculosis and other diseases multiplied in dirt and dust. Doctors writing in Soviet journals therefore prescribed clean, well-ventilated, and sunlit apartments as a means to minimize the danger of contagious airborne diseases.[17]

While purportedly scientific and objective, medical interventions in the home throughout Europe entailed the value judgments of experts regarding the lifestyle and morality of the people they sought to reform. A historian of medical efforts to combat tuberculosis in French working-class slums around 1900 concludes that government inspectors and doctors inherited a desire to pass moral judgment on the poor, common before the role of bacilli was understood, and to control and reorder their living space. These health officials did not scientifically analyze all the features of slum housing to prove direct correlations between dirt and disease; they simply portrayed overcrowding, foul odors, and filth as part of an overall repulsive environment where diseases bred and disseminated. The lower classes, already seen as uncivilized and politically dangerous, were now classified as a biological threat as well.[18]

The writings of Soviet doctors, while more benevolent and politically favorable to workers, also reflected the revulsion of educated medical per-

"The sun is a child's best friend. Bright sunlight is the worst enemy of all diseases." (Poster identification number RU/SU 905, Poster Collection, Hoover Institution Archives.)

sonnel when they observed lower-class housing. Ia. Trakhtman condemned the population's "unculturedness" and "darkness." He went on, "We live in filth, and are untidy and unfastidious. Because of this we get sick and die from infectious diseases, many of which no longer occur among cultured peoples."[19] Medical specialists condemned peasants' living conditions even more stridently. One Soviet commentator noted that peasants inhabited dark huts "without windows" and slept on beds covered with such "soot and dirt that every parasite and microbe lives in clover."[20] Thus experts grafted scientific explanations onto their disdain for the lifestyles of the lower classes.

The condescension of specialists toward national minorities was still more pronounced. Soviet authorities created "cultural stations" and traveling medical detachments in the far north to reform the traditional lifestyles of ethnic groups in the circumpolar regions.[21] Soviet medical personnel in Kazakhstan focused on Kazakh culture and habits as the source of disease transmission. Here again scientific awareness of germs did not prevent Russian doctors from identifying "backward" Kazakh customs as the conduit or even the cause of disease. Medical supervision thus became a form of cultural imperialism, which used the authority of science to denigrate the customs and traditions of national minorities.[22]

The Commissariat of Health set up an extensive system of housing inspections. During the 1920s it formed "health cells" in housing units to assist sanitary doctors in conducting inspections and enforcing regulations.[23] In Moscow by 1935, fifty-eight "housing sanitation inspectors," ninety-two doctors, and several hundred assistants worked full-time inspecting the city's housing. They had the authority to order hygienic improvements and institute "sanitary measures" in any housing they deemed unclean. Soviet housing inspectors also had the authority to fine residents who did not maintain adequate hygiene in their apartment or building.[24] Across the country the Workers and Peasants' Inspectorate carried out inspections of housing, hospitals, resorts, and schools.[25]

In addition to inspections, Soviet authorities held clean-home contests to instill hygienic values. Party officials in one town inspected workers' apartments every day for an entire month, and awarded 100 rubles to the family with the cleanest home. The Commissariat of Education, as part of its cultural work among peasants, organized competitions between collective farms to see which had the most hygienic and orderly households. Trade union officials conducted similar work to fix up and clean the housing of peasants and workers.[26] Other means to inculcate hygienic habits were agit-trials—mock trials performed as educational theater. These trials prosecuted characters and even objects for spreading dirt and disease, thereby conveying to the audience the importance of hygiene.[27]

Soviet officials sought to inculcate domestic cleanliness and orderliness not only for the sake of workers' health but also to ensure the efficiency of their labor. Propagandists argued that people needed cleanliness and order at home, lest they bring their "domestic chaos" to work with them.[28] A Soviet journalist similarly claimed that improvements in socialist production "demand from each person exceptional tidiness and impeccable cleanliness . . . not only in the factory but without fail at home."[29] Another journalist argued that cleanliness and orderliness in military barracks helped instill order and discipline in soldiers.[30] Many articles echoed these ideas and emphasized cleanliness, the orderly arrangement of furniture, and "hygienic habits" in the home as central to the health and progress of Soviet society.[31]

Some cultural workers stressed not only cleanliness and order but nice decoration as well. The author of a domestic hygiene article recommended decorating the home with "beautiful things" to make it more advanced and cultured. Articles on model worker apartments and peasant huts also emphasized the importance of decoration. One journal cited approvingly a peasant woman who not only thoroughly cleaned out her home but hung curtains and brought in flowers as well. The author of a book on Moscow factory workers described in glowing terms the beautiful interiors of workers' apartments. Workers had planted flowers around their building, she added approvingly: "Flowers and beauty in general—this is not petty bourgeois. Flowers must be accessible to the mass of all workers."[32] The health and efficiency fostered by cleanliness and orderliness were essential but not the sole concerns of Soviet officials; they wished to see workers and peasants transformed into cultured people, whose tasteful homes would both reflect and promote their progress from benighted masses to Soviet citizens.

Soviet health propaganda particularly emphasized the part of women in establishing a hygienic and healthy home. Drawing upon traditional gender roles, Soviet officials viewed the domestic sphere as a female realm, and the pamphlets and posters they produced portrayed health in the home as the responsibility of women. Men were depicted as having little or no role in the domestic sphere; women were expected to clean, prepare healthy meals, care for small children, and provide a restful home environment.[33] Soviet health propaganda, then, not only drew upon but also reinforced traditional gender stereotypes. Also noteworthy is the fact that women and their domestic function figured so prominently in health campaigns. Health specialists in the Soviet Union and elsewhere understood that to improve the health and physical capacity of the population, they needed to transform people's everyday lifestyle. And they saw hygiene education for women as a vehicle to renovate the home environment.

The Soviet government assigned a special acculturating role to the wives of high-ranking officials and engineers. Sergo Ordzhonikidze, the commissar of heavy industry, initiated the wife-activist (*obshchestvennitsa*) movement, whereby women volunteers taught workers about hygiene and strove to improve their living conditions. At the all-union conference to found the movement in 1936, Ordzhonikidze announced that these women would bring "cleanliness and order" to workers' residences and cafeterias.[34] The wife-activist movement was a means to mobilize the labor of nonworking elite women to improve workers' health and hygiene and to help workers to become more orderly and cultured.[35] Soviet leaders referred to the wives of factory directors and engineers as "a large cultural force" and "an enormous cultural army [that] will bring order to workers' apartments."[36]

The idea of mobilizing elite women to acculturate the masses apparently came from similar movements in other countries. At a 1935 conference of the Main Sanitation Inspectorate of the Commissariat of Health, one delegate reported that in Western Europe and the United States, non-governmental organizations played a crucial role in assisting government inspectors in upgrading domestic hygiene.[37] Countries throughout Western Europe and also Japan had women's organizations that focused on the home and strove to improve people's household organization, hygiene, diet, and child rearing.[38] These movements reflected the ambition of social reformers and state officials in many countries to penetrate people's homes and reform their habits of daily life.

The Soviet wife-activist movement, however, was distinguished by its attempt to facilitate a new and distinctively socialist home life. While women's organizations in other countries also promoted clean, neat homes, the Soviet domestic sphere was to be permeated by public consciousness. The wife-activists themselves embodied this spirit by concerning themselves not just with their own families' comfort but with the cultural progress of all society. At a wife-activist conference, one delegate described the transformation of a manager's wife who used to waste her days playing cards and gossiping with friends, but now devoted herself wholeheartedly to cleaning and decorating the factory dining hall and barracks.[39] Wife-activists, then, performed a dual societal role as both homemakers for their own families and cultural educators for peasants and workers. As such they represented liminal figures helping to achieve a new Soviet way of life.[40]

Reports on the wife-activist movement indicate that tens of thousands of elite women volunteered to inspect workers' barracks, clean cafeterias, and give lectures on the importance of hygiene, order, and culture. Leningrad alone had over one thousand wife-activist inspectors, who visited housing, cafeterias, and kindergartens to ensure that hygienic standards were maintained.[41] One article described how female volunteers improved living conditions at a construction site that initially lacked the most rudimentary amenities. The volunteers there cleaned up the squalid barracks, placed white tablecloths and flowers in the cafeteria, and raised the cultural level of workers. Wife-activists, then, clearly played an aesthetic role in addition to safeguarding the health and hygiene of workers. Indeed, at factories and construction sites throughout the country they decorated barracks and dining halls, installed curtains and carpeting, planted flowers, and organized cultural activities.[42]

The wife-activist movement had important implications for gender roles in Soviet society. The reliance on women to oversee domestic hygiene and decoration reflected and reinforced gender stereotypes. Accounts of the work done by wife-activists stressed "a woman's touch and a woman's taste"; "a woman's cultured eye," they instructed, "will bring order to all corners of our large socialist home."[43] While these formulations privileged women's judgment in the domestic sphere, they undercut women's authority in the workplace and gave them secondary status in society. Some of the propaganda for the wife-activist movement explicitly stated that women were supposed "to help their husbands in their work" by making both the home and workplace orderly and comfortable. One wife-activist declared, "All my dreams are connected with the work of my husband, for whom I want to be the first and best helper."[44]

The wife-activist movement also reinforced class inequalities. While allegedly a classless society, the Soviet Union in reality was characterized by some social differentiation—most notably between managerial elites and manual laborers. The fact that the wives of high-ranking officials and managers did not work in itself differentiated this group from female workers and peasants.[45] The wife-activist movement highlighted these distinctions by assigning elite women a benevolent and didactic role in relation to Soviet laborers. Delegates at a wife-activist conference resolved, "We all burn with a desire to make the lives of our country's laborers ever happier and ever more splendid."[46] Even though philanthropic in character, the enlightenment work of wife-activists placed their domestic values and tastes above those of workers and peasants. Evidence indicates that there was popular resentment toward elite women. Some female workers complained when wife-activists received awards, and others asked why the wives of managers and engineers had domestic servants and did not work themselves.[47]

The extensive efforts of Soviet officials and wife-activists to improve workers' and peasants' living conditions did not mean that Soviet housing in fact became orderly and hygienic. During the industrialization drive, the Soviet leadership channeled virtually all resources into building factories. Housing conditions therefore deteriorated at the very moment when rapid urbanization necessitated their improvement and expansion. As many urban residents found themselves living in overcrowded communal apartments, rat-infested barracks, and unheated shacks and mud huts, hygienic standards fell.[48] Lacking the resources to expand and improve housing, Soviet officials ordered even more regulations and interventions to safeguard the health of the population. One Moscow inspector noted that the housing in his district consisted primarily of unclean and overcrowded barracks, and he recommended an increase in the number of inspectors and fines in an effort to ameliorate the situation.[49]

Attempts to instill hygienic habits and cultured tastes also produced mixed results. Since the great majority of the Soviet population struggled to obtain basic food, clothing, and housing, particularly during the 1930s, many did not have the luxury of decorating their homes or dressing in a cultured manner. It is true that some Soviet citizens adopted the language of culturedness and aspired to its superficial trappings. In appealing to Party leaders for improved living conditions, for example, people claimed they needed resources to make their communities more cultured. Others wrote letters that mimicked official propaganda about the importance of neat and "cultured" dress.[50] Diary evidence indicates that some young people also internalized notions of culturedness and aspired to a cultured lifestyle. One former peasant in Moscow described his hopes "to dress in a cultured way," though he often lacked the money to do so.[51] Many sought fashionable clothing and decorations, though Soviet newspapers actually criticized some young people for becoming overly concerned with the latest fashions and "unnecessary" statuettes and paper flowers.[52] Soviet cultural work, then, established norms of hygiene and order to which all citizens were expected to conform. But material realities often limited the degree to which these norms could be met and lifestyles transformed.

Cultured Labor and Leisure

For all countries during the industrial age, people's labor represented a crucial resource. Political leaders, social thinkers, and industrialists throughout Europe and around the world sought to mobilize and cultivate their population's labor. To do so they promoted values of punctuality and sobriety in efforts to make workers more reliable and efficient. Soviet officials and industrial managers inculcated similar values in their efforts to forge a productive workforce. But Soviet leaders viewed people's labor as more than simply a resource. According to Soviet ideology, manual labor was a means of human transformation and personal fulfillment. The process of laboring had the potential to ennoble workers, to instill political consciousness, and to replace selfish individualism with collectivist, socialist ideals. Teaching cultured work habits was therefore integral both to state economic interests and to Soviet citizens' capacity to realize their human potential.

Labor hygiene emerged as a field through which Soviet specialists defined and promoted work habits to ensure the health and efficiency of industrial workers. Labor hygienists conducted surveys on topics ranging from the effects of industrial toxins and pollutants on workers' health to the proper posture to maintain workers' efficiency.[53] In addition to overseeing the health and safety of workers, labor hygienists and other industrial officials conducted studies on the rational organization of labor and on ways to maximize labor productivity. In special laboratories, efficiency

Для предупреждения туберкулеза наши мастерские
должны быть чисты и просторны.

"For the prevention of tuberculosis, our factory shops should be clean and spacious." (Poster
identification number RU/SU 1197.2, Poster Collection, Hoover Institution Archives.)

experts conducted physiological studies to determine optimal labor techniques for industrial workers. These studies reached far beyond questions
of lighting and ventilation in factories; they also took into account "biological and socioeconomic" influences on workers' performance.[54] The
leading journal on these issues, *Gigiena truda*, kept Soviet specialists ap-
prised of the latest European studies on industrial physiology, technology,
accident prevention, and efficiency.[55]

Soviet efficiency experts also examined the psychological effects of industrial labor and sought ways to minimize psychological and neurologi-
cal stress. A leading Soviet psychologist, Aron Zalkind, wrote in 1930 that
"socialist construction requires the maximal, planned use of all sciences
connected with questions of human psychoneurology." He hoped to up-
grade the labor performance of "the working masses" ("production psychoneurology") through psychological, motor-skills, and pedagogical
research.[56] Soviet industrial psychology was part of a broader movement
in interwar Europe. In the early 1920s psychotechnical institutes were established in England, France, Germany, Italy, Poland, and Japan, as well as

in the Soviet Union. (In fact, an international psychotechnical congress to create a unified terminology for the international psychotechnical movement was held in Moscow in 1931.) The new subdisciplines of industrial psychology and aptitude testing became part of scientific management and more general attempts to replace the chaos of the free market with rational deployment of personnel.[57]

The efforts of Soviet efficiency experts to train workers for maximum productivity were also apparent in the image of the human-machine hybrid. The machine was perhaps the most salient symbol of progress and perfectibility, and for some it became a model for human transformation as well.[58] A number of nineteenth-century European thinkers argued that the body, like the machine, was a motor that converted energy into mechanical work. They believed that society should conserve, deploy, and expand the energies of the laboring human body and harmonize its movements with those of the machine. By the 1890s the "science of work" had emerged as a field, and in the twentieth century this scientific approach to the laboring body pervaded parliamentary debates, sociological treatises, liberal reform programs, and socialist tracts.[59]

Soviet leaders adopted the ideal of human beings as machines, whose labor would be deployed rationally in order to maximize the productivity of society as a whole. In 1923 Nikolai Bukharin, a Party leader, urged the creation of "qualified, especially disciplined, living labor machines."[60] Aleksei Gastev, the leading Soviet proponent of the "scientific management" theories of Frederick Taylor, developed even more extensive ideas on human automation. His Central Institute of Labor in Moscow studied the physiological aspects of labor and trained workers to perform more efficiently. Gastev's ultimate goal was the symbiosis of man and machine: workers would adopt the rhythm and efficiency of factory equipment and become robot-like producers with perfectly disciplined minds and bodies.[61]

Gastev's ideas, while very influential, nonetheless encountered considerable opposition. Many labor hygienists feared that Gastev placed efficiency before the safety and health of workers.[62] Even more fundamentally, many workers and Left Communists opposed Gastev's Taylorist methods as capitalist exploitation. Lenin strongly supported Gastev and the creation of the Central Institute of Labor in 1920, and justified his approach by arguing that "it is necessary to grasp all the culture which capitalism has left and build socialism from it."[63] Gastev's ideas were put into practice during the early 1930s, when the industrialization drive necessitated optimal labor productivity and the rapid training of millions of former peasants for industrial labor.[64]

The Soviet industrialization drive of the 1930s and the recruitment of millions of new industrial workers made the task of disseminating cultured work habits even more urgent. Because the great majority of these new workers were former peasants with no experience in factory work, they had to learn new work routines and labor discipline. Teaching peasants efficient work habits for industrial production represented a major challenge for the Soviet government. In Western Europe, labor discipline was instilled in industrial workers only after several generations of multifaceted efforts. Managers employed bells and clocks to impress a sense of time discipline, schoolteachers taught obedience and punctuality, and the clergy preached against the evils of idleness.[65] Soviet officials promoted similar work values, but given the forced pace of the industrialization drive, they were unable to inculcate labor discipline as quickly as it was required. Reports indicate that factory workers wasted hours each day, loitering and taking smoking breaks. Labor productivity in Soviet industry actually fell sharply during the First Five-Year Plan despite extensive efforts to teach workers to be efficient and disciplined.[66]

The Soviet government also launched worker productivity campaigns that did not depend on steady, efficient labor. Socialist competition and shock work constituted one such campaign, begun in 1929. Socialist competition involved contests between workers, brigades, and even factories to see which could increase production the most. Spurred by socialist competition, brigades of shock workers began to exceed their work norms and in some highly publicized cases set production records. Rather than work steadily and efficiently, workers participating in shock work and socialist competition would work at a feverish pace for a day or two and then take several days to recover. This sort of storming was reinforced by the planned economy, under which managers and workers strained at the end of each month to meet their quotas but failed to develop regularized work routines the rest of the month.[67]

Stakhanovism represented another extrasystemic campaign to raise worker productivity. When a Donbass miner named Aleksei Stakhanov reportedly mined over one hundred tons of coal in a single shift in 1935, Commissar Ordzhonikidze ordered widespread publicity to make Stakhanov a hero.[68] Soon Stakhanovites began to set production records in other branches of industry, often by experimenting with their machinery and violating established work routines in their attempts to produce more quickly.[69] Party officials began to publicize similar record-breaking production by newly designated Stakhanovite workers in other branches of industry as well. This publicity was intended not only as an inspiration for workers but as a justification for raising production norms.[70] Stakhan-

ovism, then, also failed to inculcate labor discipline and industrial routinization. Instead it encouraged workers to set production records and
collect awards and bonuses without internalizing the steady and efficient
industrial rhythms favored by factory managers. In this sense, it was a distinctly Soviet approach to work culture—an approach that relied on revolutionary leaps forward rather than routinized progress.

Shock work and Stakhanovism both reflected a strong strain of Promea-
theanism in the thinking of Soviet leaders. Because they sought the revolutionary transformation of the economy and society, Soviet leaders were
not content with gradual industrial progress. Instead they sought to break
the bounds of economic and technological limitations and to leap ahead
toward socialism and communism. Time itself, they believed, could be
transcended or accelerated, so that it would be possible for Soviet workers
to, as their slogan said, "fulfill the Five-Year Plan in four years."[71] The labor values they sought to instill in Soviet workers were therefore somewhat contradictory. While in most periods they promoted efficiency and
routinization, during shock work and Stakhanovite campaigns officials ex-
horted workers to violate their routines and exceed their quotas. Campaigns and storming did result in spurts of economic growth, but they did
not establish regularized work discipline or an efficient and routinized system of production.

In addition to productivity campaigns, the Soviet government resorted
to coercion to try to enforce punctual work habits. In 1932, with tardiness
and absenteeism among workers rampant, the Soviet government decreed
that workers would be fired for any unexcused absence and deprived of
their ration cards and factory housing. One article justified such harsh legislation as necessary to discipline "new workers from the countryside who
have not developed a collectivist spirit of labor."[72] In 1938 the Soviet government issued even more repressive labor legislation, and in 1940 it mandated prison sentences for workers who quit their jobs.[73] Repression,
however, proved largely ineffective at instilling labor discipline in workers.
Given the severe labor shortages of the industrialization drive, managers
were loath to enforce the laws that required them to fire or imprison workers. And workers for their part could generally find new jobs without being questioned about their previous work record, so they often evaded the
effects of these decrees.[74]

Soviet authorities also employed coercion to force people it regarded as
social parasites to work. Labor in the Soviet Union was both a right and an
obligation.[75] According to the Soviet constitution, everyone had the right
to work, but no one had the right not to engage in socially useful labor. Beginning shortly after the Revolution, the Soviet government established a

labor camp system, expanded greatly during the 1930s, where "social parasites," "class enemies," and common criminals could be incarcerated and forced to perform work. Soviet labor camps were located in remote regions of northern European Russia, the Urals, Siberia, and Kazakhstan, where labor resources were scarce; they provided crucial labor in the extraction of raw materials for the Soviet industrialization drive.[76]

But Soviet labor camps represented more than a coercive mechanism of labor mobilization. Even as the Soviet government adopted the new view that the laboring body was an instrument whose energies could be scientifically deployed to maximize production, socialist ideology also perpetuated the ancient craft ideal of labor as an ennobling accomplishment. Soviet leaders believed in the power of manual labor to instill proletarian consciousness and even to redeem those whom it regarded as social parasites. The White Sea Canal, for example, dug by forced labor in the far north, was heralded as a project that built not only a new transportation link but new people as well.

The Soviet government espoused cultured leisure as well as efficient labor. Whereas productive labor clearly served to augment state economic and military power, the purpose of cultured leisure is not so immediately apparent. Soviet officials' efforts to regulate people's free time stemmed in part from their desire to guarantee or even augment workers' ability to work well. By preventing drunken or decadent leisure activities, they could ensure workers' health and physical capacity. Some Soviet thinkers also argued that physical culture activities would enhance workers' labor capacity. But in addition to serving these more pragmatic concerns, the campaign for cultured leisure once again reflected Soviet leaders' aesthetic vision of what socialist society should look like. Healthy and edifying entertainments fitted their vision of a progressive and enlightened society, where all aspects of life, including leisure, were rationalized, orderly, and harmonious.

Because the traditional leisure activities of Russian peasants and workers centered so much on alcohol, Soviet officials made drinking a particular target of their reform efforts. Many Party members in fact wished to continue the complete prohibition against any alcoholic beverages initiated during the First World War, but the Soviet government chose instead to institute a state monopoly on the sale of vodka, which Stalin justified in 1927 as necessary to generate revenue for industrialization.[77] While the government produced and sold alcohol, it simultaneously fought against drunkenness and conducted anti-alcohol propaganda. Party leaders such as Bukharin strongly condemned the use of alcohol and tobacco and called for "a conscious battle" against them. Komsomol reports on cultural

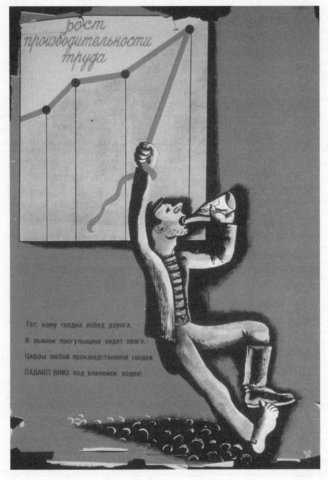

A drunk lowers labor productivity. "Those who seek a winning report see drunk absentees as the enemy. . . ." (Poster identification number RU/SU 1942, Poster Collection, Hoover Institution Archives.)

work in the countryside recommended healthy activities such as films and sports to replace the "hooliganism and drunkenness" that characterized peasants' leisure.[78]

Soviet officials also condemned card playing, billiards, and dancing as uncultured and decadent pastimes. Just after the Revolution, the Soviet government made some attempts to outlaw card playing completely, and while it relaxed these efforts by the 1920s, it continued to campaign against both cards and billiards.[79] Dancing, and particularly Western dances such as the waltz and foxtrot, posed an even greater danger in the eyes of Soviet authorities. Throughout the 1920s and 1930s, Komsomol officials warned of dancing's decadent influence on youth.[80] During the Great Purges, they even portrayed dancing as an activity that could lead to political as well as moral degeneration. A 1938 Komsomol report on dance schools in Moscow decried the "vulgar dances" that took place there and declared that lack of supervision allowed "hostile elements to engage in anti-Soviet work." A similar account announced that the director of a Leningrad dance site had been uncovered as an enemy of the people, and concluded, "The enemy knows that often we poorly organize young people's leisure, and he takes advantage of this."[81] According to this view, failure to organize healthy alternatives to dancing left young people vulnerable to moral and political corruption.

To replace uncultured and decadent leisure, Soviet authorities provided a range of enlightened activities and entertainments—films, plays, public readings, art circles, and physical culture. The Commissariat of Education organized cultural events, literary readings, and physical culture activities in the countryside with the explicit aim of distracting peasants from drinking and fighting. Party officials sponsored artistic circles that gave peasants and workers the chance to learn about painting and handicrafts and to create their own art.[82] Amateur theater groups provided people the opportunity to organize and act in plays and spectacles. In the 1930s, these groups particularly emphasized teaching their participants to be cultured. Amateur actors were to learn not only the classics of world drama but also important lessons in fashion, diction, manners, and comportment. Group leaders even organized excursions to libraries and museums so their members could become more knowledgeable and cultured.[83]

Soviet authorities built special sites at which cultured leisure activities were to take place: workers' clubs, "palaces of culture," and "houses of leisure." Emel'ian Iaroslavskii, a Party leader, emphasized the need to have attractive workers' clubs and orderly palaces of culture, with the implication that neat, well-organized sites would guarantee orderly activities. Other officials similarly stressed that houses of leisure be neat and comfortable, with bright paintings and new furniture, so as to attract and inspire workers and peasants. They also insisted that houses of leisure have baths to promote hygiene and a daily regime of activities and exercise to ensure that people's free time would be well organized.[84] "Parks of culture and leisure" were also created to provide settings conducive to edifying entertainment. These parks, well patrolled to prevent drinking and fighting, were to inspire their visitors to enjoy the outdoors in an orderly environment, amidst exhibitions and symbols of Soviet technological progress. As

Lewis Siegelbaum has noted in connection with workers' clubs, the Soviet organization of leisure had inescapable parallels with Italian Fascist mass culture in that both regimes sought to control and link recreational pastimes with state beneficence.[85]

Physical culture received special attention because it both expanded participants' labor capacity and allegedly guarded against immoral and decadent activity. In the preface to a 1932 pamphlet advocating healthy and cultured lifestyles, former commissar Semashko wrote:

> The correct organization of everyday life (especially of leisure and rest) has enormous cultural-educational significance. After all, it is one thing if a worker spends his free time engaged in drinking, hooliganism, or the church. It is something else if he spends it doing physical exercises, going on excursions, and benefiting from the sun, water, and fresh air. . . . Everyday life must be organized so as to best realize this goal: to produce working strength.[86]

Semashko and other officials believed that physical culture would prepare people for labor and expand their work capacity.[87] One physical culture expert, K. Mechonoshin, argued that exercise would instill in youth an appreciation of labor's importance and would increase work efficiency.[88] And the labor hero Aleksei Stakhanov endorsed physical culture as something that "disciplines people and instills in them new strengths and enthusiasm."[89]

Beyond the practical aim of increasing the population's labor capacity, physical culture offered a means to transform people's attitude toward work. Soviet physical culture specialists developed new fields of labor gymnastics and labor sports in the 1920s.[90] Soviet physical culture pageants sometimes combined labor and sports images in an allusion to Marx's prophesy that work would become pleasurable.[91] Of course Marx's vision of unalienated labor was based primarily on the fact that workers would reap the benefits of their own work. But it also relied on a notion of labor as voluntary, recreational, and fulfilling. By portraying physical labor as akin to recreational exercise, Soviet authorities sought to instill a new attitude toward work.[92]

The renowned Soviet theater director Vsevolod Meierhold applied these ideas about labor in his techniques to train actors. In a 1922 lecture titled "The Actor of the Future and Biomechanics," Meierhold argued that the actor "will be working in a society where labor is no longer regarded as a curse but as a joyful, vital necessity." To prepare workers and actors alike for continuous, efficient, and aesthetic labor, Meierhold prescribed a regimen to perfect the body. He stated that "the actor must train his material (the body), so that it is capable of executing instantaneously those tasks which are dictated externally." In response to his own question, "How do we set about molding the new actor?" Meierhold replied, "If we place him in an environment in which gymnastics and all forms of sport are both available and compulsory, we shall achieve the new person who is capable of any form of labor."[93] Physical culture, then, offered a means not only to ensure the health and labor capability of the population but also to promote labor efficiency and, according to some, transform work into a recreational, fulfilling, and joyous enterprise.

Laboratory research by Soviet physiologists also established norms for exercise and leisure. One such study determined that "active leisure" in the form of rhythmic exercises was the most efficient way to restore the body's energy and labor ability.[94] Research focused particularly on the health and fitness of children. Another specialist, S. I. Kaplun, linked "proper leisure" with high labor productivity, citing both physiological studies (on the benefits of healthy leisure for the nervous system and blood circulation) and industrial productivity experiments.[95] Commissar Semashko himself had recognized in 1926 the need for leisure "to cleanse" the bodily organism "from the harmful substances that accumulate in it as a result of work."[96] And the Commissariat of Health, noting that working-class children were not as healthy as peasant children because they lacked fresh air and sunshine, recommended "excursions, walks, and other means of natural health improvement" for children.[97]

The Soviet government's emphasis on the scientific organization of leisure reflected the Enlightenment belief that all aspects of life should be ordered and rationalized. In contrast to traditional leisure activities (which might include drinking, card playing, and other vices), Soviet leisure was to be part of a balanced lifestyle that improved the health and vitality of the human organism. As one Soviet health journal stressed, proper leisure could revitalize the human organism as effectively as sleep and restore to "the human machine" the energy that would allow continued work and productivity.[98] Soviet officials in fact stressed the division of daily life into equal eight-hour segments of work, sleep, and leisure. This approach, also common to Fordism and international workers' movements, reflected an interest not only in leisure to maintain workers' health but also in the comprehensive ordering of everyday life.[99]

Physical culture also served the Soviet government's larger aspiration to restore social harmony. A 1920 Commissariat of Health report titled "The Tasks of Physical Culture" stressed the necessity of physical culture both "to make the population healthy" and "to create the harmonious and com-

Physical culture at a Young Pioneer camp, 1935. "The Pioneer camp—a base of cultured and healthy leisure." (Poster identification number RU/SU 1818, Poster Collection, Hoover Institution Archives.)

plete individual from whom one can expect qualities of most benefit for the common good."[100] Soviet officials also saw physical culture as a means to cultivate harmonious individuals who would contribute to the perfect society. A 1919 report on children's well-being explained that a healthy body also meant a "healthy spirit," and it went on to link a proper physical upbringing with "the harmonious development of the individual."[101] In 1920 the Commissariat of Health admitted that "medicine, with all its scientific discoveries, is not in a position to create the new individual." It went on to argue that of all means available ("new social conditions, cultural enlightenment work, a new upbringing, sanitary-hygiene measures"), physical culture "has perhaps the most important place" in creating "an individual with the harmonious development of mental and bodily strengths."[102]

Physical culture was championed partly because it seemed to present a bulwark against the decadence of modern life.[103] Lenin himself recommended "healthy sport—gymnastics, swimming, excursions, physical exercises," concluding that "in a healthy body there is a healthy spirit."[104] A 1926 Komsomol resolution stressed physical culture as a means to divert young people from the evil influences of alcohol and prostitution.[105] And one Soviet commentator, after observing sporting exercises, contrasted their "freshness, vibrancy, and healthy strength" to the decadence of "Americanized dances."[106]

Despite Soviet officials' extensive efforts to make leisure cultured, rationalized, and healthy, they succeeded only partially in transforming popular pastimes. Throughout the 1920s and 1930s, a large proportion of Soviet citizens continued to drink, play cards, and engage in other officially discouraged activities. Many peasants and workers observed religious holidays by gathering with friends and drinking heavily. After work they would also congregate to drink, sing songs, play cards, brawl, and engage in other "hooligan" behavior.[107] One Komsomol report from the late 1930s complained that students skipped meetings to drink and gamble, while another decried young people's degenerate activities, from playing cards in cafés to joining gangs and holding drunken orgies.[108] Anne Gorsuch has shown that throughout the 1920s many Soviet young people rejected organized leisure activities in favor of Western fads such as dancing the foxtrot, and even in 1941 commentators noted the continued influence of Western dances and fashions on Soviet youth.[109]

The complete transformation of everyday life and leisure was an ambitious goal. While Soviet cultural officials had a clear vision of rational, sober, edifying leisure, they generally lacked the resources to organize such activities in a compelling manner. Many workers' clubs and palaces of culture had poor facilities and little money to arrange activities. The club for workers constructing the Moscow metro was a small shack that could hold only two people at a time; the metalworkers' trade union reported having several good proposals for cultural programs "but not one kopek" to pay for them.[110] Cultural facilities in the villages were even more poorly funded. One rural club had no films, drama productions, lectures, or books, and owned nothing more than a broken accordion.[111] The top priority for Soviet leaders throughout the 1930s remained industrialization, and the resources they invested in building steel mills left relatively little for cultured leisure.

It is not clear that even if greater resources had been available, Soviet citizens would have embraced the officially prescribed leisure activities. Such a change presupposed people's willingness to alter their daily routines and pastimes. Some people who aspired to join the Party and advance in the system conformed to the government's standards of cultured leisure, but the majority of the population continued the drinking and socializing long established in peasant and worker culture, much to the dismay of cultural officials.

Cultural Revolution

While the effort to civilize and acculturate the masses was common to all modernizing societies, this cultural mission carried a particular urgency in Russia, even before the Revolution. Because the Russian intelligentsia were acutely aware of their country's backwardness and felt a sense of responsibility to serve the people, Russian liberals and radicals alike were eager to transform Russia's political and social order, not only by overthrowing the autocracy but by uplifting the population as well. As scholars have noted, prerevolutionary Russian intellectuals across the political spectrum emphasized culture as a means to achieve social transformation, and each group assumed that their own cultural code provided a model for the lower classes to adopt.[112] Enlightening the masses would not only uplift them but overcome the social rifts within Russian society and restore its wholeness under the leadership of the intelligentsia. Russian intellectuals might thereby overcome the mixture of guilt and apprehension they felt toward the lower classes.

While the Bolsheviks focused primarily on the political and economic aspects of revolution, they shared an interest in culture. The Vpered (Forward) group—a branch of Left Bolsheviks—in fact stressed cultural revolution over sociopolitical revolution, insisting that cultural transformation needed to precede political or social change. In contrast to intellectuals who wanted to instill in the lower classes an appreciation of existing high culture, the Vperedists, led by Aleksandr Bogdanov, wanted to create a unique proletarian culture, complete with new art, literature, habits, and ethics, as well as a proletarian intelligentsia to take power after the Revolution. But as Lynn Mally notes, the Vperedists' emphasis on cultural preparation of the working class echoed other Russian intellectuals' belief in culture and education as the keys to emancipate the people and prepare them to participate in civic life.[113]

After the Revolution, the Vperedists' mission was taken up by the Proletkult movement—a network of proletarian culture organizations largely shaped by Vperedists and their ideas. Proletkult members saw radical cultural transformation as vital to the survival of the Revolution, and they sought to create a new proletarian culture and a proletarian intelligentsia. By 1919 the movement ran afoul of Lenin, who announced his opposition to "all kinds of intellectual inventions, all kinds of proletarian culture." A cultural conservative who favored the classics of Russian literature, Lenin disapproved of many avant-garde experiments and instead advocated taking the best elements of existing culture. His opposition to Proletkult ended the Soviet government's support for the movement and spelled its ultimate demise.[114]

The idea of cultural revolution, however, survived and flourished during the 1920s. Even as the Politburo reduced Proletkult's independence and funding, it expanded cultural education programs for workers. As Michael David-Fox has argued, the idea of cultural revolution was absorbed into the Bolshevik mainstream and became the avenue by which broader, non-Bolshevik intelligentsia ideals of cultural transformation became a central part of the Bolshevik project. In his last writings of 1922–23, Lenin again stressed cultural progress—overcoming backwardness, inculcating habits of hygiene and efficiency, and the mastery of science and technology. Other Bolshevik leaders in the 1920s took up cultural themes as well. Bukharin advocated cultural revolution, which he defined as changing people's habits, feelings, desires, and manner of life. Trotsky, in his book *Questions of Everyday Life,* called the acquisition of culture a revolutionary task and championed hygiene, efficiency, sobriety, and cultured speech.[115]

While the Vpered-Proletkult goal of creating a unique proletarian culture was lost, Party militants continued to push for the replacement of "bourgeois specialists"—the prerevolutionary technical and cultural elite—with a proletarian intelligentsia. At the end of the 1920s, the Stalinist leadership enacted just such a policy through a combination of show trials to remove old specialists and a massively expanded training program to prepare workers to become engineers and factory directors. This policy, carried out against the background of the industrialization and collectivization campaigns, unleashed a wave of "class war" militancy in both economic and cultural realms. Non-Marxist cultural and intellectual figures were denounced and removed from positions of authority, while radicals gained the upper hand in universities, institutes, theaters, and other cultural institutions.[116]

The "Great Break," as Stalin termed it, lasted from 1928 to 1931, and amounted to a wholesale assault on nonparty specialists and intellectuals in the economic and cultural spheres—an assault that both politicized these realms and undercut existing professional hierarchies. But despite its antiestablishment character, the Great Break did not destroy behavioral norms and in some ways even reinforced them.[117] Industrial supervisors intensified their efforts to instill punctuality and discipline in workers, and cultural officials vastly expanded hygiene and literacy campaigns. Educational institutions emphasized practical and technical training over theoretical learning, but they nonetheless recruited and educated hundreds of thousands of workers and peasants, greatly raising the overall educational level of the population. Cultural policy during the Great Break, then, was distinguished not by a new cultural program but rather by the speed and militancy with which officials pushed modern cultural norms.[118] In a sense the Stalinist leadership enacted half of the original Vpered-Proletkult program by creating a new proletarian intelligentsia, but not a unique proletarian culture.

Stalin's speech "New Conditions—New Tasks of Economic Construction" in 1931 signaled an end to the antiestablishment militancy of the Great Break. Stalin announced that most of the prerevolutionary technical elite could now be trusted. Whereas "wrecking" had been widespread among these specialists just two years before, according to Stalin, "a significant part of the old technical intelligentsia . . . has now sided with Soviet power." Stalin attributed this shift to the country's great strides toward socialism. Citing the success of collectivization, he explained that with the elimination of "capitalist elements in the city and countryside" and the crumbling of the bourgeois specialists' hopes for foreign intervention, the old technical elite had accepted the permanence of Soviet power. Because most of these people could now be trusted, Stalin decreed a new policy of recruiting and caring for these specialists rather than persecuting them. Stalin also noted the "tens of thousands of worker and peasant youths" now studying in institutions of higher education, and heralded the fact that the working class was thereby creating its own intelligentsia.[119] The rapid training and promotion of workers into positions of authority from 1928 to 1931 was another reason for the reassertion of hierarchy. Not only was the nonparty technical elite now more trustworthy after the elimination of "capitalist remnants," but increasingly they were becoming outnumbered by newly trained specialists of working-class origin, who owed their training and their loyalty to the Soviet government.

A similar logic applied to cultural and intellectual institutions. The Great Break had demoted or eliminated many nonparty intellectuals in these realms and replaced them with Marxist militants and Party loyalists. Once the "bourgeois specialists" were no longer predominant and those who remained had largely accepted Soviet power, antiestablishment militancy was no longer appropriate. Respect for cultural authorities now meant support for Soviet socialism. After Stalin's speech, Komsomol militants and self-proclaimed proletarian culture groups were reined in. In April 1932 a government decree dissolved independent proletarian culture organizations such as RAPP, the association of proletarian writers.[120]

Shifts in Soviet education illustrate both the newfound respect for cultural authorities in the 1930s and the continued priority given to enlightening and acculturating the masses. During the 1920s, many teachers remained suspect in the eyes of Soviet authorities. While most of them were socialist in orientation, rural teachers in particular often harbored populist rather than Marxist sympathies, and relatively few teachers were Party members. Soviet educational policy during the 1920s in many ways challenged and undermined the authority of teachers. Moreover, the Commissariat of Education instituted progressive educational approaches that undercut traditional curricula and decentralized authority in the classroom.[121]

But beginning in 1931, the Soviet government began to bolster teachers' authority. Like the old technical specialists, nonparty teachers could now be trusted, given the country's progress toward socialism. Moreover, in a way that paralleled the training of new technical specialists, the Commissariat of Education at this time was hiring hundreds of thousands of new teachers who had been trained under the Soviet regime and were therefore politically reliable.[122] In 1931 the Party Central Committee resolved that schools should not indiscriminately apply theories of progressive education, and the Commissariat of Education subsequently introduced a more structured curriculum. The Central Committee resolved in 1935 that teachers' standing in the classroom should be strengthened further and that students should be taught to obey their teachers and respect their elders. Teacher conferences organized to discuss this resolution emphasized the importance of instilling discipline and obedience in students.[123]

Throughout the second half of the 1930s, Party and educational officials continued to emphasize student discipline. At a school directors' conference in 1935, one director called on all schools to issue rules of behavior for students to follow at home as well as at school. He stressed that parents had a responsibility to work with teachers to teach children to be "cultured," and to follow rules and routines to ensure their health and discipline.[124] Party Central Committee reports in 1938 and again in 1941 also emphasized the importance of student discipline in schools. As "rules of student behavior," the second report stated that students should be prompt, clean, properly attired, orderly, polite, and respectful (rising when a teacher entered the classroom), and that they should "fight against displays of indiscipline, hooliganism, and rudeness by their comrades."[125] In 1940 the Commissariat of Education presented special awards to a number of veteran teachers, none of whom were Party members, commending them for their ability to maintain strict discipline in the classroom.[126]

Discipline was a major theme of Anton Makarenko, the leading Soviet pedagogue of the 1930s. Makarenko became famous as the founder and director of a colony for juvenile delinquents. The techniques he developed there for rehabilitating these young people focused on discipline and regimentation. Makarenko justified discipline in terms of the larger social good, arguing that "defiance of discipline means that the person is acting against society." But he also believed that precise rules and a strict regimen would make children feel more secure and hence, paradoxically, more "free" to go about their lives with a clear sense of right and wrong.[127] Makarenko saw the school and the family as key institutions in the proper upbringing of children, and wrote widely about the ways teachers and parents should inculcate values of respect and obedience.[128] He asserted that students' outward discipline and politeness "determines the inner content of behavior as well . . . for it mobilizes the will, gives one a feeling of efficiency and smartness."[129] In his widely popular 1937 handbook on child raising, *A Book for Parents,* Makarenko condemned slovenliness and a lack of structure in family life as extremely harmful to children. "From the very earliest age," he wrote, "children should be trained to keep exact time and clearly defined bounds of conduct. . . . Punctuality means being in reach of discipline and parental authority."[130]

Makarenko also advocated discipline in language. Noting that even "highly cultured people, holding responsible posts," frequently resorted to swearing, he wrote, "It is hard to understand the cause of this stupid and abominable tradition." He warned that children who heard swear words would think of the sexual meaning of the terms and turn to "perverted daydreaming," and recommended "a resolute and persistent struggle against foul language, if not from aesthetic considerations, then from purely educational ones."[131] Komsomol officials also campaigned against foul language. Some young people in the 1920s, as part of their rebellion against bourgeois culture, deliberately cultivated a coarse manner of speaking, with swear words and street slang.[132] In reaction, in 1923–24 the Komsomol participated in a campaign for "cultured speech" that taught young people to avoid vulgarisms and make their language clean and grammatical. As one scholar has argued, this campaign against swearing was intended not just to overcome cultural backwardness but to control the disorder of popular speech, which was seen as an expression of the libidinal energies of the body.[133] Disciplining speech, therefore, became a means to discipline the mind and the body as well.

Official efforts to clean up language continued into the 1930s. As an editor told one cultural worker, "It is necessary to struggle not only for clean rooms and beds but also for clean, cultured language."[134] Another cultural critic called for the elimination of vulgar expressions in film scripts, arguing that the arts and literature "help raise the cultural level of the laboring masses," but warned that this mission would be hampered if works contained crude words.[135] One peasant woman even sent a letter to the 1936 constitutional commission complaining of pandemic swearing in the countryside and asking that it be legally banned.[136] As this letter suggests, swearing did not cease despite official campaigns. In fact, evidence from the late 1930s indicates that vulgar language remained widespread in schools and factories.[137] Nonetheless, official efforts to eliminate swearing at a minimum made people aware that proper speech was a crucial component of cultured behavior.

The campaign for cultured speech sought not only to eliminate swear words but to make language more rational and efficient. In his *Questions of Everyday Life* Trotsky included a chapter on cultured speech that condemned both folk expressions and bureaucratic language. He advocated rationalized, standardized language, with "more precise and dynamic expressions" for efficiency and clarity. He wrote, "Precision and correctness of speech are necessary prerequisites for correct and precise thought."[138] His ideas were echoed by others, including Boris Arvatov and the Productionists, a subset of the Constructivist movement in the mid-1920s, who believed that it was possible to change people's thinking by making their language cleaner, clearer, and more efficient. In 1934 Gorky similarly denounced folk expressions as "language pollution," and got the Union of Soviet Writers to ban the use of folk language in literature. As a consequence, socialist realism portrayed common people as speaking in formal, cultured language. In this sense, socialist realism was a form of classicism— a normative system that emphasized purity and decorum not only through character and plot development but through the language it used as well.[139]

The campaign for cultured language illustrates several key dimensions of cultural revolution. Soviet officials revealed their aesthetic sensibilities by working to eliminate vulgar speech and swearing; like the new society, language was to be clean and pure. They also sought to modernize speech by abolishing folk language and slang, much as they sought to transform the peasantry by encouraging the abandonment of "backward" customs and beliefs. The campaign for cultured language also entailed rationalization and discipline to make speech and life more efficient and productive. All these efforts reflected an underlying faith both in the importance of culture and in the possibility of molding human beings. Rather than relying simply on economic transformation to change people's consciousness, Soviet authorities continuously promoted cultural education in the belief that changing people's behavior and speech would change the way they thought.

One other crucial area of cultural education was the teaching of literacy. In 1929 more than half of Russian peasants were still illiterate, and rates among some national minority peasants were even higher. The Soviet government made literacy one of its top priorities, both through mandatory primary education and through the creation of adult literacy classes. The number of adults enrolled in such classes rose to over 14 million by 1932, and illiteracy declined dramatically as a result.[140] Cultural workers also organized reading circles and published special books and newspapers, with simplified stories and large print, for the newly literate.[141] Literacy represented enormous cultural progress in the eyes of Soviet officials. It allowed peasants and workers to become enlightened, to gain political consciousness, and to live up to their human potential.

In view of the high rates of illiteracy that persisted among the Soviet population even at the end of the 1920s, Soviet cultural education made enormous gains during the 1930s. To transform a predominantly illiterate peasant society into a largely literate, urbanized population in the course of just one decade was a tremendous accomplishment. But literacy itself did not guarantee that Soviet peasants and workers developed the political consciousness or appreciation of high culture the authorities prescribed. Librarians reported that few workers requested political books or literary classics, preferring popular fiction and adventure novels.[142] When reading circles assigned political literature, so many words lay outside their vocabulary that newly literate peasants and workers found much of it incomprehensible.[143] One collective farm director ordered that every household subscribe to a newspaper, but it is unclear whether peasants actually read and understood the newspapers they received.[144]

The overall results of Soviet authorities' attempt to acculturate the masses were similarly mixed. Some peasants and workers, particularly those with ambitions and opportunities to advance within the economic and political hierarchy, consciously strove to adopt Soviet models of cultured thought and behavior.[145] Others tried to conform to these models, but did so only partially or superficially. One Moscow worker wrote in his diary that he wanted to become cultured, but he recounted lectures and books in a manner that parroted official phrases without demonstrating any comprehension of them.[146] Soviet citizens who wrote to Party leaders often mimicked cultural education slogans, agreeing that everyone should "raise their cultural level," and that building socialism required "more highly cultured people."[147] These letters, which often contained appeals for government money, reflected an awareness of official cultural norms but not necessarily their internalization. Finally, it is clear that some Soviet citizens rejected official cultural norms. Particularly in the countryside, where even in the late 1930s many villages had no books, newspapers, or cultural facilities, many peasants maintained traditional cultural forms and entertainments.[148] And even peasants who moved to cities, many of whom lived in unlit barracks where they could not read if they wanted to, often preserved versions of their old culture—peasant songs, village networks, and passive resistance to authority.[149]

The New Soviet Person

Thus far I have emphasized the teaching of cultural norms common to all modernizing societies—hygiene, punctuality, literacy. But the Soviet cultural project involved more than producing clean, efficient, and literate citizens. It aspired to create new people, whose values and ways of thinking would be qualitatively different from those who lived under capitalism. The New Soviet Person was to be free of egotism and selfishness, and was to sacrifice personal interests for the sake of the collective. In their attempt to create the New Person, Soviet authorities relied on control of the living environment, education, and inculcation of the practice of working on oneself. It was their belief in the plasticity of humankind that heightened their ambition to transform not only people's daily habits and culture but their modes of thinking and human qualities as well.

Scholars have frequently depicted the Soviet system as one that sought to subjugate or even obliterate individuals' selfhood. But Soviet power was productive as well as repressive, and strove to foster a strong sense of self in order to create the New Soviet Person.[150] Because people think and act according to an understanding of themselves and their place in the world, their sense of self determines their ability to become personally motivated subjects, or actors, in everyday life. Subjectivity—the capacity to think and act on the basis of a coherent sense of self—received considerable attention in the Soviet system. Soviet authorities sought to fashion a certain type of subject—the New Person whose thinking and actions would be based on an awareness of his or her role in building socialism. Through education, propaganda, and subjectivizing practices, Party officials constantly strove to instill this awareness, or consciousness, in Soviet citizens.

The Soviet system was not unique among modern political systems in promoting a sense of self among its citizens. While autocracies of the old regime expected the population simply to obey the monarch, modern systems were based on the ideal of popular sovereignty, in which all citizens were to play an active part in politics. Even nondemocratic political systems in the modern era have required their citizens not simply to obey orders but to participate on the basis of an understanding of the national interest and their role in attaining it. In fact, the very notion of the self in modern European thought is one in which people develop an awareness of their moment in history and of themselves as historical agents. At the same time that the Soviet system shared with other modern political systems an emphasis on its citizens' sense of self, it was distinguished by the type of self it sought to cultivate. This self was not to be individualistic; instead, according to Soviet ideology, individuals could find fulfillment only by joining the collective. In contrast to Western societies, where the liberal self was constituted by ownership of private property and a system of legal protections and individual rights, the Soviet system promoted an illiberal subjectivity, in which private life was eradicated and individuals reached their full human potential through participation in social life.

In spite of the extreme brutality of their policies, Party leaders actually emphasized people's realization of their humanity. Trotsky wrote:

> The Revolution is most of all the awakening of the human personality in the masses, who previously were supposed to be without personality. The Revolution, despite the occasional toughness and bloody ruthlessness of its methods, is first and foremost the awakening of humanity, its forward movement, increasing attention to one's own and others' self-worth.[151]

The awakening of people's humanity was to come in part from the transformation of economic relations. The abolition of private property and capitalism would end human exploitation and alienation. In Marx's vision, described in *The Communist Manifesto,* the advent of communism would free people to pursue a range of activities that would restore the organic wholeness of their personalities and allow them to realize fully their humanity.

But this liberation was not to come at the expense of one's obligations to society. On the contrary, individuals could achieve their human potential only by performing socially useful labor and participating in the life of the collective. One of Makarenko's moral principles was that "the interests of the collective are superior to the interests of the individual." Members of a collective, he argued, have a duty to one another that goes beyond friendship and that requires joint participation in the work of the collective.[152] Analyzing Makarenko's writings and Soviet pedagogy, Oleg Kharkhordin concludes that the Soviet system sought to advance the individual through the collective, and that the Soviet ideal became "collectivist individuals"—fully developed individuals who espoused collectivist values.[153]

Other values and qualities followed from the principle of collectivism. Makarenko emphasized "the real solidarity of the working people," "the abolition of greed," and "respect for the interests and life of [one's] comrades."[154] Other Soviet leaders stressed the elimination of egotism and selfishness. In 1933 Politburo member Lazar Kaganovich said to a Young Pioneer leader, "I am asking how much our children have progressed in truly human terms with respect to how they relate to one another, with respect to getting rid of the mentality of the past, egotism, vanity, selfishness, with respect to getting rid of all the bad elements that have lingered from the past." Kaganovich went on to express doubt that the population had progressed very far in eliminating these "vestiges of the past," but the fact that he was so insistent on the need for children's transformation demonstrates that even the most ruthless Stalinists hoped to cultivate lofty human qualities.[155]

A lead *Pravda* article in 1937 highlighted modesty as an essential Communist quality. It contrasted Party leaders' modesty with the "vanity, . . . pride, [and] haughtiness" of capitalist society, and stated that modesty presupposed "respect for labor, people, and the masses, and a faith in the moral and creative strength of the collective."[156] A Komsomol journal in 1940 boasted that the Soviet Union was creating "a generation of new people, for whom lying, deviousness, chauvinism, hypocrisy . . . and other abominations of bourgeois society are foreign."[157] The New Soviet Person, then, was supposed to be free of the selfish egotism and hypocrisy of capitalist society. Devotion to the collective would bring out in people the highest human qualities—selflessness, modesty, honesty, and sincerity.

Antireligiosity was another central value for the New Soviet Person. In contrast to Western societies, where religion was often used to reinforce obedience, sobriety, and other respectable behaviors in the lower classes, the Soviet system vehemently opposed religion and promoted atheism instead. Rationality and science were supposed to triumph over religion and superstition in people's thinking, and the Soviet government conducted a protracted campaign both to prevent organized religious worship and to teach peasants and workers not to believe in God. The tactics employed by Soviet antireligious organizations, such as the League of the Militant Godless, fluctuated between overt repression and educational work to undermine religion and teach atheism. But throughout the 1920s and 1930s, antireligiosity and atheism remained central values of Soviet official culture.[158]

Soviet authorities' belief in the plasticity of human beings was very much in accordance with Marxism, which stressed the environmental determinants of people's thinking and behavior. Yet it also reflected a more general predisposition in prerevolutionary Russian disciplinary culture, which favored nurture over nature as an explanation of human behavior. Russian

РЕЛИГИЯ-ЯД
БЕРЕГИ РЕБЯТ

ШКОЛА

An old woman dragging a girl to church, while the girl tries to go to school. "Religion is poison. Protect your children." (Poster identification number RU/SU 650, Poster Collection, Hoover Institution Archives.)

physicians and social scientists, as well as Soviet officials, maintained that changing the socioeconomic environment of peasants and workers would also change the way they thought and behaved. While Soviet authorities placed great emphasis on education and enlightenment as a means of transformation, they relied on fundamental changes in the economic system to alter people's mentalities.

By abolishing the "remnants of capitalism" at the end of the 1920s, Party leaders created an environment that was supposed to foster socialist values and thinking. Collectivization, for example, altered peasants' relation to the means of production, transforming them from petty landowners to rural laborers with a more proletarian consciousness. According to Semashko, peasants who joined collective farms lived "a collectivist life," which altered their individualist way of thinking.[159] One speaker at the 1935 Second All-Union Congress of Collective Farm Shock Workers hailed the "reeducation of collectivized peasants," millions of whom were learning to place "social interests above personal ones."[160]

At the Seventeenth Party Congress in 1934 Stalin had warned against immediately collectivizing all possessions, stating that for the present collectivization should entail only collective ownership of the means of production. But he heralded this step as a means to educate peasants "in the spirit of collectivism" and help their progress toward the ultimate goal of communism.[161] Collectivization, which involved an enormous amount of coercion directed at the peasant population, was an attempt by Party leaders to accelerate evolutionary time toward communism. Peasants who were collectivized laborers rather than landowners would shed their petty bourgeois mentality and adopt a socialist consciousness. Those peasants who resisted collectivization were labeled kulaks and deported to labor camps, where they would be reeducated through forced labor.

In the cities as well, Party leaders eliminated small-scale capitalism at the end of the 1920s, thereby creating a completely socialist socioeconomic order. In the planned, state-run economy, no market relations or private ownership of the means of production existed to corrupt the consciousness of workers. No longer subject to capitalist exploitation, workers allegedly would enjoy the fruits of their own labor and would take on voluntarily all the tasks of building socialism. The Soviet government sought to reinforce this socialist mind-set by glorifying manual industrial labor. As an allegedly working-class state, the Soviet Union propagandized the virtues of the proletariat and institutionalized this labor ethos by giving industrial workers top priority in the rationing system, in educational opportunities, and in admission to the Party.[162] In the most fundamental sense, then, the creation of a socialist socioeconomic order was supposed to facilitate the creation of the New Person.

Another environmental means to inculcate a collectivist consciousness was to refashion people's living arrangements through city planning, model communities, and communal housing. Unlike the Soviet economy, these approaches were not uniquely socialist, and in fact Western architects such as Le Corbusier and Ernst May actually worked on several Soviet projects.[163] Le Corbusier was a mentor of Soviet Constructivist architects, who believed that the New Person could be created by establishing a completely new environment, with carefully planned cities, buildings, furniture, clothing, and utensils. By restructuring every aspect of everyday life both in the workplace and at home, the Constructivists aspired to transform people's conduct and mind-set. To them a fully rationalized, collectivized, and aestheticized existence would instill in people efficient, collectivist, and virtuous patterns of thought and behavior.[164]

Other Soviet architects and urban planners, such as Leonard Sabsovich and Konstantin Melnikov, also conceived of a planned, structured living environment as a vehicle for social transformation. They believed that well-lit and orderly streets, wide squares and boulevards, and community-oriented housing complexes with communal cafeterias and cultural centers would produce the New Person. For them, as for urban planners around the world, the elimination of chaos, congestion, and other urban problems would imbue people's lives not only with rationality and efficiency but with a harmony and interconnectedness that would overcome the alienation of most modern cities.[165] In practice, Party leaders never committed the resources necessary to enact the vast majority of urban planners' and architects' plans. They instead gave priority to industrial production and allowed economic planners to violate the urban plans that were in place.[166] In theory, however, the ambition to refashion people by restructuring their living environment very much animated the ideas of Soviet architects and urban planners.

On a more micro level, some Soviet thinkers promoted communes and collectives as an environmental means to reorganize people's lives and thinking. Zalkind recommended communal housing, dining halls, and nurseries "to emancipate the family from the petty details of everyday life and direct the freed energy to social activism."[167] Other social commentators also championed communal forms as a mechanism to eradicate individualism and replace it with collectivism.[168] A number of students and workers in the 1920s and 1930s put these ideas into practice by forming communes and other collective living arrangements. These communes and collectives varied in degree of communalism—some simply pooled wages to purchase food collectively while others required that all possessions, including clothing, be held and used in common.[169]

While Soviet authorities placed their faith in the power of the environment to reshape individuals' thinking and behavior, they also relied on cultural and educational means to create the New Person. Culture in the narrow sense of artistic and symbolic expression was supposed to help transform culture in the broader sense of beliefs and values interwoven into everyday life. Stalinist art and literature communicated collectivist, socialist values by depicting factories and collective farms in a positive light. Soviet symbols, such as the hammer and sickle, and new festivals and holidays, such as May Day, advanced socialist values and thought. Both real-life and fictional heroes in Stalinist culture embodied the qualities of the New Person—selfless service and sacrifice for the good of the collective.[170]

Soviet authorities also developed new bases of self-identification, designed to attach peasants' and workers' identities to larger, collective units and to connect them to the building of socialism. The factory history project, for example, called upon workers to describe their past and present roles in the factory. This ritual encouraged them to identify with a laboring collective and to derive their validation and self-actualization from their contribution to the larger tasks of industrial production and building socialism.[171] The Red Army engaged in similar efforts to teach soldiers the history of their unit in order to make them identify collectively with that unit and with the army as a whole.[172]

Education offered the most important means for molding children into the New Person. Zalkind had written in 1924 that children are "an extraordinarily plastic material," and that they yield to educational pressure "much more flexibly than the adult part of the population . . . and constitute the richest soil for the growth of exactly those principles which are necessary to a revolutionary education."[173] Soviet pedagogues hoped to implant a collectivist mentality in children from an early age and to instill in them the qualities of selflessness, modesty, and honesty. A special congress on children's literature in 1936 encouraged writers to act as "engineers of the human soul" by writing books "to help form the consciousness and character of the future citizens of a classless socialist society." One speaker at the congress, V. Bubenkin, called children's literature "a state matter." Noting that Soviet society "is giving birth to a New Person with healthy ideas, tastes, and habits," he concluded that writers should produce literature to imbue children with "new, noble communist qualities."[174]

Organizations such as the Young Pioneers and the Komsomol were also to teach children and youth to think and act in a collectivist manner. D. B. Elkonin, writing in a 1931 primer for pedagogical students, compared the Young Pioneers with the Boy Scouts in Western countries and concluded that whereas Boy Scouts were individualists who cooperated only to get individual merit badges, Young Pioneers had "collectivist aspirations." To build a collective, he argued, the following are required: "an expressed class collectivist attitude; a goal common to all participants . . . [and] mutual help in work; and a socialist attitude to labor."[175] Actually, the Young Pioneers emphasized many of the same values as the Boy Scouts do—hygiene, fitness, discipline, preparedness, and patriotism. But they also differed in important respects, opposing religion and stressing collectivism and help for one's comrades over self-sufficiency.[176] The Komsomol similarly paid a great deal of attention to the lifestyle and values of its members, seeking to foster the collectivist attitudes deemed essential to the New Person.[177]

While education focused primarily on children, classes for adults also sought to inculcate new values and qualities. Most adult education focused on fundamentals such as literacy and job skills, but Soviet educators sought to convey socialist ideals and ways of thinking. In 1923 Commissar of Education Anatolii Lunacharskii told readers that the greatest goal of self-education should not be to acquire specialized skills but rather "to turn oneself into a conscious citizen."[178] At the height of the First Five-Year Plan, when factory training programs struggled to prepare thousands of new recruits for industrial labor, an article in a Party journal reminded factory officials that they must also raise the cultural level of workers and create the New Person, on whom the socialist system could be based.[179] In spite of enormous pressure to meet production goals, Party officials throughout the industrialization drive took time to hold political lectures for workers to promote socialist thinking. Even gulag prison camps were equipped with libraries and other educational facilities to help refashion the prisoners into New People.[180]

Individuals were encouraged to take a hand in transforming themselves. Soviet publications urged people to test their knowledge, to become more cultured, and "to work on yourself."[181] To induce people to reflect on their lives and understand their role in building socialism, Soviet authorities encouraged and even required people to engage in autobiographical writing and speaking. Requiring such autobiographical reflection represented an important subjectivizing practice in that it sought to shape people's sense of self and transform them into fully conscious Soviet subjects. Communist Party members in particular but many other Soviet citizens as well were obliged to answer questions and tell their life stories in ways that made them understand themselves in terms of official ideological categories and the larger revolutionary narrative of building socialism.[182] Autobiographical reflection also encouraged self-improvement by getting people to recognize petty thoughts and selfish habits and to refocus their attention on the heroic, collective task of socialist construction.[183]

While Party leaders clearly stood to gain social support by inducing people to understand their lives in these terms, they also believed that such an understanding was necessary for people's own sense of personal growth and fulfillment. At a 1935 conference of rural Stakhanovites, when one combine driver described his cultural development and growth as a human being, Politburo member Viacheslav Molotov interjected, "It is necessary to grow further."[184] The Stalinist leadership wanted all Soviet citizens to become more educated and cultured, and to attain the highest human qualities by eliminating petty bourgeois instincts and selfishness. The Stalinist system was enormously repressive, imprisoning and even executing those who did not conform, but its power was also productive. For those citizens who chose to embrace socialist values and join the collective, Stalinism offered a means of self-fulfillment—a means of escaping the competition and alienation of the capitalist system, of participating in the world-historical task of building socialism, and of discovering and cultivating the best qualities within themselves.[185]

It is difficult to assess the degree to which Soviet citizens actually accepted the ideal of the New Soviet Person. Diary evidence provides some insight into the thoughts of average citizens. One collective farm member wrote in a 1933 diary entry:

> There is not, there was not, and there will not be in world history a generation more happy than ours. We are the participants in the creation of a new epoch! . . . Had the October Revolution not happened, could I have conceivably understood life in this way, and could I have conceivably exchanged my personal life for the struggle for common goals? No! I would have remained a half-animal, but now I am happy. . . . I am prepared to confront any difficulties and to bear any sacrifice in the name of the great goals of the building of the Communist society.[186]

Another diarist, Galina Shtange, expressed the Soviet collectivist ethos in the following 1938 entry: "Man is a social animal. He can be happy and joyful only in a collective. . . . Only an awareness of his usefulness to society can bring joy and satisfaction." Moreover, Shtange, Stepan Podlubnyi, and other diarists took seriously the injunction to work on oneself, and strove consciously to replace their selfish thoughts and impulses with collectivist, socialist convictions.[187]

One Moscow institute student recorded in his diary a 1934 incident that reflected students' internalization of collectivist values. In a pedagogical class, the teacher stated that each student should have "his own library" and be able to study "independently." But students in the class challenged these ideas, accusing the teacher of fostering private property and individualism instead of collectivism. The teacher responded that "all books are intended for society as a whole, and are therefore social property [obshchestvennaia sobstvennost']," even if they are owned individually. The diarist did not fully accept this answer, however, and wondered why all books should not be held in public libraries where they could be used collectively.[188]

Letters from Soviet citizens to Party leaders also indicate that some people adopted at least the language of collectivism. Such letters are less reliable as evidence of the authors' true beliefs, because they may have involved posturing for Party officials, but they nonetheless reflected a degree of acceptance or at least comprehension of socialist values. The engineer M. Iu. Panov, in a 1940 letter to Mikhail Kalinin, the chair of the Presidium of the Supreme Soviet, described his understanding of culturedness in terms of a person's commitment to the collective and to socialist construction. He wrote, "Culturedness is defined first of all by the degree to which a feeling of collectivism is developed within a person, the degree to which he places the interests of laborers, the Party, the state, and his motherland above his own personal interests."[189] While we cannot know if Panov actually believed what he wrote, his letter reflects a comprehension of Soviet values that went beyond mere mimicry of official slogans. For those who aspired to rise within the Soviet system, such comprehension was crucial.

Other evidence, however, indicates that a great many Soviet citizens rejected the ideal of the New Person and the values associated with it. People continued to identify their own personal interests apart from and in conflict with the interests of the state. In this time of extreme hardship and scarcity, peasants and workers in particular had to struggle to obtain basic food and housing, and proved unwilling to sacrifice for the collective or the state.[190] Other people faulted the Soviet government for not living up to the values it propagated. The engineer Ia. Sorin wrote to Kalinin regarding his statement that people must be taught "absolute honesty." He pointed out that the Soviet system did not allow honesty, and that "if you try to call things by their name and act as your conscience (honesty) dictates, then you are soon fired from your institution."[191] Much of the population also maintained their religious beliefs and continued religious worship, either passively or actively resisting official efforts to promote atheism.[192] In fact, both the 1937 census and more anecdotal evidence such as letters to Red Army soldiers during the Second World War reveal the persistence of religious values and the limitations of official efforts to eliminate religion.[193]

Many peasants and workers did feel a sense of collectivism, but their allegiance was to their own voluntary collectives instead of to the Soviet state. Peasants, for example, showed solidarity in their opposition to collectivization, engaging in collective action to resist Soviet officials and activists.[194] The millions of peasants who migrated to the cities and became urban workers during the 1930s relied heavily on artels—groups of laborers who traveled, worked, and lived together. But these artels often defied Soviet authorities and instead pursued the economic interests of their members, even if such action increased labor turnover and undermined the Soviet industrialization drive.[195] Kaganovich blamed extremely high labor turnover (150 percent in industry nationwide in 1930 and still 90 percent in 1936) on "the mass of new workers entering the ranks of the proletariat who frequently bring petty bourgeois attitudes to enterprises."[196] Many established industrial workers also pursued their own interests and engaged in collective action, including strikes against the Soviet government, during the 1930s.[197]

Some citizens rejected Soviet rule altogether and denounced official policies and values. Vladimir Aref'ev, a Moscow factory worker, in a 1934 letter indicted the Communist Party for "enslaving" and "destroying" the Russian people, and called Party leaders, including Stalin, "enemies of the people and monstrous criminals."[198] Sarah Davies has shown that many Soviet workers and peasants, instead of identifying with the Party and its values, established their identity in opposition to Party officials. Some called officials "the rulers" or "the new bourgeoisie," and accused them of deceiving the people. Others took the Great Purges as an occasion to express their hatred of the elite, rejoicing at Grigorii Zinoviev's and Lev Kamenev's death sentences and declaring that "all the leaders in power and Stalin should be shot."[199] The Soviet government prosecuted countless cases against people for "anti-Soviet agitation" during the 1930s, a reflection of widespread dissent.[200]

Soviet efforts to remake everyday life and create the New Soviet Person, then, met with mixed results. In economic and social terms, Party leaders made considerable progress, albeit at great human cost. In little over a decade they collectivized agriculture, industrialized the country, and transformed an overwhelmingly rural society into a predominantly urban one. In conjunction with nonparty professionals, Soviet officials also promoted education and hygiene, making enormous strides in the elimination of illiteracy and disease. In many ways their efforts paralleled those of government officials and social reformers throughout Europe and around the world who similarly sought to bestow literacy, cleanliness, and sobriety upon the laboring populations of their respective countries. But if Soviet efforts to change people's behavior reflected a more general modern ethos of social intervention, those efforts also included particular Soviet values, such as collectivism and personal sacrifice for the larger goal of building socialism. Soviet authorities sought to reinforce collectivist values through official culture and institutions, such as socialist realist literature, the factory history project, and labor camps. And some Soviet citizens embraced this new system and its values, working on themselves to expunge individualist thinking and attaching their identity to the collective socialist ideal. But as with all totalizing projects, the Soviet system failed to refashion all people in all ways. Most citizens, even as they inhabited a world of Soviet norms and values, continued to hold their own beliefs and pursue their own individual interests.

It would be a mistake, however, to conclude that Party leaders' failure to remake every Soviet citizen into the New Person caused them to abandon socialist ideology. Party leaders saw themselves as a vanguard that derived its mandate not from popular opinion but from the laws of history as expounded in Marxist-Leninist thought. Far from retreating from socialism, they continued their drive to transform the country and every person in it. As Catriona Kelly concludes in her study of Soviet advice literature, the mid-1930s witnessed no Great Retreat from socialist values. Propaganda on proper conduct and behavior throughout the 1930s continued to stress hygienic living, efficiency, and collectivism.[201] The determination of Party leaders to promote and defend Soviet socialism was also apparent in their continued use of state violence—violence that, as we will see, the Stalinist leadership deployed on a massive scale against those it considered opponents, both within the Communist Party and among the population as a whole.

CHAPTER TWO

A Code of Behavior for Communists

Our generation was born with October. It is the first generation
in Russian history which does not have predecessors. We are
children without fathers.
—L. BALABANOV, "Forsaken Values," 1921

Official Soviet culture propagated behavioral norms and values not only for the general population but for the Communist Party elite as well. The cleanliness, sobriety, and order prescribed to ensure workers' and peasants' productive labor were expected to mold Party officials into an efficient bureaucracy. In fact, the values conveyed by the Soviet ideal of culturedness went beyond basic hygiene and order to include politeness, neat dress, and a sense of decorum. Any bureaucratic or managerial elite needs commonly held norms of decorum in order to work together smoothly and to solidify their sense of common identity and purpose. The seemingly insignificant details of a person's speech, dress, and manners actually communicate in a subconscious yet crucial way their legitimacy and reliability.[1] More fundamentally, Party leaders wanted new officials to adopt habits that would guarantee their effectiveness in ruling the country and conducting the country's industrialization drive. The official discourse on culturedness thus served an integrative and disciplinary function for Party leaders who sought to shape new officials into efficient managers and bureaucrats.

While a code of behavior is important for any administrative elite, it was particularly crucial for the Communist Party, which identified itself as a vanguard leading the country toward communism. Party members considered themselves the elect—a self-proclaimed elite whose sense not only of leadership but of history-making required them to demonstrate their worthiness through a high standard of comportment. But determining what precisely those standards should be presented a formidable problem. The October Revolution had seemingly wiped away everything from the past, including all preexisting morals and values. In fact, most Bolsheviks derided the very idea of morality as a bourgeois strategy to control and subordinate the laboring classes under capitalism. When the question of ethics and morality in the Soviet Union was debated in the 1920s, Communist theorists asserted that there existed no absolute moral code for Communists; whatever advanced the cause of the proletarian state was morally correct.

Yet it soon became clear that the Party needed some sort of moral and behavioral guidelines. Communist leaders sought to police the behavior of Party members in order to guarantee that they remained worthy of their vanguard position in society, and to identify any "elements" that had degenerated so that they could be purged from the Party. Simultaneously the Party rank and file sought more concrete ethical rules and repeatedly requested a code of behavior, but no such code was issued. The need to delineate proper behavior grew even stronger in the 1930s with the promotion of hundreds of thousands of new cadres into positions of authority. These "promotees" (*vydvizhentsy*), as they were called, were largely lacking in education or experience, and accordingly were insecure in their new status. They sought not only a moral code but also guidance in how to dress, speak, and act in a manner befitting their elite position.[2] And the Party leadership, which remained suspicious of the rank and file's worthiness and loyalty, also sought to establish behavioral norms for Party members.

The process by which these norms were delineated, however, was complex. Since Party leaders refused to issue a concrete code of behavior throughout this period, a kind of unwritten code emerged instead. Party pronouncements and etiquette manuals provided some guidelines, but Party control commissions actually played a greater role in policing members' behavior and establishing an unwritten code of conduct. As we will see, the work of these commissions was highly politicized, involving the purging of Party members deemed deficient on either political or moral grounds. In fact, Party leaders equated moral infractions with political disloyalty, so that ethical misconduct in a Party member's personal life could be taken as a sign of ideological deviation.

Communist Morality

Long before the Revolution, members of the Russian intelligentsia had challenged the legitimacy of morality and ethics. Some Russian radicals found notions of morality in a deeply hierarchical and unjust society to be nothing more than hypocrisy. The nihilists of the 1860s rejected wholesale traditional culture, religious beliefs, and values. As Dmitrii Pisarev wrote, "What can be smashed should be." He and other nihilists sought to eliminate existing culture and values and replace them with a pragmatic code of behavior based on science and materialism. In their rejection of traditional culture, many nihilists adopted simple dress and coarse manners, as well as more general social rebelliousness and political radicalism.[3]

Russian Marxists, following Marx himself, dismissed morality and ethics as part of the superstructure—a product of the economic organization of social relations. They denied the existence of any absolute ethical standards; morals, they argued, were devised by members of the ruling class to perpetuate their domination and exploitation of the laboring masses. Some Marxist theorists sought to develop Communist ethics in the 1890s, but these efforts were not conclusive.[4] Instead most Marxists, and the Bolsheviks in particular, denounced the falsity of ethics and morality under the tsarist regime as instruments of subjugation and control.

The October Revolution seemed to offer the opportunity to invent an entirely new moral code untainted by the hypocrisy of the old regime's ethical strictures. But the attempt to formulate prescriptive ideals contradicted the ethical relativism of Marxism, which viewed morality as superstructural elements derivative of material conditions.[5] Many Bolshevik leaders, their own ethical sensibilities notwithstanding, therefore remained distrustful of moral codification and continued to espouse a relativist or utilitarian understanding of morality. In his only substantive proclamations on morality, Lenin denounced the idea of a universal morality as "a deception" perpetrated in the interests of landowners and capitalists. Speaking at the Third All-Russian Komsomol Congress in 1920, he went on to declare that for Communists, "morality is subordinate to the interests of the proletariat's class battle." Morality, he said, was "that which promotes the destruction of the old exploitative society and unites all laborers around the proletariat, which is creating a new society of Communists."[6]

During Soviet debates about ethics in the 1920s, many Party theorists repeated Lenin's pronouncements and argued against concrete ethical guidelines. In his 1924 speech "On Party Ethics," Iaroslavskii, the Party's leading authority on morality, stated that a specific moral code could not be issued because Communist morality consisted of whatever advanced the cause of the proletariat.[7] Nadezhda Krupskaia, a leading Party member and Lenin's wife, wrote that "a Communist must always conduct himself in the interests of Communism."[8] In response to a call for "a new morality"

and "concrete ethical rules" under socialism, the Party theorist M. Neznamov declared that such rules did not exist and that even to search for
them would be harmful.[9]

Other Party officials, however, worried that some form of moral and ethical guidelines were needed. During the Civil War and the 1920s, many
Party and Komsomol members adopted a crude manner and dissolute
lifestyle. Partly in rebellion against the moral strictures of the old regime
and partly under the influence of a cult of toughness spawned in wartime,
Communists took as their prototype the crass commissar in a leather jacket
who swore, spat, drank heavily, and engaged in casual sex. Komsomol
members in particular became known for their dissolute ways and sexual
frivolity.[10] Some Party leaders feared that nihilistic tendencies had gone
too far, and that energies vital to the construction of socialism were being
dissipated in immoral behavior. For other Party leaders the disorder and
debauchery they witnessed simply did not correspond to their aesthetic vision of a perfectly ordered, rational, and harmonious life under socialism.

Trotsky was among those who advocated greater order and responsibility in everyday life. In *Problems of Everyday Life,* published in 1923, he put
forth guidelines for proper behavior, civility, and cultured speech.[11] Another Party moralist, L. Balabanov, decried the "sexual dissoluteness"
among youth and wrote that "it is necessary to construct consciously a new
lifestyle and a new morality."[12] Bukharin, while he was against the term
"Communist morality," did see a need for "rules of behavior" for Komsomol youth in particular. In addressing the Fifth Komsomol Congress in
1922 he argued that while smoking and drinking had been a legitimate
means to flout discipline under the old regime, after the Revolution it was
necessary to avoid tobacco, alcohol, and sexual dissoluteness as harmful to
the body and detrimental to the building of socialism.[13] Even Iaroslavskii,
despite his resistance to the idea of a moral code, wrote extensively about
Communist morality and condemned excessive or corrupt behavior among
Party members.[14]

Despite the profligacy of some Party and Komsomol members, many
rank-and-file members also favored a strict moral code. Some simply
wanted to have a clear set of guidelines for their own behavior. One Komsomol cell in 1926, for example, resolved that the Komsomol "should have
its own class morality, that is, well-known rules."[15] Other Party members
wanted to rein in excess and debauchery because it could discredit the
Party as a whole. They favored the ascetic model of revolutionary life put
forward by Nikolai Chernyshevsky in his classic novel *What Is to Be Done?*
and they believed that a specific code of behavior should be issued to enforce it.[16] Purification of Party members' personal lives represented a

means to guard against NEP-era degeneration and to prepare the Party for a revolutionary advance.[17]

While Party leaders refused to issue a specific moral code, they did create mechanisms to police the behavior of members. They held that the Party, as the vanguard of socialist construction, needed to maintain the highest standards of ideological and ethical purity. In 1920 they created a hierarchy of control commissions, overseen by the Central Control Commission, to combat bureaucratism, abuse of authority, and "breaches of Communist ethics" among its members. At the time, Zinoviev called the Central Control Commission "the court of Communist honor."[18] Delegates to the Tenth Party Congress in 1921 passed a resolution that said control commissions were to "strengthen the unity and authority of the Party" by battling "bureaucratism, careerism, abuse by Party members of their positions, [and] violations of comradely relations within the Party."[19]

The Eleventh Party Congress in 1922 both strengthened the power of the Central Control Commission and provided a more specific list of infractions for it to guard against. It resolved that control commissions must purge "all those who disgrace the Party with their behaviors and actions," including "alien, harmful, and degenerate elements" and those who adopt an "uncommunist way of life" through "private trade, drunkenness, or moral dissoluteness."[20] The impetus for this increased emphasis on ethics was Party leaders' fears that with the introduction of the New Economic Policy, small-scale capitalism and the resulting petty bourgeois milieu would corrupt the Party rank and file. Aaron Sol'ts, the chair of the Central Control Commission, warned in his report at the Eleventh Party Congress that it was time for the Party to discuss ethics and "pay attention to those deficiencies, those elements of degeneration" within the Party. The New Economic Policy, he pointed out, raised the danger that the Party's weak "elements" would fall into petty bourgeois ways.[21]

By the mid-1920s, the Party control commissions had firmly established the place of ethics and morality within Party discussions and practices. While the Central Control Commission still declined to issue a moral code or specific rules of Party behavior, it declared in its 1924 proclamation "On Party Ethics" that it would "decisively fight against flagrant repudiations of proletarian class morality." It called for more uniform enforcement of moral behavior and specified the permissible limits of Party members' property ownership in this "transitional period."[22] Sol'ts provided an even more detailed discussion of ethical and unethical behavior in 1925. In addition to forbidding drunkenness, personal enrichment, and observance of religious rituals, he insisted that Party members do nothing to distance themselves from the working class they represented. Under capitalism, he explained, dress and manners were intended to flaunt success and arouse envy. While he admonished Communists to dress well, not in rags, he declared that jewelry aroused "aesthetic indignation" and that Party members' appearance should not indicate a complete break with manual labor.[23]

Sol'ts's admonition to dress well but not to distinguish oneself from the working masses reflected a tension within the Party that would persist into the 1930s. On the one hand, it was important for Communists to dress and conduct themselves in a manner that befitted and projected the authority they were to have in society. On the other hand, some Party members sought not only to legitimate their status but to enrich themselves and acquire the material symbols of success. Party leaders such as Sol'ts tried to establish a fine line between respectable and lavish behavior. They found it necessary to fight against nihilistic and iconoclastic tendencies that denied the need for morality, manners, and neatness altogether. At the same time they sought to prevent materialism and embourgeoisement among Party officials.

The process of defining Communist ethics and morality became even more urgent during the 1930s as hundreds of thousands of new Party members were promoted into positions of authority. In the continuing absence of a written code of behavior, Iaroslavskii began in 1935 to speak of "our unwritten Communist morality," and he argued that it was impossible to separate morality from the political tasks of the Party. Party members' personal lives, he added, should be subject to scrutiny both to prevent any discrediting of the Party and to ensure that they served as "a model for the nonparty masses."[24] And indeed, Party members' personal lives did come under investigation, often with deadly consequences, during the Great Purges of the late 1930s. As we will see, the process of purging ultimately played as important a role in defining Party morality as did theoretical debates on the topic. But before turning to the purges, we must examine dynamics within the Party, including the large-scale promotion of new Party members and their struggles to secure their status through respectable behavior.

Culture for the New Elite

In a 1934 report, S. Kotliar, the head of the union of government officials, declared, "We have in our apparatuses thousands and tens of thousands of new people from the working class . . . , who are already contributing to the new system of administration."[25] Indeed, it was true that tens if not hundreds of thousands of workers had been recruited into the Communist Party and promoted into positions of authority within the Soviet bureaucracy. Between 1927 and 1932 the number of Party members increased from 1.1 million to 3.6 million.[26] The great majority of new recruits were from the working class, as the overall percentage of Party members of working-class origin grew in the same period from 55 percent to 65 percent.[27] Most of these new Party members also received either educational opportunities or promotions within their factories or within the Soviet bureaucracy. Some 1.5 million workers moved out of manual labor and into administrative positions or full-time study in this period.[28]

The education and promotion of workers into positions of authority within industrial management and the Soviet bureaucracy was a conscious policy of the Party leadership, championed by Stalin himself. Stalin had never trusted the old technical intelligentsia, the so-called bourgeois specialists, and he repeatedly stressed the importance of training new specialists from the ranks of the working class. In his 1931 "New Conditions" speech he had called upon workers to form a new technical intelligentsia, capable of representing "the interests of the working class."[29] At the same time that the Party promoted manual workers into managerial and bureaucratic positions, it also purged "bourgeois specialists" and, during the Great Purges, older Party members. As Sheila Fitzpatrick has concluded, the Stalinist leadership's policy of educating and promoting workers, combined with purges of older cadres, resulted in the creation of a new elite.[30]

This new elite, lacking experience and hastily trained, was not well prepared for the new status and responsibilities thrust upon it. A 1936 Party report noted that half of the factory directors in one branch of industry had only the lowest level of education and that 70 percent of them had been in their positions no more than two years.[31] One promotee, in an ungrammatical letter to the Industrial Department of the Party's Central Committee, described the discomfort he felt at being appointed to a deputy directorship just two years after he graduated from a technical institute.[32] A newly appointed shop head at a large Leningrad factory described how being thrown into a position of such responsibility with so little preparation "provoked doubt as to whether [he] could cope with the work."[33] Another newly promoted industrial manager requested both "moral help" and "organizational directions" to assist him in his new responsibilities.[34] The newly promoted elite clearly needed guidance in the workplace.

As one might expect, this new elite needed guidance in their conduct outside of work as well. Having risen so quickly in the social hierarchy, and coming from working-class origins, the new managers and bureaucrats had little knowledge of the type of dress, speech, or behavior that would be expected of them in their privileged positions. And the insecurity they felt, given their inexperience and low levels of education, only heightened their desire to conduct themselves in a way that would legitimate their new status. One new official assigned an important position in the industrial bureaucracy recalled in his memoirs how "dazed" he felt when called to Moscow, put up at a fancy hotel, chauffeured about town in a foreign car, and handed a thousand rubles as spending money after his meeting with the commissar of heavy industry, Sergo Ordzhonikidze. Life among the elite in Moscow was so far from his humble working-class life in Ukraine that it was difficult to adjust to the new environment.[35]

In the face of the new officials' uncertainty about proper conduct and decorum, the Party leadership stepped in to teach administrative and cultural norms—norms that corresponded to its own managerial needs and notions of propriety. A 1934 Party conference resolved that special seminars should be held to teach new Party and Komsomol officials how to act.[36] In 1938, after further promotion of young officials in the wake of the Great Purges, the Industrial Department of the Party's Central Committee held a special conference on the challenges facing newly appointed industrial managers. It concluded that they should receive assistance and support from higher bureaucrats in every aspect of their jobs.[37] At the same time that Soviet leaders sought to provide technical and administrative help, they also offered new officials guidance in how to conduct themselves through cultural education, etiquette pamphlets, excursions to museums, and outings to the theater.[38]

Already in the 1920s the Soviet government had published conduct guides that instructed new managers and bureaucrats how to perform their jobs and live in an efficient and cultured manner.[39] A 1929 pamphlet titled *How to Become Cultured* prescribed both professional and personal habits for Party and government officials. The pamphlet stressed organization, neatness, and efficiency.

> A cultured person is first of all an orderly person. Contemporary technical culture requires even a certain "passion for order." A professional official not only orders the forces of nature, he himself is ordered. . . . He himself strives to work optimally, with maximum productivity.[40]

From a pragmatic standpoint, the dictate to manage one's behavior consciously in order to maximize productivity served the Party leadership's interest in forging an efficient bureaucracy. The pamphlet went on to criticize "unproductive," "unhygienic," and "uneconomical" ways as a "squandering of one's own and social forces."[41] Throughout the 1930s, numerous government reports condemned inefficiencies and violations of bureaucratic procedure. A report on the local court system in Archangel noted irregularities and improper procedures, and concluded that the courts were operating in an "uncultured" way.[42] An order of the Main Military Procuracy announced that its bureaucracy needed to be rationalized and systematized through the "strengthening of the political-moral condition" of its officials.[43] And in 1934 the Commissariat of Justice denounced the Komsomol's "Light Cavalry," which previously had been applauded for raiding government offices to uncover bureaucratism, but which now was chided for "hooligan actions" and told not to disrupt normal bureaucratic functioning.[44]

The effort to forge an efficient bureaucratic machine focused not only on the workplace but also on new officials' personal lives. The author of *How to Become Cultured* admonished managers and bureaucrats to develop a daily routine by allocating a certain number of minutes to eat breakfast, read the newspaper, work, go to the movies, and sleep.[45] Rationalization and ordering of all aspects of life, one of Party leaders' larger goals, was seen as particularly important for the efficiency of Party and government officials. A conference on collective farm administration sharply criticized the lack of daily routine among some Party officials, who were said to wake at ten o'clock in the morning, waste time breakfasting, sit around chatting with one another, and end their workday without accomplishing anything.[46] To order one's personal life efficiently was considered the best guarantee that such efficiency would be carried into the workplace.

Reading received special emphasis as a crucial leisure activity for Party members. Members were expected to read widely, and they had to respond to a questionnaire indicating which journals and newspapers they subscribed to and what political books and novels they read. The questionnaire also asked how they read—whether they took notes, whether they studied texts either alone or in reading circles, and how much time they devoted to self-education through reading. If their answers indicated a lack of culture, Party members could be categorized as "politically illiterate" and assigned to do additional reading.[47] A 1936 pamphlet titled *What to Read to Become Cultured* recommended not only the works of Lenin and Stalin but also books on science, economics, agriculture, and atheism, as well as classic Russian novels.[48] The same year the head of the Komsomol, Aleksandr Kosarev, declared that young Communists should read the works of Pushkin, Gorky, Shakespeare, Balzac, and Goethe, among others.[49] With the publication of a new history of the Communist Party (the

Maxim Gorky and workers gather books for a literacy campaign, 1932. "'Without a book, there is no knowledge. Without knowledge, there is no communism' (Lenin). We will implement the Komsomol Central Committee's decision and M. Gorky's call to gather books. We will gather and send millions of books to the countryside!" (Poster identification number RU/SU 1752, Poster Collection, Hoover Institution Archives.)

Short Course), this volume too became required reading for Party and Komsomol members. A Central Committee decree in fact prescribed individual reading of the *Short Course* as the correct method of mastering Marxism-Leninism and of attaining a high level of political consciousness.[50]

On a more practical level, Party campaigns to educate officials focused on health and hygiene in Party members' daily lives. The pamphlet *How to Become Cultured* stressed the importance of health for Party bureaucrats, asserting that "a cultured person is first of all a healthy person." It encouraged bodily and domestic hygiene as a means to ensure health. It also pointed out the importance of sports to promote health and "strong nerves," and concluded that only healthy people can become "useful cultured officials."[51] The pamphlet furthermore prescribed the golden mean—all things in moderation—and recommended the sublimation of sexual energy in problem solving and practical activity.[52] In a similar vein, Ordzhonikidze told factory managers, "The white collar and the clean shirt are necessary work tools for the fulfillment of production plans and the quality of products."[53]

The code of cultured behavior for officials also included politeness and decorum. An article in a journal for Party bureaucrats explained that each Communist "is obliged to demonstrate through his own behavior and external appearance an example of cultured work. . . . He must in the most merciless way eliminate rudeness. . . . Polite and attentive relations with visitors—this is the first obligation of each Communist."[54] Another article, "The Manners of Bureaucrats," deplored the discovery that despite "cultural-political growth," many bureaucrats related to people in a "heartless, imprecise manner."[55] One Party report sharply criticized a raikom secretary whose "rudeness and cries" had undermined his political authority and discredited all local Party officials.[56] Another report implored officials not to "address people rudely," because such behavior reflected the "unculturedness" and "immodesty of Party members."[57]

In view of the brutal policies that Party members carried out, it seems ironic that the Party placed such emphasis on politeness. During collectivization and dekulakization Party officials dispossessed and deported millions of peasants. In subsequent grain requisitions they took food from starving peasants and left millions to die. As part of the industrialization drive they oversaw the extensive use of forced labor in extremely harsh conditions. Throughout the 1930s officials were repeatedly instructed to use coercion and violence, so the fact that the Party reprimanded them for rudeness seems odd. Yet it was precisely the emphasis on propriety and decorum that helped legitimate these extreme coercive acts. In the same way that European colonialists maintained spotless uniforms and careful protocol while engaging in the brutal subjugation and exploitation of indigenous peoples, Party officials were urged to carry out murderous policies in a civil and morally upright manner.

Civility and protocol received special emphasis in the Soviet legal system. Just as the Great Purges were beginning, the Commissariat of Justice published an article titled "On Culturedness in the Operation of Courts," stressing the importance of maintaining clean, well-furnished, and orderly courtrooms. Magistrates should "judge in a cultured way" by starting on time, deciding cases promptly, and avoiding rudeness in dealing with defendants.[58] On the surface it seems strange that courts involved in the imprisonment and execution of millions of innocent people would concern themselves with the cleanliness of the courtroom and politeness toward prisoners, but again propriety and decorum served to legitimate these extremely immoral and unjust acts in the minds of observers and of officials themselves.

The Party as the Elect

The discourse on culturedness aimed at more than molding efficient and polite bureaucrats; it also strove to shape Party members into a vanguard for the building of socialism. The Party was supposed to be made up of an elect group of the most conscious, most capable, and most exemplary people in society. Stalin declared, "We Communists are people of a special brand. We are made of a special material. We are those who constitute the army of the great proletarian strategist, the army of Comrade Lenin. There is nothing higher than the honor of belonging to this army."[59] To be part of this vanguard, one had to live up to very high standards in all realms of life. It was for this reason that, through Party admissions, propaganda, and purging, a strict code of behavior for Communists was developed.

The admission process for Party members was long and rigorous. It required a strong work or military record, three personal recommendations from current Party members, knowledge of Party history and ideology, and satisfactory responses to oral and written questions (made more exacting after 1933) on one's family and personal life.[60] Party members were admonished to take extremely seriously the recommendation of a person for membership, and to do so "in the spirit of Bolshevik Party allegiance and discipline."[61] Those admitted were initially only candidate members of the Party, until they had proved their worthiness and could ascend to become full members.[62] Even then Party members were subject to constant scrutiny through a range of Party practices—verification campaigns, comrade trials, and self-criticism—to ensure their loyalty and worthiness.[63]

One had to merit Party membership through exemplary behavior in private as well as public life. As early as the 1920s, the Party cell had the responsibility to oversee the morality of its members' personal lives. The cell would question members about their families and categorize them according to the degree to which they had reeducated family members on political and religious questions.[64] Party cells in the 1920s also scrutinized members' relationships with their spouses and issued reprimands for "uncomradely relations and rudeness" in private life.[65] Indeed, the Party never distinguished between public and private life. Party leaders attacked the very notion that private life could be separated from the public realm. Speaking at the Sixth Komsomol Congress in 1924, Krupskaia argued that "personal life cannot be separated from social concerns. . . . A division between private life and public life sooner or later leads to the betrayal of communism."[66] As Sol'ts was to say in 1932, Communists "are not simply a political party—we are the avant-garde that is building socialist society and our behavior . . . is part of the construction of a new way of life." It was the task of the Central Control Commission to ensure that the behavior of Party members was "worthy of the title they hold."[67] The absence of a private sphere meant that no aspect of Party members' behavior was off limits, and with the increasingly strict moral norms of the 1930s, more and more Party members were criticized or purged for behavior in their personal lives.

In the 1920s Party control commissions were already reprimanding large numbers of Party officials—particularly those newly promoted from the ranks of the working class or peasantry. Many of these promotees registered their surprise at being called before the commissions for personal habits and pastimes they did not realize were inappropriate or under scrutiny.[68] During the 1930s, even stricter moral norms were imposed. Iaroslavskii denounced drinking as a violation of "the avant-garde, advanced, leading role of the Communist."[69] Drinking seemed to reflect a lack of control or self-discipline, and because Party members were supposed to maintain the highest standards of behavior and discipline even during their leisure time, it was deemed unacceptable. Throughout the 1930s, Party members' drinking was chastised as "moral degeneration" and "anti-Party behavior."[70] As we will see, by the time of the Great Purges the charges of "systematic drunkenness" and "moral degeneration" were frequently invoked against purge victims.

The Party also focused on the personal qualities of members, and constantly urged them to work on themselves to transform and improve those qualities. The pamphlet *How to Become Cultured* stressed the importance of selflessness, benevolence, and orderliness for Party officials. The achievement of such a character "requires intricate work on oneself: the mastery of one's nature, the conscious management of one's behavior."[71] Another pamphlet, published in 1933, emphasized modesty, calling it "something of great value for a Communist official," and quoting Stalin as saying that "not conceit but modesty decorates a Bolshevik." The pamphlet also encouraged Party members to recognize their weaknesses and to work constantly to improve themselves.[72] Indeed, Party members were supposed to work on themselves incessantly in all aspects of their lives, so that they would be not only ideologically correct Party personnel but also conscientious citizens, exemplary workers, good family members, and honest and discreet people.[73]

As we have seen, the idea of working on oneself was deemed important for all Soviet citizens, but it was particularly emphasized for Communist Party members. The fashioning of worthy Party members required introspection and self-work to realize individual transformation and the creation of the New Soviet Person. The Party's concept of culturedness was similar to the German concept of *Bildung* in that it urged members to examine their behavior and improve themselves. But the ultimate Communist goal went beyond this idea to include a transformation of human nature: the New Person would possess all the highest human qualities and hold a strong collectivist spirit, which would rise above narrow individual desires and interests.

From the time of the Revolution, Party leaders and theorists, as well as many nonparty professionals, had believed in the plasticity of humankind and the great transformative power of education and enlightenment work. In the mid-1930s, partly because of the promotion of thousands of new officials, the Party increased its emphasis on transforming individuals. Stalin signaled this greater emphasis with his 1935 speech "Cadres Decide Everything." His objectives were partly economic; he argued that cadres' expertise and initiative were crucial to further industrial progress. But Stalin also used the speech to focus the Party's attention on individuals. Over the next three years the Party passed six resolutions stressing a meticulous "individual approach" to the recruitment and purging of Party members.[74] The "Cadres Decide Everything" speech triggered a variety of efforts to scrutinize and improve official personnel (and it also prompted the Stakhanovite movement, aimed at manual workers). The Soviet government's Central Executive Committee sent out a directive shortly after Stalin's speech calling for increased attention to judicial cadres, with emphasis on ensuring their responsible behavior and disciplined character.[75] Commissar of Justice Nikolai Krylenko subsequently announced that every judge needed a high level of "political development" and "moral quality." The report quoting Krylenko concluded that the "primary deficiency among judicial cadres" was "a lack of culturedness," noting the low levels of education among judges.[76]

Local Party organizations also responded vigorously to Stalin's speech. One Party cell in Smolensk oblast resolved that "people are the principal element for edification. . . . We must mobilize all our efforts to form the sort of person who will not stop working."[77] The secretary of the Gorky Party committee, Ivan Pindiur, wrote that "the political and cultural level" of Party officials should be raised. He announced the creation of new seminars for officials on Russian language and literature, asserting that "in the matter of Party members' cultural growth, literature plays a significant role." He also praised collective outings for Party members to the theater and cinema.[78] Another official in Gorky wrote that local Party leaders needed to know each individual member. He recommended "personal, close communication" between the Party secretary and each member, and he stressed the importance of "uncovering their many personal qualities," because these qualities had importance for the entire Party.[79]

The reference to "uncovering" and the insistence that members' personal lives and qualities were the domain of the Party had ominous meaning on the eve of the Great Purges, when Party members' character and lifestyle came under even greater scrutiny. A lead article in *Pravda* in February 1937 said that the Party demanded "honesty and truth" from each Communist, and that members were entitled to hide nothing from the Party or the working masses. It condemned double dealing, hypocrisy, and fraud, and declared that Party members who did lie or deceive people were Trotskyists, Zinovievists, and other "anti-Soviet swine."[80] In this case, then, the definition of proper behavior and personal qualities for Party members became intertwined with Party purges. As the Stalinist leadership sought to root out enemies and potential oppositionists, it used principles of honesty and transparency to purge Party members.

Communists' code of behavior therefore developed in a particular social and political context. The newly promoted elite were insecure in their status and ready to embrace the Party leaders' dictates in a literal and dogmatic way. While Communists, as the vanguard of socialist construction, were expected to have an array of outstanding qualities, the particular qualities emphasized by the Stalinist leadership also served specific political purposes: not only the formation of an efficient bureaucracy but the elimination of all potential opponents within the Party elite. To pursue this agenda, Party leaders elevated modesty to an essential Communist quality during the Great Purges. As we shall see, the proper qualities and behaviors of Communists were defined as part of overall political processes and in a context of purging and political terror.

Communist Party Purges

The Great Purges were an extremely complex and politically motivated phenomenon, orchestrated by the Stalinist leadership to eliminate enemies and potential opposition within the Party and the country as a whole.[81] I will not discuss here the genesis of the Great Purges or all aspects of their unfolding. Instead I will limit my analysis to the ways in which alleged moral failings were used to purge Party members and the extent to which these uses of a moral discourse actually defined and solidified definitions of Communist morality. The Party's discourse on morality and purification was intended to justify the purges in the eyes of Party members. To explore such justification is not to exonerate Stalin for the mass murders he perpetrated. It does, however, help explain why fellow Party leaders and many of the rank and file went along with Stalin's bloody drive to eliminate any opposition or deviation within the Party.

Purging was a Party practice long before the mass arrests and executions of the late 1930s. The perceived need for purging stemmed in part from the nature of the Soviet project as a utopian enterprise. To progress from an imperfect reality to a perfect world, the leadership had to guard against the transmission of present imperfections to the future. Any sort of historical link brought with it the danger of contaminating the utopia with impurities of the past and present. To prevent such contamination required not only constant work to transform individuals and society but constant vigilance and purging to eliminate impurities and imperfections.[82] In less prosaic terms, Communist Party leaders remained constantly wary of the danger posed by past class aliens and oppositionists who may have wormed their way into the Party. Indeed, the entire mind-set of Party leaders and lower-level officials was geared to imagine themselves surrounded by enemies and conspiracies.[83] Rooting out enemies and purifying the Party required periodic membership purges.

Purges were considered necessary to maintain the Party's moral as well as ideological purity. As early as 1921 the Party leadership had the secret police monitor local Communists' behavior—a fact that in itself reflected the Party leaders' doubts about their lower ranks. Secret police reports revealed widespread drunkenness, harassment of women, bribery, and embezzlement among local Party officials.[84] Such failings seemed to confirm the need to purify the Party. In the 1920s purges often focused on the moral failings of Party members and cited immoral behavior as the reason for exclusion from the Party. As we have seen, Party control commissions had the specific function of monitoring members' behavior, and these commissions expelled members who did not live up to their position as society's vanguard. While Party members could be expelled at any time, purging in the 1920s came in three distinct waves.

The first purge, in 1921, focused on the expulsion of former tsarist officials and opposition party members, as well as of "kulak elements" and persons of bourgeois origin. From 1924 to 1926, when Party leaders recruited a large number of workers into the Party, they also purged "corrupted elements."[85] In particular, the Central Control Commission and regional Party control commissions excluded members for drunkenness, squabbling, careerism, participation in religious rituals, and violations of Party discipline and Party ethics. Indeed, a 1925 Central Control Commission report indicated that drunkenness, violations of Party discipline, and violations of Party ethics were the three most common reasons for expulsion.[86]

A third round of purging, during 1929–30, was partly political, as it aimed to exclude "right oppositionists," persons who opposed Stalinist collectivization and rapid industrialization. It also, however, expelled members for drunkenness, extramarital affairs, and other unspecified moral abuses, as well as for alien class background.[87] At the Sixteenth Party Congress in 1930, Iaroslavskii declared that of those expelled, 22 percent were purged for "defects in personal life and conduct."[88] In all, 116,000 members were expelled during this purge, the majority of them peasants, in contrast to the Great Purges, which focused much more on mid-level and high-ranking Party officials.[89]

In the 1930s another series of Party purges culminated in the Great Purges of 1936–38. In January 1933 the Party Central Committee and Central Control Commission resolved to suspend recruitment into the Party and to carry out a large-scale purge of its membership—a purge that led to the expulsion of 800,000 members in 1933 and 340,000 more in 1934.[90] The purge was to target "class alien elements," "double dealers," violators of Party discipline, degenerates with bourgeois origins, careerists, and "moral degenerates."[91] Some of those purged for moral degeneration had specific charges of "drunkenness," "sexual debauchery," or "swindling" leveled against them, while others were purged for a "degenerate lifestyle" or "behavior that discredits the Party."[92] In March 1933 Iaroslavskii explained the need for the purge in moral terms, pointing out that there were many "swindlers" in the Party who should be excluded. Noting that the Party should have only members who served as examples to others, he stated that "this Party purge should raise the authority of Party members to the highest degree." The following year Iaroslavskii again justified the purge by arguing that "we cannot tolerate a situation where one Communist or another lessens Bolshevik dignity with his behavior, . . . with his drunkenness, with his mercenary use of his position."[93]

After the assassination of Sergei Kirov, the Leningrad Party boss, in December 1934, the character of Party purging became much more highly politicized. Earlier that year, at the Seventeenth Party Congress, Stalin had warned that despite the attainment of socialism, Party members should not let down their guard; on the contrary, he urged them to sharpen their vigilance. Kirov's assassination seemed to prove Stalin correct. In May 1935 the Central Committee called for the verification of all Party documents, saying that inadequate security had allowed "enemies" to infiltrate the Party. The checking of membership documents also entailed purging, as 9 percent of members checked in 1935 were expelled from the Party.[94] Nikolai Ezhov, the future head of the secret police, announced at a September 1935 conference on the verification of Party documents that the

Party should focus on rooting out Trotskyists, other former oppositionists, former members of other political parties, and class alien elements who had wormed their way into the Party. However, he also held up as an example of the type of member that needed to be purged a collective farm director whom he accused of drinking, playing cards, and embezzling money. Thus, while he focused on political enemies, he also included immoral and corrupt Party members among those who should be purged.[95]

Andrei Zhdanov, a Politburo member, sounded a similar theme in December 1935, when he called the verification of documents a means to purge "swindlers, adventurers, and spies" and to "restore order in our Party home." He added that all Party members should keep their documents in order, and that they should also "raise the productivity of their labor and raise their cultural level."[96] The results of the verification of documents also show this purge as serving a dual function of eliminating both those suspect on political grounds and those who seemed morally corrupt or unworthy of Party membership. Members purged included those accused of being Trotskyists, former Mensheviks or Socialist Revolutionaries, and kulaks, as well as swindlers, violators of Party discipline, and those deemed morally degenerate.[97]

While the 1935 verification of Party documents placed political and moral deviation side by side, a case the same year explicitly linked the two, equating moral degeneration with political degeneration and treason. At a Central Committee plenum in June 1935, Avel Enukidze, the head of the Soviet Central Executive Committee that was responsible for security at the Kremlin, was denounced and expelled from the Party. This denunciation came in the wake of the Kremlin affair, when dozens of Kremlin employees were arrested for conspiring to commit "terrorist acts" against the government. In his speech denouncing Enukidze at the plenum, Ezhov began by accusing Trotsky, Zinoviev, and Kamenev of organizing Kirov's assassination, and then went on to call Enukidze a "corrupt and self-complacent Communist" whose lack of vigilance made him an involuntary accomplice to similar terrorist conspiracies being organized within the Kremlin. Enukidze tried in vain to defend himself against charges of personal corruption, including "cohabitation with certain women," and was strongly condemned for his immoral behavior as well as for his lack of vigilance.[98]

When the Politburo confirmed Enukidze's dismissal from his post, it cited "political and lifestyle degeneration" as the reason.[99] Nikita Khrushchev, at that time head of the Moscow Party organization, explained Enukidze's disgrace to a Moscow Party plenum by saying that Enukidze had to have been "politically and morally corrupted" not to see the infiltration of enemies into the Kremlin.[100] The Enukidze case thus linked moral with political degeneration. Such a linkage was not new in Party thinking. Throughout the 1920s and 1930s, Party leaders had associated improper conduct in one's personal life with political unreliability and deviation. During NEP, moral degeneration was often seen as petty bourgeois, revealing the presence or influence of class enemies. Once dekulakization and the end of NEP eliminated overt class enemies, a Party member's moral and political deviance signaled something even more ominous— the presence or influence of "enemies of the people." This was a new type of enemy—not simply a person corrupted by NEP, who might be reformed, but an inveterate opponent of socialism, who had to be eliminated altogether. It was the search for "enemies of the people" within the Party that characterized the Great Purges.

The Great Purges of 1936–38 were distinct not only in their sweeping scope but in that those purged from the Party during this period were subsequently arrested and either executed or sent to a prison camp for alleged treason. At the February–March 1937 plenum of the Central Committee, Stalin provided a justification for the Great Purges: the resistance of defeated enemies was increasing as the final victory of socialism drew near. He chided Party members who had become complacent in the glow of Soviet economic successes. Pointing to the threat of capitalist encirclement, Stalin argued that the struggle against internal and external enemies must be continued and intensified. Stalin's argument was apparently persuasive to a crucial segment of the Party leadership and the secret police, who carried out the Great Purges. For them the rising threat from Germany and Japan seemed to confirm the presence of enemies bent on destroying socialism and the need to eliminate any enemies within the Party itself.[101]

For our purposes here, the Great Purges were significant for their continued linkage of moral degeneration with political treason. While these purges were much more explicitly political, charging the majority of those expelled from the Party with being "enemies of the people," the purge process also focused on the lifestyle and morality of those accused.[102] Articles published at the time stated that "lifestyle degeneration, in the final analysis, inevitably leads to political degeneration," and that "moral purity of officials is a reliable guarantee against political degeneration."[103] In case after case of Party officials who were purged, charges of immorality were leveled alongside Trotskyism and sabotage, and in many instances immoral conduct was shown to be the first indication of political treason. One Party official in Voronezh was first accused of "moral and lifestyle degeneration," "rudeness," "bureaucratism," and sexual misconduct, and only then was he uncovered as a Trotskyist. Local Party leaders were reprimanded for failing to probe his political reliability immediately once they knew of his immoral behavior. In another case, officials who squandered state money on drunken banquets were also found to be accepting bribes and embezzling state funds for Trotskyist work.[104]

At first glance, it appears gratuitous that Party members accused of Trotskyism, spying, and wrecking were also indicted for such things as drunkenness and sexual misconduct. Political treason would seem to be cause enough to purge and arrest a Party member. But because Party leaders linked moral and political degeneration in official discourse, it became part of the logic of the purges to find moral failings as well as political treachery among those who were purged. Charges of moral degeneration, drunkenness, illicit sexual affairs, and corruption served to discredit and thus further undermine Party members accused of political treason. But even more than discrediting the accused, these charges confirmed the Party line on the matter—Communists who were unworthy of their vanguard role, as shown by their immoral behavior, were also those who succumbed to political degeneration and had to be eliminated from the Party and from society.

Moral behavior was thus imbued with political meaning, and for those arrested and executed during the Great Purges, it had deadly consequences as well. Because of the enormous importance of morality, definitions of proper and moral behavior became even more rigid during the Great Purges. Indeed, while standards had already been established through debates on Party ethics in the 1920s and early 1930s, the moral relativist strains of earlier thought (Communist morality is whatever advances the interests of the proletarian state) gave way to very strict and dogmatic definitions of propriety. And as one can imagine, when Party members' lives came to depend in part on their conformity to moral standards, they sought to conform, at least outwardly, as closely as possible to the unwritten moral code.

Drunkenness was the most common charge leveled at those accused of moral degeneracy. Accusing a Party official of drunkenness in order to discredit him had been a long-standing tactic in the Party.[105] During the 1920s, however, the act of drinking in itself was not so clearly identified as a misdeed. Some Party members argued that drinking with other Communists was no cause for condemnation, and that it was only Party members who drank with NEPmen and kulaks who should be denounced.[106] By the late 1930s, however, charges of drinking in any setting constituted immoral behavior and grounds for purging. Countless Party officials were purged for "systematic drunkenness," a charge that was sometimes leveled in connection with Trotskyism and other crimes, but that also served in itself as evidence of "degeneration" and as a basis for purging.[107] Some officials' drinking was said to have been the first sign of the degeneration that led them to political mistakes.[108] For other officials, drinking was highlighted as part of a more general pattern of moral and political misconduct.[109]

Immoral sexual behavior was another charge made against victims during the Great Purges. A Party official in Voronezh was accused of having trysts with young women and was expelled from the Party and subsequently arrested.[110] An official in Kazakhstan, allegedly known to be "a drunkard," was purged because of "his sexual depravity," while a collective farm chair in Kursk was purged for having an extramarital affair.[111] A Party official in Orel, assigned to educate and train Komsomol members, was denounced and purged for "anti-Soviet relations toward young women" after he burst into a women's dormitory at night and sexually harassed women there.[112]

The importance of Party members' moral behavior during the purges led to a focus on their home lives. One 1937 Party report claimed that Trotskyists could have been uncovered sooner had their home lives been more carefully scrutinized. It cited one "Trotskyist" whose apartment was "like a club," where all sorts of decadent activity, including card playing and drunken singing, took place.[113] A Party cell in Smolensk conducted an inquiry into one member's alleged wife-beating. Concluding that "the family life of a Communist is not a private matter," the cell severely reprimanded him for his "petty bourgeois lifestyle" and "degeneration in family relations."[114] Another Party cell, this one in Voronezh, conducted an inquiry into one member's failure to take his wife to the movies and the poor upbringing he was giving his children.[115] The Party organization at Sverdlovsk University in Moscow likewise reminded Party and Komsomol members to monitor all aspects of one another's lives, including their home lives.[116] The emphasis on moral behavior as a criterion for judging not only Party members' worthiness but their political reliability as well thus resulted in even greater intrusion into their personal lives.

The Stalinist leadership also attacked high-ranking Party officials for their lavish and decadent lifestyles. In doing so, it mobilized the enormous resentments of common people and low-ranking Party members to attack and purge local Party bosses. One 1937 article urged Party members to be more critical of their leaders and to denounce those who had "degenerated in their everyday life."[117] During the Great Purges, rank-and-file Party members frequently did come forward at orchestrated meetings to criticize local leaders' excessive lifestyles and abuses of power. Stalin and his supporters in the Politburo thereby used such resentments to unseat local and regional Party bosses, some of whom had built up powerful fiefdoms. It was in this connection that Party propaganda began to stress the importance of modesty for Communists. A lead article in *Pravda* in 1937 defined modesty as an essential quality for Party members, and denounced "vanity, arrogance, swollen pride, haughtiness, boastfulness, [and] self-promotion" as capitalist characteristics unworthy of Communists.[118]

Stalin finally took measures to halt the Great Purges in 1938. At a Central Committee plenum that January he and other Politburo members expressed concerns about mass expulsions of Party members. In November the Politburo admonished the secret police and procuracy for excesses and prohibited them from carrying out further mass arrests. Later that month Ezhov was forced to resign, and he was subsequently arrested.[119] In an effort to reassure members of the Party elite that mass repressions against them had ended, Andrei Zhdanov in his speech at the Eighteenth Party Congress in 1939 sharply criticized those who, under the guise of vigilance, had denounced "honest officials."[120] The same year, Party officials reviewed purge cases and condemned numerous excesses and procedural irregularities of the secret police, thereby securing a halt to the Great Purges.[121]

While the Great Purges themselves were halted, their bloody legacy endured. The arrest and execution of millions of innocent people, from high Party officials to common citizens, spawned a deep sense of fear and distrust at all levels of society. Especially significant for our purposes here was the way the purges signaled to Party members the importance of proper conduct and moral behavior. The elimination of thousands of high-ranking Party officials actually created opportunities for members of the Party rank and file to be promoted to positions of power. But these promotees, even more than those who had preceded them in the early 1930s, were naturally insecure in their status. Not only did they lack the cultural upbringing and expertise to know how to conduct themselves in their positions, but they were also aware that misconduct could lead to purging, arrest, and execution.

The Great Purges solidified the belief that Communists' morality and personal lives were inseparable from their political reliability. In fact, the Komsomol Central Committee said as much explicitly when it decreed that each young Communist should be "instilled with an understanding that lifestyle is inseparable from politics, and that moral degeneration leads to the ruin of a Komsomol member."[122] And after the purges, Party efforts to oversee members' morality and lifestyle continued. At the Eighteenth Party Congress, Zhdanov not only condemned the purging of honest officials but also proposed including in the Party rules a number of responsibilities for members, such as "conducting oneself in a Communist way in one's lifestyle."[123] The Party and Komsomol organizations at Moscow University held debates on "the moral countenance of a Communist," which prompted large-scale discussions of morality, manners, and ethics, while Soviet legal scholars began to cite morality as a basis for socialist legality.[124]

The Politburo went so far as to dictate guidelines as to the maximum size for Party officials' dachas, in order to prevent material excesses uncovered during the purges.[125] And though the Great Purges were drawn to a halt, the Party continued to expel members for such moral infractions as "lifestyle degeneration" and drunkenness. Indeed, some secret police agents who during the purges had busily arrested Party officials for the formulaic charges of Trotskyism and drunkenness found themselves charged with a similar formula—"violations of revolutionary legality and systematic drunkenness."[126] The equation of moral and political infractions, then, became a permanent part of Soviet rhetoric and practice. Begun with debates on Communist morality in the 1920s and completed in the highly politicized atmosphere of the Great Purges, the unwritten code of Communist behavior was quite puritan and rigid. Whether Party members actually internalized it or only conformed outwardly to its strictures remains to be investigated.

The Internalization of Values

Gauging the degree to which Party members internalized values is extremely difficult. Nonetheless, memoirs and diaries do provide evidence that permits us to draw some tentative conclusions. As we will see, some Party members genuinely adopted official values as their own. Others attempted to live up to the ideals of the New Soviet Person, but fell short. Still others outwardly conformed to Party behavioral norms but inwardly rejected them, retaining personal beliefs and behaviors quite contrary to official values.

Letters of Party members make it clear that at a minimum they adopted the rhetoric of Party honor. One member in 1924 wrote to thank his instructors in a Party education course, saying that as a Communist "I feel myself to be an important person."[127] A member who had been expelled from the Party wrote in 1926 to request reinstatement, asking that officials return "my lofty title of Communist." He added that "nothing would be dearer to me than your just, Party-line word that my happiness will be returned to me."[128] The same year another former Party member who pleaded for reinstatement called the Party his "purpose and life."[129] And in 1934 a Party member wrote to refute charges of drunkenness, claiming, "I am first of all a Communist, and the honor of this is higher than anything else."[130] At least in their rhetoric, these people adopted such official values as Party honor.

As members of a self-identified elite, most Communists accepted the need to behave in a cultured manner, and indeed many of them sought respectability as a means to legitimate their high status. Because many of them were of humble origins, however, they often lacked an inherent grasp of respectable behavior and instead conformed only superficially and clumsily to official etiquette. Kosarev acknowledged as much when he complained at the Tenth Komsomol Congress in 1936 that some Komsomol and Party members mistook superficial symbols of culturedness for true cultured living.[131] A remarkable document written by a Soviet scientist who vacationed for three summers, 1936–38, at a health resort for high-ranking Party officials reveals a great deal about the behavior of the Communist elite. The scientist, Mikhail Kitaev, emigrated from the Soviet Union, so his account may contain some anticommunist bias, but overall it provides a quite nuanced and insightful portrayal of Party officials' social interaction and behavior.

Kitaev describes one high-ranking official as taking very seriously the emphasis on culturedness in Party propaganda. This official came from peasant origins and thus lacked a cultured upbringing, but he compensated for this deficiency by carefully studying etiquette manuals, through which he learned to help women with their coats and to kiss their hands upon greeting them. Kitaev also writes that Party officials took seriously the charge that they attend cultural events regularly. But he notes that when they did go to the theater, they conducted themselves very unnaturally. They looked awkward and uncomfortable, and though they felt compelled to comment on the play, they did not really know what to say.[132] A Komsomol member in Moscow during the mid-1930s described a similar phenomenon in his diary. He wrote that at a classical concert he and other students from his institute felt "uncomfortable," afraid to mingle with other audience members and uncertain what to say about the music.[133]

Because so many Party officials came from humble origins, they generally had not been brought up with good table manners. According to Kitaev, many officials conducted themselves rudely, chewing their food loudly and with their mouths open. Some prided themselves on eating properly, though in an overly self-conscious way. One official, for example, carefully ate his chicken dinner without using his hands and at the end of the meal proudly announced, "I am able to eat not only chicken but also herring without getting my fingers dirty."[134]

Reading newspapers and journals was another prescribed norm for a "cultured person." Party officials did in fact read many newspapers, according to Kitaev. In the dining hall of the health resort they would all be reading not only publications of the central press but local newspapers as well, despite considerable overlap in content. The fact that they read newspapers in public suggests that mealtime reading may have been something of a public ritual to impress fellow officials. But Kitaev offers another explanation as well. Noting the vital importance of adhering to the Party line on all matters, he speculates that the Party elite needed to peruse all newspapers carefully and to read between the lines in order to determine what ideological and policy positions they should take. He also describes a "typical promotee"—a Party official from a working-class family—who was poorly educated and thus tried to learn as much as possible from newspapers in order to fulfill his responsibilities.[135]

The Party elite's careful reading of newspapers did not mean, however, that all of their leisure time was spent in healthy and edifying activity, as prescribed by official culture. At the health resort for high-ranking Party members, dominoes was the most popular pastime, and everyone followed the domino tournaments held there. Not only the game but the manner in which they played was far from refined. Players would slam dominoes down on the table, and often they would get into arguments that ended only when one player scattered his dominoes and quit the game. Some Party bureaucrats also played poker or other card games. They ignored entirely the sports equipment available at the resort for volleyball, croquet, and other prescribed leisure activities.[136] An article on the life of Komsomol members revealed a similar tendency to squander leisure time playing cards or gossiping. The article, written by a student at the Iaroslavl' pedagogical institute, stated that "we ourselves must become cultured people," but he noted that few films or cultural activities were available and that Komsomol members rarely read literature or newspapers.[137] One diarist described a fellow Komsomol member who claimed to be an expert on Russian literature but could not answer a single question about the authors he allegedly knew the best.[138]

Party officials often fell short of prescribed norms of morality as well. Ample evidence suggests that despite campaigns to reduce smoking and drinking, Party officials continued to smoke and drink heavily. Indeed, it seems clear that most did not even take seriously the pronouncements that smoking and drinking were violations of Party ethics. When the head of the Khar'kov Party Control Commission claimed in a speech that "drunkenness is a crime against our class" and that "smoking is unethical behavior," the audience laughed heartily.[139] Of course once drunkenness became such a pervasive charge during the Great Purges, and one with such deadly consequences, it became important for Party officials to avoid public drunkenness. But drinking and smoking continued to be widespread habits among the Party elite, official norms notwithstanding.

Cultured leisure, 1936: reading the newspaper, playing chess, and playing volleyball. "Bring cultured living to camp." (Poster identification number RU/SU 1970, Poster Collection, Hoover Institution Archives.)

Some Party officials also violated norms of sexual morality. In the appraisal of Kitaev, members of the Party elite who vacationed at the health resort saw it as "a vacation from their marital commitments," and they engaged in numerous extramarital affairs. One Party official there spoke often about ethics, and insisted that Communists had the highest standards of morality anywhere in the world. He prided himself on his own moral behavior and "cultured" manner with ladies. In practice, however, he cynically tried to "buy" nurses and female dining hall employees.[140] There is also evidence that Communist officials in national minority republics did not conform to the uniform moral standards being defined at the center. Party investigators in Kazakhstan found that some local officials had up to seven wives. Because these investigators assumed a uniform (though still unwritten) moral code, they viewed polygamy as "sexual debauchery" rather than as a difference in cultural and religious traditions.[141]

Despite violations of officially defined moral and respectable behavior, most Party officials did conform at least outwardly to behavioral norms. More difficult is the question whether they internalized official values and genuinely sought to live by them. Through his analysis of Stalin-era diaries,

Jochen Hellbeck has shown that some Party members did internalize the official value system and worldview. The diary of Aleksandr Afinogenov, a prominent Soviet playwright who was expelled from the Party in 1937 but later reinstated, reveals that he approved of the purge that victimized him. In fact, he understood the purge as an effort to cleanse "our Soviet house from all impurity," and he resolved to pursue personal asceticism to purify and improve himself and thus be worthy of reinstatement in the Party.[142] Another diarist, a collective farm activist named Zhelezniakov, wrote, "There is nothing greater than to be a member, a citizen of the Soviet land and to belong to Lenin's Communist Party, hardened in battles and led in our days by the beloved leader, Comrade Stalin."[143] With these and other examples, Hellbeck has dramatically demonstrated that some Party members both internalized the official worldview and derived their sense of identity and self-worth from it.

Nataliia Kozlova reached similar conclusions in her analysis of the diary of a peasant named Vladimir who moved to Moscow in the 1930s, joined the Communist Party, and eventually became a Party official. She describes Vladimir as a promotee who did in fact internalize official values and understand his world according to official ideology. In his diary Vladimir wrote that he left behind the life of a petty bourgeois peasant and instead chose the path of "a new person, with a Communist worldview." He compared his father's peasant hut, which represented the "old world" of capitalism, with his own apartment in Moscow, which he described as the "new socialist world." In accordance with Soviet propaganda, he sought to imbue his life with order, rationalism, and discipline. Moreover, he adopted as part of his self-image the Communist ideal of an honest, open, and loyal Party member. He recounted that in his letters to Stalin, he would "write from his soul with sincere filial feelings, and without any shade of falsity."[144]

Other evidence, however, indicates that some Party and Komsomol members outwardly conformed to official values while inwardly rejecting them. A Moscow institute student in the 1930s conveyed the humiliation he felt after being reprimanded for his behavior and views at a Komsomol meeting. He concluded that in the future he would keep his thoughts to himself. In fact, he described his diary as the one place where he could express himself freely, and in its pages he dissented from official Soviet values.[145] As Oleg Kharkhordin argues, many Party functionaries also learned to hide their personal views and behavior. Dissimulation among Party members became widespread, as some consciously detached their public statements and actions from their hidden personal lives.[146] It is clear, then, that some Party and Komsomol members did not internalize official values, though it is still significant that they learned to conform outwardly to officially defined norms of behavior.

In addition to the values promoted in Party propaganda, there were some unofficial values among Party members. One unofficial rule among Party officials was the reciprocal loyalty of patrons and their clients and their interconnected fate. Each new head of a Party or government bureau had the tacit right to appoint his own people to leading staff positions, and conversely, when a high official was demoted or purged, his clients suffered the same fate.[147] In national minority republics, family and clan alliances also played an important role in the formation of Party networks, and these alliances were also governed by unwritten traditions outside of official discourse. Referring to these strong patron-client and clan networks, Stalin criticized regional Party leaders as "feudal princes," and he sought to eliminate these links during the Great Purges. Indeed, many Party officials were expelled and arrested during the purges simply because of their association with someone accused of being a Trotskyist or wrecker.[148]

How did Party members respond to the Great Purges? Did they believe the charges of treason and immoral behavior leveled against purge victims? Some Party officials did believe such charges, at least initially. Evgeniia Ginzburg's husband, a high-ranking Party official, said when an innocent colleague was arrested, "Perhaps he really was mixed up in something or other."[149] Given the extreme international and domestic tensions of the period and the nature of the postrevolutionary situation, when oppositionists and former members of other political parties were numerous, Party members genuinely believed in conspiracies and hidden enemies.[150]

It is also true that some Party officials had ethical lapses, such as drunkenness, sexual impropriety, and material greed. Of course such "moral degeneration" did not lead inevitably to political treason. Nonetheless, resentments among peasants and workers, many of whom expressed satisfaction that their bosses were being purged, were shared to some extent by low-ranking Party members, who also resented the lavish lifestyles and abuses of authority by some Party elites.[151] A few of the Party rank and file even wrote to say that the purges had not gone far enough, that more officials needed to be expelled from the Party.[152]

A number of Party members, however, vigorously protested the purges, at great risk to their own lives. One member wrote to Stalin on behalf of those wrongly purged, saying that they had been "cut off from their dear party," and that they should be quickly reinstated.[153] A local Party leader in Voronezh stated at a Party plenum in 1937 that accusations against officials were greatly exaggerated, and that no wrongdoing had occurred.[154] One Party member who spoke out to defend Zinoviev and Kamenev was quickly purged himself.[155] The fact that some members were willing to speak out actually indicates their belief in the Party and in Soviet justice. Had they recognized the Great Purges as an effort by the Stalinist leadership to eliminate any potential rivals whether guilty or not, they would not have risked their own arrest to protest the innocence of their colleagues.

The futility of these protests and the execution and imprisonment of millions of innocent people, however, clearly undercut such belief, not only among Party members but among average citizens as well. One worker, who eventually was executed, wrote in his diary that "if hundreds of sincerely devoted, battle-hardened Communists . . . turn out to be scoundrels and spies, then who can guarantee that we are not surrounded by swindlers."[156] Evgeniia Ginzburg found her faith in the Soviet system deeply shaken by the purges even before her own arrest. She recalls that when innocent colleagues were arrested and others criticized for not denouncing them, "I came up against that reversal of logic and common sense which never ceased to amaze me."[157] The purges, then, were disillusioning for many people who believed in the system, and provoked doubt and cynicism toward Soviet ideals. And whereas official Party ethics called for honesty, openness, and initiative, the purges taught precisely the opposite—the need to be secretive, to trust no one, and to avoid responsibility. Even while compelling outward conformity, the purges thus undermined belief and the internalization of values.

Perhaps it was in the realm of morality that the Great Purges in fact did the most to undermine ideals and promote cynicism, for it was here that the greatest contradictions occurred. The fact that in the name of morality (combating moral degeneration) acts of extreme immorality were committed—the arrest and execution of millions of innocent Party members and citizens—could only have the effect of discrediting the Party and the entire concept of morality. Much as extreme coercion and killing in the name of achieving a socialist utopia discredited the entire idea of socialism, the moral discourse used to justify the purges only undercut the legitimacy of the system. And indeed, when first Khrushchev and later Gorbachev exposed the crimes of Stalin's purges, their revelations sharply undermined the system itself.

By the end of the 1930s, the official values of the Communist Party had developed considerably beyond the moral relativist or even nihilist strains present before the Revolution and during the 1920s. No longer did Party leaders define Communist morality as whatever advanced the cause of the proletariat. Instead they established a strict definition of the proper values and behavior of Party members: sobriety, sexual propriety, honesty, openness, and loyalty. The emergence of an unwritten moral code emphasizing such values should not be seen as a retreat from Soviet socialism. With the elimination of the bourgeoisie, nihilistic attacks on bourgeois morality were no longer necessary, and Communists' adherence to a strict code of behavior was supposed to strengthen the cause of socialism. Also indicative of the Party leadership's steadfast commitment to Soviet socialism was its continued emphasis on the collectivist, anticapitalist ethos of Marxism and the vanguard role of the Communist Party.

The development of an unwritten moral code for Communists was part of the process by which Soviet socialism and its vanguard were defined. Marxist ideology provided no such code and it emerged instead from a number of other inputs. Party leaders' own moral propensities certainly played a role. Lenin and Stalin both held rather Victorian notions concerning morality, and some other Party leaders shared not only their values but their concerns that sexual liberation and ethical nihilism could distract from the tasks of socialist construction. Party control commissions formed the institutional basis for defining and enforcing moral and ideological standards among Party members. Another factor was the large number of newly promoted Party officials who were anxious to behave in a manner that would legitimate their status. While these promotees did not themselves determine a code of behavior, their dogmatic adherence to official values contributed to the cultural orthodoxies of the Stalin era. Finally, political developments and historical conjunctures played important roles in the delineation of Communist values. During the Great Purges, when the search for internal enemies reached fever pitch, the Stalinist leadership frequently charged "enemies of the people" not only with political treason but with moral transgressions as well. Thus many purge victims were accused of moral degeneration in addition to Trotskyism, spying, and wrecking.

The code of behavior for Communists went beyond adherence to moral strictures. It included norms of neatness and efficiency required of officials in any modern bureaucratic system. And as the vanguard of Soviet society, Party members were held to high standards of respectability and cultured behavior as well. To be worthy of their elite status, Party officials were to dress well, speak politely, read widely, and attend the theater. At the Eighteenth Party Congress in 1939, one Politburo member after another praised the progress of new officials who had risen from humble origins. Stalin boasted about the creation of a new intelligentsia from the ranks of workers and peasants, calling it "one of the most important results of the cultural revolution in our country." He went on to say that in time all workers and peasants would be made "cultured," but in the meantime the education and promotion of this new elite was a major achievement.[158]

In his speech at the congress, Andrei Andreev heralded the replacement of old cadres by newly promoted Party officials. He claimed that "our Party home has become cleaner and fresher," and that "elements of moral degeneration have largely disappeared." He called the new cadres "more cultured" and said that unlike the old (purged) officials, they "are not infected with bureaucratism, dictatorial tendencies, conceit, and self-aggrandizement." Instead, according to him, they were "more connected to the masses, and more honest and devoted to their Party."[159] The Soviet project had always entailed creating not only a new socioeconomic order but new people as well, and Andreev's praise of the new cadres seemed to indicate that they were the embodiment of the New Soviet Person. Not only were they more cultured and educated than their predecessors, but their character was more lofty and pure.

Andreev also sought to justify the purge of thousands of old Party officials, and he did so in moral terms:

> The entire Party has come to the Eighteenth Congress with a feeling of deep moral satisfaction with its work. How, comrades, could we not be satisfied, when the Party with the support and participation of the entire people succeeded in crushing and annihilating the Trotskyist-Bukharinist cadres and all other conspirators, wreckers, murderers, and spies.[160]

But did the congress delegates indeed feel a deep moral satisfaction at that moment? Or did they instead secretly recall the thousands of innocent Party officials arrested and shot in the Great Purges? The hypocrisy of justifying actions of extreme immorality through a moral discourse could only discredit the very notion of morality and the ideals of socialism as well.

CHAPTER THREE

Stalinist Family Values

The old family is dying out. . . . Every woman will be freed from
the chains of domestic slavery and will be saved from the cross of
motherhood.

— ALEKSANDRA KOLLONTAI, 1918

In our life there must be no gap between the personal and the
social. Even in such seemingly personal matters as the family and
the birth of children the personal coincides with the social. . . .
The Soviet woman is not free from the great and honorable duty
that nature has given her: she is a mother, she gives birth. And
this is undoubtedly not only her personal affair but one of
enormous social importance.

— AARON SOL'TS, 1936

A fter the October Revolution, the family in Soviet society appeared to
be headed for extinction. The leading Bolshevik feminist, Aleksandra Kollontai, blamed the family for the enslavement of women
and denounced it as a bourgeois institution. In its place she proposed love
freed from the confines of marriage and state-funded child care to spare
women the burden of child raising. Legislation in 1918 in fact facilitated
divorce and thereby greatly weakened marriage and the family as institutions. Kollontai and others predicted that the family would soon wither
away. Yet by the 1930s, official Soviet culture endorsed strong families,
glorified motherhood, and strove to raise the birth rate. The Soviet government also enacted legislation that made divorce more difficult and outlawed abortion. The country that had embarked on the great socialist
experiment reverted to a very traditional family model and an essentialized notion of women's "natural role" as mothers.

Timasheff highlighted this shift in family policy as one prominent feature of what he called the Great Retreat. According to him, Soviet leaders recognized that the vast majority of the population still venerated the family as an institution and opposed its dissolution. He saw the renewed emphasis on the family as a concession by Soviet leaders to the wishes of the population and to the state's need for social stability.[1] While Timasheff's analysis was pathbreaking in its day, there are several problems both with his characterization of Soviet family policy as a "retreat" and with his explanation for its reorientation. Many Party leaders, including Lenin, never wished to dissolve the family in the first place. Apart from those who agreed with Kollontai that the family was an obstacle to sexual liberation and women's emancipation, most leading Communists feared family disintegration and sexual frivolity as distractions from the building of socialism. Before accepting Timasheff's claim that "the disintegration of the family did not disturb the Communists," we should examine debates about sexual liberation and sexual control in the 1920s.

We must also place Soviet family policy in comparative context in order to appreciate fully the reasons for its shift in the mid-1930s. Pro-family legislation and propaganda similar to that in the Soviet Union occurred in countries throughout Europe during the interwar period. The similarity in family policies suggests that the impetus behind them went beyond Soviet leaders' "retreat" from revolutionary values. Pro-natalist concerns stemming from the demands of mass warfare and a sense of demographic competition among political leaders greatly influenced family policies throughout Europe. Through a comparison of these policies and the motivations behind them, we will gain additional perspective on similar as well as distinctive features of Soviet family policy and norms of sex and gender.

Finally, before we accept the characterization of Soviet family policy in the mid-1930s as a retreat, we need to examine the family model promoted by the Soviet government. "Retreat" implies a return to a previously existing type of family, which in the Russian context would mean the prerevolutionary patriarchal family. But the Stalinist family had neither exclusive property and political rights for the patriarch nor protection from state interference. Despite rhetoric about strong families, the Soviet state actually encroached upon family autonomy and used this traditional institution for modern mobilizational purposes. By exploring the family in relation to the state, we will arrive at a more complete understanding of Soviet family policy, as well as of its consequences for sexual norms and gender roles in Soviet society.

Sexual Liberation and Sexual Control

Questions of sex, gender, and the family were hotly debated in the Soviet Union during the 1920s. The Revolution opened up the possibility of completely restructuring norms of sexual behavior and gender roles, and some social commentators seized this opportunity to advocate the dismantling of marriage and the traditional family. But alongside advocates of sexual liberation and women's emancipation were political leaders and medical professionals who feared sexual and social anarchy, and who demanded increased discipline in sexual matters as a means to preserve and cultivate the human resources necessary to build socialism. Many Soviet leaders also found sexual liberation distasteful and clearly harbored an aesthetic sensibility that understood long, stable marriages to be the basic unit for sexual and social organization.

The Revolution's most immediate effect on family law was to take jurisdiction over marriage away from the Orthodox Church and transfer it to the Soviet state. The decree of December 20, 1917, elaborated in the Soviet Family Code of 1918, gave the Civil Registry Office sole authority to sanction and dissolve marriages. The primary author of the decree, the jurist A. G. Goikhbarg, heralded the new law as "almost completely free of male egoism," and indeed, the decree incorporated the language and principle of sexual equality in marriage. The new code also made divorce, virtually never granted under the old regime, very easy to obtain. Goikhbarg criticized the old system, saying that without divorce, "people alien to each other were chained together like prisoners to a wheelbarrow." His decree allowed marriages to be dissolved immediately if by mutual consent and after a brief court hearing if only one spouse sought divorce. Full freedom of divorce made Soviet marriage law the most liberal in the world.[2]

Kollontai supported this legislation not only as a means to free women from the subordination and economic dependency of traditional marriage but also to clear the way for romantic unions based on love and equality. Before the Revolution she had written that marriage often became "a funeral service said over the corpse of dead feelings," inasmuch as women bound themselves to men to ensure monetary support for their children.[3] In the Soviet period, Kollontai endorsed "a new form of relationship between men and women: a comradely and heartfelt union of two free, independent, wage-earning, equal members of communist society." In place of bourgeois marriage she envisioned a "higher union of two loving and mutually trusting souls."[4]

To permit this higher union and to free women for participation in economic and social life, Kollontai advocated collective responsibility for the raising of children. In her 1923 tract *Women's Labor in the Development of the Economy* she called for "the removal of all cares connected with mother-hood from the individual woman's shoulders and their transfer to the collective, thus recognizing that the upbringing of children goes beyond the parameters of the family and becomes a social and state institution." Collective child raising would be accomplished, according to Kollontai and others, through the establishment of children's homes, child care, and communal dining facilities, all of which would free women from child-raising responsibilities and domestic chores.[5] Significantly, Kollontai did not seek to free women from childbearing itself. Noting the Soviet Union's need to expand its "laboring forces," she called childbirth "the social obligation of women." She added that women would not shrink from this obligation if state support for maternity and child raising were provided.[6] A leading Soviet sociologist in the 1920s, S. Ia. Vol'fson, believed that in view of the shortage of children's homes and communal facilities, the state would be forced to use the family temporarily as "an auxiliary social formation," but he looked forward to the day when the family "will be sent to a museum of antiquities."[7]

While her focus was on women's emancipation, Kollontai had another motive for championing collective, state-sponsored child care over parental responsibility for children. She and other Communists feared that traditional families would perpetuate petty bourgeois ways, as parents passed on to their children the selfish individualism of capitalist society. Kollontai wrote, "The narrow, closed family, with its parental squabbles and its habit of thinking only about the well-being of relatives, cannot educate the New Person." Only state institutions with "wise educators," she argued, could raise a child to be "a conscious Communist who recognizes only . . . loyalty to the collective."[8] The 1918 Congress of Working-Class and Peasant Women urged social education for newborn children up to age sixteen, and delegates to the 1919 Congress on the Protection of Childhood argued that only the state could create the necessary environment to develop the communist personality.[9]

Some Soviet ideologists' opposition to the family assumed a more misogynist tone, as they concentrated on women as a bad influence on children. In warning about the continuation of bourgeois habits, they depicted women as less politically conscious than men and hence more likely to contaminate children. Several commentators insisted that all parents, and mothers in particular, should isolate themselves from their children to guard against the perpetuation of individualist and anticollectivist attitudes.[10] Communist Party cells showed particular concern that the wives of some Party members were politically backward, and feared they might infect both their husbands and their children with retrograde ideas and petty bourgeois ways.[11]

For a variety of reasons, then, the family came under attack during the 1920s. Ideologists and commentators such as Kollontai sought to eliminate the traditional family as a means both to liberate women and to guarantee the proper collectivist upbringing of children. In place of the traditional family, Kollontai articulated an alternative model for the sexual and social organization of Soviet society: unfettered romantic unions and collective responsibility for child raising. But Kollontai's model was not widely accepted by Communist leaders, and in fact it was not even well understood. Commentators frequently misrepresented Kollontai's writings as a call for unrestrained sexual gratification and multiple partners, and many people rejected her ideas as leading to sexual anarchy.

Lenin and other Communist leaders held rather Victorian notions about morality and the importance of marriage. They regarded sexual liberation and the elimination of the family as distractions from socialism, if not perversions of it. Lenin criticized the excesses of the sexual revolution in a 1920 interview with Clara Zetkin (published only in 1925). "Promiscuity in sexual life is bourgeois: it is a sign of degeneration," Lenin declared. He warned that the sexual libertinism common among urban youth after the Revolution destroyed young people's health and wasted their energy. He sought to redirect this energy toward "healthy sport" and the tasks of socialist construction. Lenin thereby espoused an idea repeated by many social commentators throughout the 1920s—the need to sublimate sexual energy and preserve it for the building of socialism. Lenin also criticized bourgeois marriage, "with its difficult dissolution, its freedom for the husband and bondage for the wife, and its disgustingly false sex morality." But at the same time he believed in monogamy and the institution of marriage. Under socialism, he assumed, marriage would be voluntary and equal, in contrast to bourgeois marriage, but he nonetheless disapproved of frequent divorce or multiple sex partners. Lenin clearly maintained a sense of propriety about marriage and accepted long-term, monogamous, heterosexual relationships as the only appropriate form of sexual behavior.[12]

Other Party leaders echoed Lenin in expressing concern about sexual liberation. Iaroslavskii, for example, also questioned "the senseless waste of young energy on sex," and stated that "a flippant attitude toward the family" was "a social evil." Commissar of Health Nikolai Semashko argued that sexual activity wasted energy that otherwise could be used for socially productive work, and a series of newspaper articles reinforced his position and advocated the sublimation of sexual energy in other tasks. The Central Control Commission resolved that the Party should combat "sexual carelessness and sexual depravity, which harmfully and destructively waste the energy of youth."[13]

The Soviet medical profession buttressed these political arguments with scientific studies that allegedly showed the ill effects of excessive sexual activity. Endocrinologists demonstrated that abstinence would preserve gland secretions within the body and thereby store up internal bodily resources. Physicians and professors argued that the young generation would be healthy and productive only if its sexual life was orderly and rational.[14] The psychologist Aron Zalkind, a leading Soviet sexologist and founder of the Society of Marxist Psychoneurologists, also argued for the rationalization and control of sex. He decried the "disorganization of sexual life" under the old regime and blamed it for "nervous-psychiatric disorders." He described sexual energy as a working-class resource that should be preserved for the sake of proletarian creativity and production. In his attempt to promote sexual control, Zalkind even issued twelve commandments of sexual behavior. His strictures included sexual abstinence until marriage (at age twenty or twenty-five), monogamy, moderation in the frequency of sex, a prohibition against sexual perversion, and the right of a class to interfere in the sex lives of its members.[15]

Soviet sexologists depicted masturbation not only as a waste of energy but as an individualistic act that detracted from one's collectivist spirit. One sex education specialist, G. N. Sorokhtin, claimed that masturbation and other autoerotic processes cause "a pathological increase in egocentrism and produce shy loners imprisoned in themselves and unconcerned with the life of society."[16] Using the language of science, Sorokhtin and others passed normative judgments against masturbation and linked this "deviant" behavior to social dysfunction. Subsequent medical specialists warned against masturbation and implored parents and educators to discourage adolescents from engaging in it.[17] Soviet sexologists, then, sought to control and limit all sexual activity, even when it did not involve promiscuity.

Soviet political leaders and social commentators argued vigorously for the control of sexuality in part because of their fears of political as well as moral degeneration. Particularly during the New Economic Policy, they worried that small-scale capitalism and decadent cafés and casinos might corrupt society. As Eric Naiman has argued, alarm about the possibility of ideological corruption was expressed through discussion of sex. The very concept of pleasure became associated with the bourgeoisie, and some commentators warned that the hedonistic lives of NEPmen might seduce young workers and lead them to stray from the ideals of the Revolution.

Soviet officials and professionals saw the control of sexual urges and the limitation of pleasure as a means to guard against such corruption.[18]

Katerina Clark has also noted that sexual license in the 1920s became identified with ideological deviance. In the same way that Party members' moral degeneration would be linked with political degeneration during the Great Purges, Soviet social thinkers and cultural producers in the 1920s associated promiscuity with bourgeois corruption and ideological transgressions. Clark points out that writers and filmmakers of the period became obsessed with bodily purity and hygiene, and that increasingly bodily, sexual, and linguistic purity were linked with ideological conformity.[19] In this climate, it is not surprising that Soviet authorities sought to control sexuality.

While condemnation of the bourgeois family was nearly universal among Communist thinkers, most were unwilling to abandon the family and morality altogether. Those who prioritized sexual liberation and the freeing of women from the bonds of marriage, as Kollontai did, were in the minority. A majority of Soviet officials and specialists saw a continued need for the sexual organization of society, and they envisioned the family, freed of its bourgeois oppression, as the institution to realize this organization. Particularly during the New Economic Policy, when fears of ideological degeneration became associated with sexual licentiousness, political leaders and doctors alike sought to control rather than to liberate sexuality. They saw abstinence until marriage as a means both to preserve young people's energy for the tasks of socialist construction and to prevent the corruption of socialist principles by sexual hedonism. While many students in the 1920s rejected traditional sexual morality, they did not deny that sex was a matter of state concern, and in fact they looked to the government to solve sexual problems and establish sexual norms.[20]

Marriage and the family also provided a way to deal with widespread social problems of the 1920s and 1930s by controlling sexual behavior and its consequences. Soviet leaders had not anticipated the enormous social problems that faced them after the Revolution. They had assumed that prostitution and venereal disease were evils of capitalism and so would vanish under socialism. Instead, given the social upheaval of the Civil War and widespread unemployment during the 1920s, these problems in some ways actually got worse. Many Soviet officials saw increased government control of sexuality as the only way to deal with these problems.

Prostitution was one of the most embarrassing social and sexual problems for the Soviet government. The 1918 Congress of Working-Class and Peasant Women resolved that "the woman citizen of Soviet Russia must never be the object of buying and selling."[21] But prostitution did not disappear, and by some measures the number of prostitutes increased in the early years of Soviet power.[22] In a report issued in January 1921, "in the interests of the entire population's physical and moral health," the Soviet Interdepartmental Commission on the Battle against Prostitution called for swift measures to eliminate the conditions that were causing prostitution. It blamed famine, poverty, and the remnants of capitalism for prostitution, and recommended full employment for young women as a means to prevent it. Commission members primarily blamed socioeconomic conditions for prostitution and sought noncoercive means to prevent it. But the commission also noted the existence of "professional prostitutes"—"social parasites and labor deserters" who should be brought to justice.[23] This resolution concurred with the Soviet government's Civil War compulsory labor policy, under which prostitutes were arrested and incarcerated in labor camps. A women's camp outside of Petrograd in 1920 had 6,500 inmates, 60 percent of whom had been imprisoned for prostitution.[24]

During the 1920s prostitution increased in tandem with inequities in the distribution of wealth and with high female unemployment. In 1924 Soviet officials established prophylactories where prostitutes could receive housing, "sexual enlightenment," and medical attention to help them change their lives and obtain legitimate jobs. These attempts to reduce prostitution through aid and education rather than coercion enjoyed some limited success, but they remained badly underfunded and did not solve the problem as a whole. In 1929 the Soviet government reverted to a more coercive approach to prostitution, and by the mid-1930s it closed most prophylactories and sent apprehended prostitutes to labor camps. This shift was partly a response to the end of unemployment, which meant that all women who continued to practice prostitution could be considered "labor deserters." But it was also characteristic of Soviet social policy during the 1930s, which enforced moral norms primarily through coercion rather than through education and medical treatment.[25]

Soviet health officials viewed venereal disease as equally dangerous and often connected with prostitution, and they cited it as another reason to control sexual activity. Soviet doctors stressed that sex was a public rather than a private matter and argued that the new society could not be achieved until the masses were sexually healthy.[26] In 1918, facing what seemed to be a venereal disease epidemic, the Soviet government formed a special commission that reported the following:

> hundreds of thousands and even millions of those with venereal disease have returned to Russian cities and villages and (intentionally and unintentionally) have tirelessly spread a grave disaster for the country. They spread death

and the extinction of the people. It is necessary to take quickly the most en-
ergetic, broad, and active measures in the battle with this grave disaster.[27]

The Commissariat of Health compiled statistics on venereal disease and
analyzed these data to determine the scale of the problem and also the patterns and behaviors behind its spread.[28]

The Soviet government conducted extensive propaganda work against
the spread of venereal disease. As early as June 1918 the venereal disease
commission issued a plan for lectures, discussions, and "tens of millions
of brochures and posters" to educate the public about the dangers of
venereal disease. The Commissariat of Health also established an extensive network of venereal disease clinics, which were to conduct "sanitary
enlightenment work" as well as treat patients. Officials found the best way
to draw an audience for education to be "sanitary trials"—mock trials held
to condemn those with venereal disease who infected others.[29]

Alongside educational work, Soviet authorities turned to legal and interventionist means to prevent the spread of venereal disease. The Soviet
Criminal Code mandated up to six months' imprisonment for anyone who
knowingly infected another person.[30] Venereologists focused on prostitution and chance sexual encounters as a major cause of the spread of venereal disease. One doctor noted that during the summer, parks in Moscow,
particularly Sokol'niki, were "hot spots" of sexual activity and disease transmission. He advocated not only the policing of parks but also the distribution of prophylactics, in case chance sexual encounters could not be
prevented. Another specialist cited the residences of migratory workers as
sites where venereal diseases were commonly spread, and recommended
that doctors visit these places to conduct medical checks and educational
work. Indeed, interventions in people's residences and homes became a
part of the government campaign. The director of a Moscow venereal disease clinic, noting that patients did not always tell their families of their ill-
ness, sent medical personnel to the homes of patients to check whether
other family members were infected and to educate them about the dangers of venereal disease.[31]

Soviet medical specialists viewed sex primarily as a health issue to be
managed through education and treatment. But the fact that these specialists employed a highly normative approach to sex, and one that emphasized sex in marriage with the object of procreation as the only legitimate
form of sexual behavior, paved the way for a more repressive approach in
the 1930s. By then Soviet officials abandoned extensive medical discussions of sexual behavior and adopted police measures rather than education to enforce sexual norms. During the Great Break of the early 1930s,

the discipline of social venereology came under attack, and open discussion of sex and sexual behavior ceased. The lively theoretical debates of the 1920s thus gave way to a more practical and coercive approach to sexual problems. As Frances Bernstein has pointed out, the 1930s in a sense saw the realization of medical sexology experts' vision of normal sexual behavior—abstinence except for the sake of procreation, the elimination of deviance, and an emphasis on reproductive needs of the collective at the expense of the individual.[32] The Soviet government no longer permitted scholarly debate or discussion about sex in the 1930s, but it enforced norms of sexual behavior and reproductive health all the more vigorously.

The other major social problem associated with sexual behavior was men's irresponsibility. During the 1920s some young men took advantage of the lax moral climate and ease of divorce; "Red Don Juans" seduced young women with false promises to marry, or they married and divorced multiple times. Many Soviet citizens, peasant women in particular, complained of the large number of "unpleasant and unscrupulous divorces," and called for limitations on divorce and an end to "serial marriages."[33] Wendy Goldman has demonstrated the extent of popular sentiment for the strengthening of marriage in the 1920s. But it would be a mistake to attribute the shift in Soviet family policy to this sentiment, because Soviet leaders were not guided by public opinion. In fact, after considerable discussion, the new family code issued in 1927 actually simplified the procedure for divorce. It permitted one spouse to abrogate a marriage at the registry office, without a court hearing; the registry office would notify the other spouse of the divorce by mail (hence the nickname "postcard divorce"). When Soviet leaders finally did strengthen the family and make divorce more difficult in 1936, they did so not to appease public opinion but to serve state interests of population growth. As Goldman concludes, "the state pursued its own agenda through the 1936 law, which was not necessarily shared by the Soviet population."[34]

Soviet Pro-natalism in Comparative Perspective

To explain the Stalinist emphasis on the family in terms of a Thermidor—a reversal of revolutionary policies either to stabilize society or to appease a conservative population—is to overlook the fact that European countries that had not undergone any revolutionary upheaval placed equal emphasis on the family during the 1930s. All across Europe governments began to champion the family and motherhood, and to offer people incentives to have children. Soviet policies paralleled those in other

European countries. In fact, the 1936 Soviet decree that made divorce more difficult also outlawed abortion. To understand the reasons behind these pan-European pro-natalist concerns and the pro-family policies that accompanied them, we must examine state population concerns in the interwar years.

The First World War had an enormous impact on thinking about population in Europe. Mass warfare required huge numbers of troops, and made clear the link between population size and military power. Moreover, the horrendous casualties of the war prompted fears in many countries about their populations' capacity to sustain military action in the future. Political leaders came to see the size of the population as a critical resource, necessary for national defense, and they focused on reproduction and the family as central to sustaining the population. The German General Staff, in a 1917 memorandum on the German population and army, stated that the falling birth rate was "worse than the losses through the war" in causing population decrease, and resolved, "The basis of the State is the family; it depends on the number and fertility of marriage."[35] When fighting ceased, the major combatants were faced not only with the frightful human cost of the war but with a demographic catastrophe. And though World War I casualties cried out for more births to replenish the population, they actually accelerated the decline in fertility after the war. The loss of young men reduced the number of potential fathers so sharply that Britain's birth rate fell by roughly 40 percent between 1914 and 1930, leading one member of Parliament to declare that population decline constituted "a danger to the maintenance of the British Empire."[36]

Russian casualties in the First World War proved as severe as those in Western Europe, and when deaths during the Civil War and the ensuing famine are added, they totaled 16 million.[37] Despite horrendous wartime losses, the postwar birth rate declined less in the Soviet Union than in the countries of Western Europe. Because Soviet society was still largely made up of peasants in the 1920s, its birth rate remained high despite the loss of young men during World War I and the Civil War. Nonetheless, Soviet officials and demographers monitored population trends closely and were alarmed by the precipitous drop in fertility that accompanied industrialization, collectivization, and the 1932–33 famine. The Central Statistical Administration tabulated annual fertility and mortality rates for every administrative district in the country, so Soviet officials knew, for example, that there were nearly ten times as many deaths as births in Khar'kov oblast in 1933 as a result of the famine in Ukraine.[38] An extensive demographic study in 1934 revealed that the Soviet birth rate overall had fallen from 42.2 births per thousand people in 1928 to 31.0 in 1932. Moreover, S. G.

Strumilin, the author of the study and one of the country's leading statisticians, demonstrated that the drop in fertility correlated with urbanization and the entrance of women into the industrial workforce—trends that had to continue if industrialization were to move ahead.[39]

Strumilin's other major finding was that groups with higher wages had lower fertility. Not only did workers have lower fertility than peasants, but urbanized workers had lower fertility than peasant in-migrants to the city, and white-collar employees had the lowest fertility of all. This discovery contradicted previous research that had identified economic hardship as the primary cause of low fertility.[40] Soviet officials now had to revise their assumption that the birth rate would rise as material conditions improved. Increasingly they saw low fertility as the result of women's choices to have abortions—choices made by women who, in their view, could afford to have children but chose not to out of personal preference. One other factor that exacerbated the decline in fertility and Soviet officials' concern was the abnormally small population cohort that entered its childbearing years in the mid-1930s. The First World War had not only decimated a generation of young men but greatly reduced the number of children born between 1915 and 1920. It was this reduced cohort that reached childbearing age in the mid-1930s, depressing the birth rate even further.[41] Consequently Soviet officials became as obsessed with declining birth rates as did their counterparts in Western Europe.

Political leaders' consternation at population trends led them to contemplate ways to increase the birth rate. Once populations could be represented statistically and fertility trends explained on the basis of demographic studies, it became possible to conceive of state and expert control of fertility. Governments in France, Italy, and Germany took steps against contraception and tightened anti-abortion laws during the 1920s and 1930s.[42] The Soviet Union, after a period of laxity in the 1920s, also discouraged contraception, outlawed abortion, and began to promote motherhood and families to raise the birth rate in the mid-1930s. The Soviet government legalized birth control in 1923, and two years later it established the Central Scientific Commission for the Study of Contraceptives. Physicians were split between those who supported contraception as a means to reduce the number of abortions and prevent the spread of venereal disease and those who argued that it would depress the birth rate and threaten the country's welfare, and perhaps even its survival.[43] Soviet leaders resolved the matter in the 1930s when they declined to allocate resources for the manufacture of contraceptives and ordered the withdrawal from sale of any remaining contraceptive devices in 1936.[44]

The Soviet government had reluctantly legalized abortion in November

1920. The decree noted the growing number of illegal abortions (due to extreme economic hardship in the wake of the Civil War), and in the interest of women's health allowed free abortions in hospitals provided that they were performed by doctors. The decree, however, never recognized abortion as a woman's right. Indeed, Commissar of Health Semashko explicitly stated at the time that abortion was not an individual right, that it could depress the birth rate and hurt the interests of the state, and that it should be practiced only in extreme cases.[45] Even before the sharp drop in fertility during the 1930s, some doctors called abortion "a great antisocial factor" and "a threat to the steady growth of the population." In an agitational mock trial published in 1925, the prosecutor asks a young woman who has had an abortion, "Do you understand . . . that you have killed a future person, a citizen who might have been useful for society?"[46] Anti-abortion propaganda, however, failed to have much effect. By the mid-1930s the number of abortions in the Russian Federation almost equaled the number of births (1,319,700 abortions in hospitals versus 1,392,800 recorded births in 1935). In large cities abortions far outnumbered births; there were 57,000 births and 154,600 abortions in Moscow in 1934.[47]

The legislative centerpiece of the Soviet government's campaign to raise the birth rate was a decree of June 27, 1936, which outlawed abortion except for medical reasons. Politburo discussion of the decree before its promulgation emphasized the importance of achieving the maximum possible birth rate. The Politburo subsequently decided "to limit as much as possible the list of medical reasons" for permitting an abortion, and this decision was promulgated in November 1936. This decree restricted the medical reasons for permitting an abortion to cases in which hereditary diseases were likely or in which a woman's life was endangered. The decree stated, "Abortion not only is harmful for a woman's health but also is a serious social evil, the battle with which is the duty of every conscious citizen, most of all medical personnel."[48]

The ban on abortion was preceded by a huge publicity campaign and public discussion of a draft of the decree, and it was followed by further propaganda on the new law's validity and importance. Numerous articles stressed the harm that abortions did to women's physical and mental health. No mention was made of the extreme danger posed to the health of women who in the wake of this law sought illegal abortions. One article asserted that the "single goal" of the decree was "the protection of the health of the Soviet mother."[49] Commissar Semashko warned not only that abortion could cause infertility but that it could have an adverse effect on a woman's other organs and nervous system. But he also justified the ban on abortion as crucial to "the state task of increasing the population of the Soviet Union." He went on to compare the fertility rate of the Soviet Union with those of other industrialized countries, and argued that the abortion ban would allow the Soviet Union to maintain or even increase its superior birth rate.[50] It is noteworthy that Semashko referred to increasing the population as a "state task." Rather than conceptualize population issues in terms of "national superiority" or "race suicide," as did leaders in other European countries, he and other Soviet leaders espoused a nonracial approach that sought to boost the birth rate in order to build socialism and prove its ideological ascendance.

Once reproduction came to be seen as a state and societal concern, governments across Europe not only intervened to regulate reproduction, they also began to provide material support for mothers. By the early 1920s, extensive family allowance schemes had been established by state decree or employer initiatives in Germany, France, and Belgium, and through collective bargaining in Austria. Governments in the interwar period also adjusted their tax codes to reward families with children and punish people with none, and Italy, France, and Germany also awarded birth bonuses to encourage people to have children.[51] Soviet policies resembled those of other European countries in both means and objectives. The Soviet government also offered financial inducements; the same decree that outlawed abortion granted women a 2,000 ruble annual bonus for each child they had over six children, and a 5,000 ruble bonus for each child over ten children. These bonuses drew an immediate response from women with seven or more children. Local officials were deluged by requests from women (primarily peasants) who qualified for these bonuses.[52]

Although Soviet pro-natalist incentives resembled those in other countries, they had important differences as well. The Soviet government encouraged reproduction among all members of the population, without distinction as to ethnicity or class. Indeed, Soviet health officials stressed the need to increase postnatal care among national minorities in order to raise their birth rates. A government report in November 1936 also clarified that mothers with seven or more children should receive bonuses regardless of their social origins, and even regardless of whether their husbands had been arrested for counterrevolutionary activity. Thus the Soviet government promoted reproduction even among those it considered class or ideological enemies, in contrast to the Nazi government, which limited the reproduction of those it considered racial enemies.[53] In practice, the Soviet government's arrests and deportations of persons it deemed class enemies and bourgeois nationalists did prevent many of these people from having children. The Soviet objective, however, was not to eliminate them and their offspring biologically but rather to remove them from society and eradicate their economic and cultural milieu.[54]

In addition to paying bonuses to individuals, the Soviet government encouraged motherhood through maternity facilities and propaganda. Within months of coming to power, the Soviet government founded a large number of maternity homes, nurseries, milk kitchens, and pediatric clinics. With the pro-natalist push of the mid-1930s, funding for maternity wards and nurseries increased even more, though not nearly enough to meet the needs of the millions of women in the workforce. Since the Soviet government channeled virtually all resources into rapid industrialization, it lacked the money for adequate child-care facilities. But in principle, the Soviet government committed itself to complete care for mothers and children.[55] The Soviet government also sought to ensure that women did not avoid pregnancy for fear of losing their jobs or wages. As early as 1921 the government decreed that pregnant women who were unable to work were entitled to receive their full salary from workers' insurance funds. Soviet labor law guaranteed women workers eight weeks of paid leave both before and after giving birth.[56]

The Soviet government also celebrated motherhood and portrayed having children as a natural and fulfilling part of a woman's life. Articles in the Soviet press stressed the happiness that children brought to women's lives. One testimonial from a woman with five children described how much her children loved her, while another article claimed that children took care of each other, so that having many children was an advantage rather than a burden. Propaganda also sought to allay women's fears about giving birth. One article discussed a new medical technique for reducing pain and making childbirth easier, and it was followed by the testimonial of a woman who found that giving birth was not at all painful and that she did "not once cry out" when having her child.[57] Governments throughout Europe and around the world launched similar propaganda campaigns to promote motherhood.[58]

In their efforts to raise the birth rate, policy-makers across Europe glorified not only motherhood but also the family. There was a sense in many countries that the family had begun to disintegrate. Industrialization and urbanization in the nineteenth century seemed to undermine the traditional family at the same time that feminist ideas and new employment opportunities for women challenged existing gender roles. The enormous social disruption of the First World War and the intense cultural ferment in its aftermath even further eroded traditional gender roles and family patterns. Governments west and east sought to bolster the family in the in-

КОРМЛЕНЬЕ РЕБЕНКА ПРИ НАСМОРКЕ МАТЕРИ.   НЕ ПОЗВОЛЯЙТЕ ПОСТОРОННИМ ЦЕЛОВАТЬ РЕБЕНКА.

"Feeding a baby when mother has a cold. Do not allow strangers to kiss your baby." (Poster identification number RU/SU 955, Poster Collection, Hoover Institution Archives.)

terwar period as a means to increase the birth rate. As we will see, however, they strengthened the ideal of the family while in fact undermining family autonomy. The family became an institution to serve the state rather than to create a separate sphere safe from state intervention.

In the nineteenth century some social commentators had already expressed alarm over the disintegration of traditional families. The influential French sociologist Frédéric Le Play warned that urbanization had undermined the family and had fostered the corrupting influences of individualism, socialism, and feminism. He held up the patriarchal family of rural societies as his ideal, noting that peasant families had very high fertility, and he proposed legal measures to strengthen the family. Particularly in France, where concerns about the birth rate and pro-family activism by Catholic organizations were both strong, his ideas resonated with many political leaders and social thinkers.[59] During the interwar period, political leaders throughout Europe began to stress the family's importance to social stability and national strength. The dictatorships of Antonio Salazar in Portugal and Francisco Franco in Spain sought to restore the family as the pillar of society.[60] Nazi leaders heralded the traditional peasant family as a bulwark against the fragmentation and alienation of modern life. They promoted an essentialized vision of women as mothers and, in contrast to most European countries, paid family allowances to fathers rather than to mothers: "a man will no longer be materially or morally worse off in competition with the so-called clever bachelor, merely because he has done his duty to the nation."[61]

Soviet attempts to strengthen the family closely paralleled those of Western European countries in content and objectives. In the mid-1930s the Soviet government took steps to buttress the family. The 1936 decree that outlawed abortion also made divorce much more difficult. It largely reversed the 1918 and 1927 family codes, which had deliberately weakened the institution of marriage by facilitating a quick and easy divorce at the demand of either spouse. The new law required that both spouses appear in court to file for divorce. It also raised the fee for divorce from 3 to 50 rubles (150 rubles for a second divorce and 300 rubles for the third).[62] The Soviet government simultaneously sought to enhance the prestige and significance of marriage in the eyes of the population. Marriage registration offices were made more dignified; officials were instructed to treat marrying couples with politeness and respect; marriage certificates were beautified and wedding rings began to be sold in shops.[63]

An enormous propaganda campaign stressed the sanctity of marriage and family. Pro-marriage propaganda countered earlier attacks on the family as a bourgeois institution. An article in *Pravda* stated: "Only hopelessly muddleheaded people and petty bourgeois 'leftists' can assert that the family and concern about it is philistinism. On the contrary, a frivolous 'tramplike' relation to the family is real philistinism."[64] Another article asserted that "so-called free love is a bourgeois invention and has nothing in common with a Soviet citizen's principles of conduct."[65] The tightening of divorce was justified as a means to counter "the many people who don't give a damn about the family, looking on marriage as a means to satisfy their own personal whims," and those who failed to conclude long, stable marriages were sharply criticized.[66]

Marxist theorists such as Vol'fson who earlier had predicted the extinction of the family were made to recant their views, and new propaganda stressed that in the Soviet Union "the family is a socialist organization."[67] The Soviet government began to alter the Pavlik Morozov story—the tale of the patriotic boy who allegedly denounced his father for hoarding grain. In the mid-1930s Pavlik Morozov was still held up as a young hero for denouncing traitors to socialism, but it was not always mentioned that the traitor was his own father. Instead, articles stressed that "respect for elders and care for parents are a component of communist morality."[68] Stalin even made a highly publicized visit to his mother in 1935, reportedly to show concern for her health and tell her about the well-being of his children.[69]

In tandem with its drive to strengthen the family, the Soviet government sought to enforce paternal obligations. A 1933 decree that required all births to be registered within one month included provisions for a mother to name the father of her child whether or not they were married or even whether he was present. Men who did not acknowledge paternity of a child would still be registered as the father if a mother named him as such and provided any evidence of cohabitation.[70] In 1936 the same law that outlawed abortion and made divorce more difficult also tightened regulations on child support. It set minimum levels of child support as one-fourth of the unmarried or divorced father's salary for one child, one-third for two children, and one-half for three or more children. It also increased the penalty for nonpayment of child support to two years in prison.[71] The Soviet government proved to be serious about paternal responsibility; it took numerous steps to track down delinquent fathers.[72]

Soviet propaganda also stressed the importance of paternity; a lead article in *Pravda* titled "Father" stated that "a father is a social educator. He must prepare good Soviet citizens." Another article stated, "A poor husband and father cannot be a good citizen. People who abuse the freedom of divorce should be punished."[73] In order to provide positive reinforcement, socialist heroes were depicted as devoted parents and family members. Whereas in the 1920s and early 1930s Communist leaders were never shown with their families and fictional heroes sacrificed family life for the higher cause of building socialism, by the mid-1930s these heroes were shown to be devoted parents and family members. Karl Marx, for example, was described as "a tender, loving father, always sensitive and attentive to his children."[74]

The Family as an Instrument of the State

It was by no means preordained that the family would become one of the instruments by which Soviet officials sought to exercise control over sexual behavior and the upbringing of children. As long as officials viewed the family with suspicion, as a possible transmitter of bourgeois values and a barrier to social transformation, they hesitated to strengthen it. But by the 1930s Soviet leaders had come to see the family as a trustworthy institution and even as a state mobilizational tool. It was then that they sought to strengthen the family as a cure for social problems and as a means to pursue state goals of population growth and social discipline.

The issue of homeless children illustrates the evolution of official Soviet attitudes toward the family. By 1922, in the wake of the Civil War and the

ensuing famine, the Soviet Union had 7.5 million homeless children—
orphans and runaways who lived on the streets and survived by begging,
prostitution, and petty theft. While these children presented an enormous
social problem, some Soviet commentators also saw them as an opportunity to bring up children apart from the potentially reactionary influence
of their parents. Raised in orphanages, these children could be instilled
with Soviet collectivist values and shaped into the New Soviet Person. The
Soviet government quickly discovered, however, that it lacked adequate resources even to begin to house and care for those millions of orphans. By
1926 officials conceded that children should be raised by families if at all
possible, "to relieve the state and local budgets of the financial burden of
supporting children and teenagers in the internment institutions."[75] At
this point Soviet officials were still suspicious of the family, but they had to
rely on it because they could not afford to raise children in orphanages instead.

By the mid-1930s, Soviet officials' perceptions of the family had evolved.
Not only did they see strong families as a means to maximize the birth rate
but they had come to believe that the family could instill Soviet values and
discipline in children, and thereby serve as an instrument of the state.
While this change may in part have been making a virtue of necessity, it is
also true that with the elimination of small-scale capitalism and the exploiting classes at the end of the 1920s, the danger of bourgeois influences
within the family seemed to recede. Parents could now be trusted to instill
socialist values and teach their children to be good Soviet citizens. By the
mid-1930s, the prominent Soviet educator Anton Makarenko, who earlier
had argued that children were better off in orphanages, stressed that the
parents' role in bringing up children was decisive; raising their children
well was "their civic duty towards Soviet society." He portrayed the family
as a "collective body," which could instill collectivist values in children.[76]

Soviet jurists' analysis of juvenile crime reflected their new view of the
family. Whereas earlier they had seen the weakening of the family as a positive development, by the mid-1930s they cited family disintegration or
parental neglect as the source of juvenile crime. V. Tadevosian, the Soviet
deputy prosecutor for juvenile affairs, argued that with the improvement
in workers' living conditions, the material basis of juvenile crime had been
eliminated. Another criminologist concurred and blamed parents' failure
to bring up their children in a responsible way.[77] In May 1935 the Soviet
government decreed that parents of children guilty of hooliganism would
be fined, publicly shamed at their place of work, and investigated for
parental neglect. In such cases, courts were empowered to remove neglected children from their parents and place them in an orphanage.[78]

The Soviet government did not champion the family as a private commitment or as a means to personal fulfillment. Instead it explicitly promoted the maintenance of one's family as an obligation to society and to
the state. Komsomol head Kosarev stated in 1934, "The stronger and more
harmonious a family is, the better it serves the common cause. . . . We are
for serious, stable marriages and large families. In short, we need a new
generation that is healthy both physically and morally." A Soviet jurist
added that "marriage receives its full value for the state only if there is prog-
eny."[79] Soviet propaganda also stressed that parents were to raise their children for the sake of the Soviet state. One official stated that "the education
of children in the spirit of communism is a civic obligation of Soviet parents," and another commentator wrote, "Hand in hand with the state's es-
tablishments, the parents must rear the children into conscious and active
workers for socialist society. . . . Parents must instill in their children . . .
readiness to lay down their life at any moment for their socialist country."[80]

Other European countries also promoted the family not as an independent entity but as an instrument of the state or, as in the Nazi case, of the
race. For all the Nazis' rhetoric about strengthening traditional families,
the model that they promoted directly violated the principle of limited
state intrusion into private life. Nazi policy strove to create a family unit
that facilitated rather than guarded against state intervention, one that
served the state's goals of population growth and racial purity rather than
individual decisions about reproduction and child rearing. Hitler had written in *Mein Kampf,* "Marriage cannot be an end in itself, but must serve the
one higher goal, the increase and preservation of the species and the
race."[81] The 1935 Marriage Health Law required people to obtain a cer-
tificate of fitness to marry, and Nazi eugenic policies intervened directly in
the reproductive choices of married couples. Moreover, despite incessant
pro-family propaganda, the Nazi government in 1938 enacted a law that
facilitated divorce in cases of "premature infertility" and "refusal to pro-
create," with the idea that divorce would free at least one member of a cou-
ple to remarry and have children.[82]

The corollary to the state function played by the family was of course the
state's right to intervene in family matters. One article criticized a local
Komsomol organization for concluding that a husband's behavior toward
his wife was a personal matter. It told the story of an unfaithful husband
who ultimately abandoned his wife and child, and chastised the Komsomol
for neglecting its obligation to oversee its members' marital behavior.[83]
The Soviet state claimed the power to remove infants and older children
from their parents, either temporarily or permanently, in order to improve
their health or safeguard their upbringing. Sick and malnourished chil-

dren were sent to special sanatoria until their health improved and they could be returned to their families. Soviet law provided for the permanent removal of children from their families "in cases of parents' failure to fulfill their responsibilities," and in the late 1930s Soviet courts invoked this law regularly to take children away from "negligent" parents.[84] Jacques Donzelot's description of French family policy in the modern era could largely be applied to Soviet policy: the family was made "a sphere of direct intervention," and there occurred a "transition from a government of families to a government through families."[85]

State intervention in family matters necessitates one qualification to our characterization of Soviet policies as "strengthening" the family. While the Soviet government encouraged marriage, discouraged divorce, and emphasized parental responsibility, it did not fortify the family's control or autonomy. On the contrary, it reaffirmed the social and civic role of the family and weakened the family as a bulwark against state intervention in private life. The family model promoted by the Soviet state heightened people's familial obligations but undercut their rights and autonomy as family members. The family was to serve the state, not provide a sphere free from state intervention.

The family as an institution was central to the entire issue of social reproduction. As in many societies, the family acted as the key institution that mediated between individual desire and state or societal interests.[86] Family values set norms of sexual behavior and social organization that determined the way Soviet society reproduced itself. The Soviet government used the traditional institution of the family to create norms of sexual and social organization, because stable marriages and large families promoted population growth. Soviet leaders also chose the family because it corresponded to their own sense of propriety. The family offered a normative model of monogamous heterosexual relationships which fit their notions of how society was to be organized.

It was just before the campaign to strengthen the family that the Soviet government recriminalized male homosexuality. In December 1933 the head of the Soviet secret police, Genrikh Iagoda, sent Stalin a draft decree outlawing sodomy, and justified it by citing "associations of pederasts" engaged in "the recruitment and corruption of completely healthy young people." The Politburo approved the ban on male homosexuality and it was issued as law in March 1934.[87] Dan Healey notes that the Soviet recriminalization of sodomy was preceded by Hitler's accession to power and a virulent propaganda war between fascism and communism, which included mutual accusations of homosexuality. In this atmosphere, homosexuality became associated with fascism in the eyes of Soviet officials, and in fact Maxim Gorky justified the antisodomy law with the slogan "Destroy the homosexuals—fascism will disappear."[88]

Healey also points out that attacks on homosexuality coincided with the Soviet government's drives in the mid-1930s to cleanse cities of "social anomalies" and promote the (heterosexual) family. In 1936 Commissar of Justice Krylenko linked homosexuality with bourgeois decadence and counterrevolution, and stated that it had no place in a socialist society founded on healthy principles. He called homosexuals "declassed rabble, either from the dregs of society or from the remnants of the exploiting classes." Employing a heteronormative discourse, Krylenko declared that homosexuals were not needed "in the environment of workers taking the point of view of normal relations between the sexes, who are building their society on healthy principles."[89] Emphasis on the family should thus be seen as part of a larger effort by the Soviet government to make heterosexuality and procreation compulsory in the interests of the state and the larger society.[90]

While the family was a traditional institution, Soviet policy should not be confused with a return to the traditional family. The family fostered by official Soviet culture of the 1930s was not the patriarchal family of Russian peasant society. Traditional patriarchalism and gender roles were rooted in village culture and based on the father's control of household property and his voice in village decisions, through the exclusive right of male elders to attend the commune gathering. Taken out of the village, patriarchy and gender roles had to be established on a new basis—in this case, legislation that strengthened marriage and child support and propaganda that promoted motherhood and paternal responsibility. That the Soviet family did not conform to traditional models was even more apparent in policy toward national minorities. In the late 1930s, Soviet authorities actually increased their prosecution of Uzbeks who followed their traditional marriage customs of bride-price and female veiling and seclusion.[91] For this reason, it is misleading to characterize Soviet family policy as a retreat. While Soviet leaders relied on the traditional institution of the family, they denied its autonomy and stripped it of its traditional organization, using it instead as an instrument of the state to augment the population.

Women's Roles and Gender Inequality

Soviet family policy had important implications for women's lives and the issue of gender equality. The emphasis on women's reproductive obligations in conjunction with women's recruitment into the workforce left women with a double burden in Soviet society—responsibility for child raising and

"Mothers, breast-feed your children. Breast-fed children are stronger and seven times less likely to die." (Poster identification number RU/SU 918, Poster Collection, Hoover Institution Archives.)

domestic chores along with full-time work outside the home. This double burden in turn affected women's decisions about having children and largely frustrated official efforts to raise the birth rate. By examining the consequences of Soviet family policy, it is possible to explain more fully the construction of gender in Soviet society and the roles assigned to women. As we will see, these roles, while they provided opportunities, also saddled women with substantial burdens and perpetuated gender inequality.

The Soviet pro-natalist drive in itself created inequality. Pro-natalism promoted an essentialized view of women as mothers, and the ban on abortion was part of an effort to enforce motherhood. Accompanying this legislation was propaganda that depicted motherhood as women's "natural role." One article asserted, "There is no physically and morally healthy woman in [the Soviet Union] who does not want to have a child." Another article claimed, "A woman without children deserves our pity, because she does not know the full joy of life."[92] By defining motherhood as a necessary part of women's lives and by outlawing the termination of unwanted pregnancies, the Soviet government restricted women's choices concerning their lives and their bodies and assigned them a social role distinctly different from that of men.

The ban on abortion was but the most visible example of Soviet efforts to control women's bodies. Soviet medical research sought more generally to rationalize and maximize reproduction through a range of studies and measures to safeguard women's reproductive capacity. Soviet medical specialists in the 1920s used the language of industrial production to discuss reproduction: a woman's ability to become pregnant and bear healthy babies was her "productive capacity."[93] A. S. Gofshtein, in his article "The Rationalization of Maternity," described mothers as "producers" and wrote that pregnancy could be "productive" or "unproductive," depending on whether it ended with the birth of a healthy child or with miscarriage, abortion, or the infant's death. Gofshtein studied the histories of pregnant women and calculated that women would optimize their productivity if they had three children at four-year intervals. He noted that more frequent pregnancies weakened "the female organism," produced sickly children, and diminished women's value in the workforce.[94] Other Soviet doctors studied reproductive capacity by combining obstetrics and gynecology with anthropometry (for example, measuring women's pelvises). One researcher warned that women who worked in factories had more narrow (and hence inferior) pelvises than women who did not.[95]

Because women in the Soviet system were expected to serve as both mothers and workers, specialists showed particular concern with the effects of industrial labor on women's reproductive abilities. They conducted studies on the effect of heavy lifting, and concluded that it could damage pelvic organs and cause problems with pregnancy. In 1921 and again in 1927 the Soviet government established employment guidelines to ensure that women were not in jobs that required heavy lifting, for fear that such work would harm their reproductive organs.[96] Health officials also promoted physical examinations and education as means to protect women's reproductive capacity. Delegates to the Third All-Union Conference on the Protection of Maternity and Infancy in 1926 stressed that young women from the beginning of their sexual maturity should have regular medical consultations, initially arranged through schools. They also noted that these consultations would give doctors the opportunity to educate the young women about the dangers of abortion and diseases. Throughout the 1920s and 1930s women's health specialists conducted studies and educational efforts that emphasized the social importance of women's reproductive capacity, and hence accentuated the physiological differences between women and men.[97]

Visual representations of women in Soviet culture also began to highlight women's difference from men. Whereas posters and films of the First Five-Year Plan presented a neutered female image—stern, broad-shouldered, plainly dressed women workers—those of the mid-1930s depicted women as flirtatious, sensual, and dressed to accentuate their femininity. Romance and motherhood became important themes in the films of the late 1930s—another shift that emphasized gender distinctions. In such films as *Traktoristy*, released in 1939, women were seen driving tractors, traditionally male work, but the hero had to rescue the heroine and men discussed political matters while women tended to the children. Such depictions promoted gender inequality even as they portrayed women working outside the home.[98]

While the Soviet effort to glorify motherhood resembled pro-natalist propaganda in other countries, it was distinguished by the fact that it encouraged women to continue working during pregnancy and to return to work after giving birth. To ensure that pregnant women could find or maintain jobs outside the home, the Politburo approved a decree in October 1936 that made it a criminal offense to refuse to hire or to lower the pay of a pregnant woman.[99] Soviet leaders constructed gender in a way that stressed women's roles as both workers and mothers, and they insisted there was no contradiction between the two. In contrast, many officials and social commentators in Western Europe blamed feminism and women's employment outside the home for the weakening of traditional female roles and the decline in the birth rate. In the early 1920s, General Maitrôt in France stated, "There are too many women typists and civil servants here and not enough *mères de famille*. With respect to natality, the German mothers have beaten the French mothers; this is Germany's first revenge against France."[100] Nazi leaders were even more opposed to women in the workforce. Central to Nazi ideology was an emphasis on traditional gender roles, and from the time they came to power they admonished women to stay at home and have children.[101]

The Soviet gender order assigned a dual societal role to women as both workers and mothers. The Soviet government had recruited women into the industrial workforce in large numbers during the First Five-Year Plan, and for the rest of the Soviet era it continued to rely on their labor outside the home. At no time during the campaign to bolster the family did Soviet officials suggest that a woman's place was in the home. On the contrary, the Soviet government stressed women's desire and indeed obligation to make an economic contribution in the workplace and as well to produce and raise children.[102] Soviet propaganda in the 1930s depicted heroines as both valiant workers and devoted mothers. Soviet women, then, were assigned the dual role of mother and worker. Soviet men were defined primarily by their labor, but also by their roles as stable but largely passive husbands and fathers.[103]

The militarization of Soviet society before the Second World War raised new gender issues. War had the potential to widen gender differences, if the front was defined as an exclusively male domain and women were confined to the "home front." The Civil War had in fact created such a gendered division of function and power. Masculine identity during the Civil War (and among Komsomol members even into the 1920s) became based on the fraternity of male soldiers and the exclusion of women. While some women served in the Red Army during the Civil War, commanders assigned the overwhelming majority to administrative and nursing positions, thereby reinforcing gender stereotypes.[104] Before the Second World War, Soviet propaganda proclaimed that if the USSR were attacked, women would fight alongside men to defend their country. Women were shown flying planes and parachuting in preparation for war.[105] But other propaganda stressed gender difference. One article described a family in which the husband was away serving in the army while the wife inculcated courage in their children.[106] Here the woman's role was shown to be raising the next generation of soldiers rather than fighting at the front. Even Soviet pilot-heroines, who provided role models for women's military preparation, were depicted as both pilots and mothers. At a Kremlin reception to honor them, they were pictured with their children and described as devoted mothers.[107]

While our focus is on officially defined gender roles and reproductive policies rather than on the popular response to them, we should pause to evaluate briefly the reaction to the Soviet pro-natalist campaign. Government reports indicated that the population received the decree banning abortion "enthusiastically." Some women who received birth bonuses did write letters to thank Stalin and promised to continue having children.[108] But in fact the response of most Soviet women was far from enthusiastic. Many wrote to newspapers to object to the ban on abortion. One student pointed out that she would have to drop out of medical school if she got pregnant and was not allowed to have an abortion. Several peasant women argued that pregnant women who were unmarried or who already had two or three children should be allowed to receive abortions. A woman engineer wrote that the abortion ban would mean "the compulsory birth of a child to a woman who does not want children," and she warned of increased deaths when women inevitably sought illegal abortions.[109]

The ban on abortion did in fact lead to a huge number of illegal abortions. Commissariat of Health reports in October and November 1936 cited thousands of cases of women hospitalized after poorly performed illegal abortions. Of the 356,200 abortions performed in hospitals in 1937 and 417,600 in 1938, only 10 percent had been authorized; the rest were incomplete illegal abortions.[110] In response the Soviet government stepped up efforts to identify people who performed illegal abortions, and in 1937 arrested and convicted 4,133 abortionists. As the law dictated, those found guilty were sentenced to a minimum of two years in prison.[111] But despite considerable efforts, Soviet authorities found it difficult to catch underground abortionists, because women who entered hospitals after botched abortions rarely cooperated with the police.[112] In oral history interviews, David Ransel found that virtually every Russian village had one person who performed illegal abortions and that self-performed abortions were also common.[113]

Despite prohibitions on abortion and contraception, and despite extensive pro-natalist incentives and propaganda about the family, a campaign to raise the birth rate failed to have a marked effect in any country, certainly not in the Soviet Union.[114] The ban on abortion did result in a rise in the Soviet birth rate, but this rise was limited and temporary. The birth rate per thousand people rose from 30.1 in 1935 to 33.6 in 1936 to 39.6 in 1937. But in 1938 the birth rate began to decline again, and by 1940 marital fertility for European Russian was below the 1936 level.[115] The enormous social disruption of the purges and mobilization for war in part accounted for the decline of the birth rate beginning in 1938. But even before these disruptions the birth rate had not even approached pre-industrialization levels, and evidence on illegal abortions indicates that Soviet women as a whole did not abide by the government's abortion ban. As Soviet authorities had noted in 1920 but then chose to ignore in 1936, the outlawing of abortion only drove women to seek illegal abortions. Repression proved ineffective at raising the birth rate in the long term.

The glorification of motherhood and birth bonuses also failed to have much effect. The women who received the bonuses were primarily peasants who already had many children before the monetary incentives were introduced.[116] The resources allotted to expand maternity wards and child care were insufficient to improve mothers' lives markedly. Government priorities continued to focus on heavy industry, while child-care systems and communal dining facilities remained woefully underfunded.[117] And given the equally underfunded consumer sector, women had enormous difficulty simply obtaining basic necessities for their children. Commissariat of Education reports to the Komsomol in 1937 noted that some children did not attend school because their mothers could not obtain shoes and clothing for them.[118] The severe shortages of food, clothing, and housing throughout the 1930s, in addition to insufficient child care and communal services, deterred women from having more children despite government exhortations.

One other crucial consideration was women's place in the workforce. Women had been recruited in large numbers into industry during the 1930s, and the official emphasis on motherhood was in no way intended to free women from their obligation to perform "socially useful labor" outside the home. Soviet fiction of the time portrayed women as both mothers and workers. As the heroine of a 1937 novel states, "a wife should also be a happy mother and create a serene home atmosphere, without however abandoning work for the common welfare."[119] Soviet law did provide paid maternity leave—a fact Stalin took care to stress publicly—but this was only another small inducement for women to have children.[120] The realities of Soviet life saddled women with the double burden of full-time work and uncompensated domestic chores. Soviet leaders wished to exploit both the labor and the childbearing capabilities of the female population, and they proved unwilling, official rhetoric notwithstanding, to allocate adequate state resources for domestic chores and child raising.

Women's double burden might have been somewhat alleviated had Soviet authorities sought to restructure gender roles within the family. Soviet propaganda could have done more to urge men to share responsibilities for raising children and maintaining the household in order to promote gender equality in the home.[121] Instead Soviet propaganda about child care and household chores addressed primarily women, indicating that these things were women's responsibilities. Soviet fiction also portrayed women as subservient to their husbands.[122] Time budget studies from the 1930s reveal that Soviet urban women, in addition to working full-time outside the home, averaged four to six hours per day on domestic chores, while men averaged only one hour per day.[123]

Women did not achieve equality in the workplace either, though Soviet leaders did seek their recruitment and promotion. At the Seventeenth Party Congress in 1934, Stalin stressed the importance of women's labor on collective farms, noting that "women make up half our country's population, they constitute an enormous army of labor," and applauding "their promotion to leadership posts."[124] While this statement reflected Soviet leaders' instrumentalist aims in the mobilization of women's labor, it is also true that they believed in the transformative effect of labor and saw it as a means for women to fulfill their human potential and reach political consciousness. The previous year at the First Congress of Collective Farm Shock Workers, Stalin had described the female delegates as "entirely new people," unlike any women he had met before. He claimed that "only free, collective farm labor could produce such heroines of labor in the countryside." Contrasting the collective farm system with petty capitalist agriculture, he called collective farm labor "an honorable matter" that had

ЧистоТа
-залог
здоровья

Содержите комнату в чистоте. Мойте руки прежде чем дотрогиваться до ребенка. Меняйте почаще ребенку белье. Купайте ребенка до полгода ежедневно, а затем до года через день.

"Cleanliness is the guarantee of health. Wash your hands before touching a baby. Change a baby's linen frequently. Bathe a baby daily up to six months of age and then every other day up to one year." (Poster identification number RU/SU 916, Poster Collection, Hoover Institution Archives.)

"eliminated inequality" and "liberated women" from subordination to their husbands and fathers.[125] For Soviet leaders, then, the shift from capitalist to socialist economic relations allowed women to achieve gender equality and human fulfillment through unexploited labor.

In reality, while women did receive greatly expanded work opportunities under Soviet power, they did not achieve equality in the workplace. The fact that Stalin emphasized women's agricultural labor (lower in status than industrial or white-collar work) in itself was indicative of a persistent gender bias in Soviet leaders' thinking. The Soviet government did recruit women into industrial and service jobs, but primarily into low-status, low-paying positions. The Commissariat of Labor, in its effort to recruit more female workers, issued lists of jobs to be filled primarily by women, and it thereby perpetuated the principle of the sexual division of labor even as it reordered this division. As a result, even in factories where the percentage of women rose considerably, female workers remained in low-status positions.[126] Ultimately, then, gender equality was achieved neither in the Soviet workplace nor in the home.

The Russian Revolution seemed to present a unique opportunity to remake society, and in the process to liberate women and achieve gender equality. Feminist attempts to restructure or eliminate the family, however, ultimately came to naught. While most Soviet leaders initially suspected the family of being a bourgeois institution that might pass on reactionary attitudes to children, they still believed in long-term, monogamous, heterosexual relationships as the proper sexual organization of society under socialism. And once socialism had been established and the remnants of capitalism eliminated in the 1930s, they came to see the family as a socialist organization—one that could raise children to be good Soviet citizens. The renewed emphasis on the family should not be seen as a retreat to the traditional family, for Soviet law and practices actually weakened the family's autonomy and made it an instrument of the state. In this sense, Soviet efforts resembled family policy in other countries that also used the traditional institution of the family to serve modern state goals of population growth and social discipline.

Soviet family policy had important implications for women's lives and gender equality. The Soviet gender system was distinguished from that of other countries in that it stressed the opportunity and obligation for women to work outside the home. But it also emphasized women's reproductive capabilities and obligations, particularly during the tremendous pro-natalist drive of the mid-to-late 1930s. This emphasis promoted an essentialized view of women as mothers and accentuated gender differences. Moreover, Soviet leaders did not restructure gender roles within the family. As a result, gender inequality continued and women ended up with the double burden of work outside the home and uncompensated domestic labor.

CHAPTER FOUR

Mass Consumption in a Socialist Society

> Nothing is too good for us. Our youth must be cultured enough
> to enjoy to the utmost the best things that life has to offer. . . .
> They want nice homes, an automobile, a gramophone. We do
> not consider these desires wrong.
> —ALEKSANDR KOSAREV, 1934

> Life has become better, comrades. Life has become more joyous.
> —JOSEPH STALIN, 1935

Industrialization created, for the first time in world history, the possibility of mass consumption—the distribution of manufactured goods to a wide range of people. With the mass production of the industrial age, material consumption was no longer the exclusive privilege of the upper classes. As the volume of goods produced dramatically increased, as populations became more urbanized and hence more aware of new forms of material wealth, and as the expansion of print media, radio, and film circulated appealing images of consumer products, people in industrializing countries aspired to acquire these products for themselves. In capitalist countries, this aspiration was increasingly realized in the twentieth century, particularly in the United States, where advertising, supermarkets, chain retailing, and systems of credit all contributed to the mass marketing of manufactured goods. Some American commentators even heralded mass consumption as the basis of a new civilization, and many people came to see consumerism as a way for all citizens to partake of the American dream.[1] But for leaders of industrializing countries, the possibility of mass consumption also presented new challenges: Should the burgeoning consumer demand be satisfied? If so, how? A tension arose between individual gratification through material acquisition and the sublimation of desires to the "higher" cause of nation or ideology.[2] The bright future of modernity could be expressed in collectivist ideological terms or in individualist materialist strivings for a better life. The ways in which various countries resolved this tension determined both the model of consumption and the distribution of wealth within their respective societies.

The Soviet Union was not immune to the challenge of mass consumption or the friction it generated between individual gratification and sacrifice for the greater good. Soviet official culture exhibited a tension between the revolutionary values of asceticism and self-sacrifice on one hand and the material aspirations of the population on the other. Alongside socialism's anticapitalist, antimaterialist strains was Marx's utopian vision of a society of abundance, where everyone's material needs would be met. Soviet leaders, then, had to define Soviet socialism partly through the establishment of official values and norms in regard to consumption. Particularly as Soviet citizens became more urbanized and educated and increasingly exposed to images of industrial progress and consumer products, they sought to acquire more material goods. But at the same time the tasks of socialist construction and national defense continued to require individual sacrifices for the sake of the whole.

The tradition of revolutionary asceticism—the sacrifice of all individual needs and material comforts for the sake of the revolutionary struggle—had begun long before 1917. This tradition was in fact strengthened during the Revolution and the desperate years of the Civil War. Communists later looked back upon the Civil War as a heroic era when they sacrificed everything for the cause of socialist victory. After the period of limited capitalism under the New Economic Policy, this ascetic revolutionary spirit was revived during the First Five-Year Plan (1928–32), partly out of a need to mobilize all available resources for the industrialization drive. But after Stalin and his fellow leaders claimed to have attained socialism in 1934, they abandoned enforced asceticism in favor of consumerism and images of prosperity. The promotion of consumerism raised the delicate matter of distinguishing socialist trade from capitalist consumption. Soviet propagandists sought to differentiate socialist trade by stressing its modern and didactic elements, and their discourse on culturedness offered a means to articulate materialist ambitions without the usual bourgeois connotation. But since scarcity continued and only a privileged few were actually able to acquire material goods, the emphasis on consumption only created further tensions within Soviet official culture.

Revolutionary Asceticism and Its Limits

The tradition of revolutionary asceticism in Russia dated from the nihilist movement of the 1860s. Not only did nihilists rebel against the existing moral order, as we saw in Chapter 2, but they repudiated all existing behavioral and cultural norms as well. In the words of a leading nihilist thinker, Sergei Nechaev, they sought to break "all ties with the social order and with all educated society, with all manners, accepted customs and morality of this society."[3] To do so they rejected fashionable clothing and material goods and purposely cultivated a disheveled appearance. Their dirty working-class clothing and uncombed hair, along with their simple and austere lifestyle, set them apart from upper-class society and indeed shocked many educated Russians.

Whereas the nihilists practiced asceticism as a form of rebellion against the existing political and social order, later revolutionaries adopted an ascetic lifestyle as a means to achieve the larger goal of political revolution. Forgoing any material desires allowed them to devote all their attention and energy to the task of organizing the revolution. Nikolai Chernyshevsky provided an example of asceticism in his character Rakhmetov, the prototypical new man of his novel *What Is to Be Done?* Rakhmetov prepares himself for the revolution with daily gymnastics, heavy physical labor, a diet of raw beef, and complete celibacy and sobriety.[4] This character served as the archetype for an entire generation of Russian revolutionaries; he embodied the ideal of complete asceticism to develop the mental strength and willpower to create a new world.

The Bolsheviks were among the Russian radicals who continued this tradition of revolutionary asceticism and iron willpower. Many Bolsheviks suffered considerable material deprivation in the revolutionary underground, and more when they were arrested and exiled by the tsarist police. To sacrifice one's personal comfort and well-being for the cause of revolution became a badge of honor for them. The Bolsheviks also shared in a more general European socialist tradition that eschewed entertainments and pleasures as distractions from the struggle for socialism. Like many on the European left, they sought to direct not only their own but all workers' energies away from the dance hall and the pub and into more serious pursuits of ideological education and political organizing.[5]

After the Revolution, the Bolsheviks found themselves in a savage civil war to maintain power, and they had little choice but to continue their ascetic ways. The Civil War in fact reinforced the ascetic strain in Bolshevism, because it was a time of great personal sacrifice. Activists who joined the Red Army and fought at the front suffered extreme hardship; many died.

Those who remained in the rear organizing munitions and supplies suffered too. The entire population had to endure rationing and deprivation as the Soviet government marshaled all available human and material resources for the war effort. The Bolsheviks later remembered the Civil War as a heroic era when they willingly risked their lives to defend the Revolution and won a glorious victory by the strength of their willpower and their readiness to sacrifice.

Many Party members experienced the introduction of the New Economic Policy in 1921 as a betrayal of revolutionary and ascetic ideals. Although they grudgingly accepted Lenin's policy of limited capitalism and free trade, they deeply resented the return of capitalists and the boorish materialism that accompanied them. These resentments only mounted as NEPmen opened expensive restaurants, casinos, and boutiques selling imported fashions and cosmetics. One Komsomol member wrote to Party leaders in 1925:

> When you walk along the street and see the satisfied well-fed faces and patent leather shoes alongside some adolescent worker, 90 percent of whom have tuberculosis, then straight away . . . you become ashamed. Was it really necessary to have the October Revolution, during which so many young people were killed, only to return to the past?[6]

In reaction to capitalist extravagances under NEP, many Communists and Komsomol members condemned material riches and fashion and strove for a proletarian simplicity or even slovenliness. These militants wore coarse clothing reminiscent of the Civil War and lived in austere and often filthy apartments and dormitories.[7] They emulated the Bolshevik hero of the Revolution and Civil War era, still portrayed in popular literature of the 1920s as a model of selfless devotion to the Party. The ascetic trappings of this archetype included "stiff leather jackets, black tobacco, straight bobbed hair, bisexual boots, and barren dormitories"—all symbols of personal sacrifice for the greater cause of the Revolution.[8] Some Komsomol members practiced these ideals by forming communes to abolish bourgeois individualism and materialism. They lived together with no personal belongings or personal space. They pooled their money and owned all items in common—clothes, shoes, sheets, even underwear—and they cooked and ate together as well.[9]

Official Soviet culture throughout the 1920s condemned interest in material possessions and portrayed it as a sign of bourgeois decadence. The newspaper *Komsomol'skaia pravda* called jewelry and feminine clothes a symptom of bourgeois contamination, and it ran a series of articles denouncing tasteless ornamentation in household objects and decorations.[10] One article, titled "Eliminate Domestic Trash!" used military language to describe a "battle" against petty bourgeois decorations in the home.[11] A Komsomol conference on home life included a display contrasting a bourgeois room with the room of an activist. The bourgeois room had family portraits and icons on the wall, a vase with flowers, a phonograph, a bed with two large pillows, a fancy dresser, and several plush armchairs. The activist's room was far more spartan; it had only a portrait of Lenin on the wall, a simple bed with one pillow, a narrow dresser, and a writing table with a newspaper on it.[12]

Although Party officials advocated a spartan lifestyle, they opposed the extreme asceticism of Komsomol militants. Fearing that a complete disregard for basic standards of hygiene and propriety would pose health risks and retard cultural progress, some Party leaders sought to moderate the militants' rebellion against norms of dress and behavior. The commissar of health, Nikolai Semashko, while he condemned bourgeois fashion as too extravagant, elegant, and Western, at the same time prescribed clothing that was neat and hygienic. He wished Russian workers to emulate the "more cultured" workers of Europe, who would change into clean clothing when they returned home from work.[13] The Bolshevik moralist A. Stratonitskii wrote that Bolsheviks were not against beauty and neatness, only against excess. He admonished Komsomol members to maintain cleanliness and to dress well, in clothing that was "attractive, but not so luxurious that you stand out from the larger working mass."[14]

Party and Komsomol leaders also sought a middle ground in leisure and material culture. Some militants, ready to sacrifice all personal pleasure to the greater task of building socialism, opposed any concession to private possessions or frivolous entertainment. Stratonitskii himself took an ascetic stand against pleasurable pastimes and called dancing "an abnormal, unnecessary and even harmful kind of entertainment," while other moralists recommended museum visits and factory tours as edifying substitutes for dancing and socializing. But in 1925 the head of the Komsomol, Nikolai Chaplin, criticized such positions as "absurd communist asceticism." It was important, he said, for Komsomol members to have fun as well as to do political work. Citing instances when Komsomol members had been expelled for playing the accordion or dancing, Chaplin said that some militants had gone too far in prohibiting pleasurable activities: extreme asceticism would only drive young people away from the Komsomol toward hooliganism and drink. Despite Chaplin's pronouncement, debate continued within the Komsomol and the Party as the tension between revolutionary asceticism and pleasurable entertainment continued throughout the 1920s.[15]

With the launching of the First Five-Year Plan, this tension was resolved in favor of asceticism with regard to both entertainment and material goods. The First Five-Year Plan required enormous material sacrifices on the part of the population. In an effort to industrialize the country as rapidly as possible, Soviet leaders channeled all available resources into building new factories, primarily in heavy industry. While the share of Soviet national income reinvested in industry in the 1920s never surpassed 10 percent (as in most societies, over 90 percent went to consumption), the share reinvested climbed to 29 percent in 1930 and to 44 percent in 1932.[16] Reinvestment on such a scale meant woefully inadequate expenditures in the consumer sector and terrible shortages of food, clothing, and housing. Industrial workers, who received priority for most goods, experienced a catastrophic fall in living standards, while other groups in the population, particularly peasants, actually starved.[17]

Party leaders accomplished their mobilization of resources by abolishing private trade and assuming state control over all sectors of the economy. They envisioned an economic system in which the state would plan all aspects of production, from investment and consumption to production and distribution. With the end of free trade in 1929, food, clothing, and dry goods became scarce, and long lines formed at poorly stocked state stores. Soviet authorities began to ration all basic foodstuffs and clothing, and by early 1930 rationing was in effect throughout the country.[18] Most Soviet leaders and economists assumed that rationing would become a permanent feature of the Soviet system, and some even foresaw the complete abolition of money.[19]

Official culture reinforced the asceticism necessitated by the industrialization drive. Parade organizers during the First Five-Year Plan jettisoned the carnival merrymaking characteristic of 1920s holiday celebrations and replaced it with militant marches that stressed discipline and asceticism.[20] Censors clamped down on "decadent" culture by banning foreign films and jazz.[21] The occasional comedies and adventure movies made during the 1920s also disappeared as Soviet filmmakers resolved "to portray on the screen issues of the five-year plan, socialist competition, and collective farm development."[22] Literature and poetry of the First Five-Year Plan also focused on industrialization and extolled asceticism and self-sacrifice for the cause of building socialism.[23]

By 1931, however, extremely high rates of labor turnover and increasing economic chaos led the Stalinist leadership to moderate its policies and to reemphasize material incentives. In his "New Conditions" speech in June 1931, Stalin admitted that the Soviet government had a responsibility to meet all of workers' "material and cultural requirements," and he called on Soviet managers to improve the supply of goods and housing to retain workers. Stalin also denounced wage leveling in the Soviet economy. "We cannot tolerate a situation where a rolling-mill worker in the iron and steel industry earns no more than a sweeper," he said, and he advocated greater wage differentials to stem labor turnover.[24] Higher wages for skilled workers meant little in an economy where most goods were still rationed, but Stalin's policy nonetheless represented a step toward material incentives and a step away from self-sacrificing asceticism.

Stalin's emphasis on wage differentials also had implications for the degree of social hierarchy in Soviet society. The period of the First Five-Year Plan had seen not only an overall drop in living standards but a general economic leveling of the population as well. The attack on "bourgeois specialists," begun with the Shakhty Trial in 1928, when a group of engineers were convicted of sabotage, precipitated a drastic decline in the status and material well-being of technical elites. At the same time, the insatiable demand for industrial labor drove up wages for even unskilled workers. Some Party members viewed these developments favorably, seeing such a socioeconomic leveling as an attribute of socialism. But Stalin argued that Marxism-Leninism posited that wage differentials would continue under socialism; they would disappear only under communism.[25] His speech was thus the first step toward greater wage differentiation and social hierarchy.

The following year the Soviet economy entered an even more serious crisis, centered on agriculture. While collectivization had increased state control of grain production, it caused enormous disruptions in agriculture, and when the government turned to requisitioning, it led to a grievous famine that killed several million peasants in 1932–33. Even before the full extent of the famine became known, the worsening food supply forced the Soviet government in May 1932 to permit peasants to sell surplus produce at market prices—a significant step back from total state economic control. By the January 1933 Central Committee plenum, Stalin was calling for slower rates of economic growth, and the Second Five-Year Plan was accordingly more moderate and more focused on consumer goods.[26]

To understand why the Stalinist leadership reoriented its economic policies so fundamentally, it is necessary to appreciate the full extent of the 1932–33 crisis. Not only had the extreme tempo of Stalinist collectivization and industrialization caused a horrendous famine, but concomitant food shortages provoked widespread unrest among workers as well as peasants. When the Soviet government reduced food rations in 1932, some industrial workers even organized strikes and protest demonstrations.[27] Food shortages also undermined economic progress, as labor turnover worsened, construction projects lagged, and industrial output fell far below the plan's unrealistic goals. Stalin even faced a challenge within the Communist Party itself, as several members of the Central Committee signed the Riutin Platform, a document that denounced collectivization and rapid industrialization and called for Stalin's removal.[28] Stalin dealt mercilessly with his opponents, both in 1932 and during the Great Purges later in the decade, but he simultaneously showed pragmatism in moderating economic policies and placing more emphasis on consumer production.

While political opposition and unrest compelled Stalin and other Party leaders to moderate their policies and placate the population, it also seems clear that the 1932–33 crisis prompted them to reassess their vision of socialism and how to achieve it. The catastrophe of the famine and the specter of worker unrest in an allegedly working-class state underscored for them the importance of attending to the consumption needs of the population. It also led them away from the extreme ascetic model of "barracks socialism," which had predominated during the First Five-Year Plan and which required people to forgo basic amenities for the sake of rapid industrialization. Once Party leaders recognized that building steel mills alone could not achieve socialism, they acknowledged the need for adequate food supplies, housing, and consumer goods. In fact, while they continued to develop heavy industry, they began to devote more resources to the consumer sector and to stress the material prosperity and abundance that could be achieved under socialism.

Another decisive factor in Party leaders' reorientation toward consumerism was their purported attainment of socialism. During the NEP period, consumption had remained associated with petty capitalists and decadence, so consumerist values were seen as a corrupting influence. Party leaders feared that an emphasis on consumption would distract from the tasks of building socialism, and this fear continued through the First Five-Year Plan, when material comforts were sacrificed for the sake of rapid industrialization. But with NEP abolished, the bourgeoisie eliminated, collectivization accomplished, and the First Five-Year Plan fulfilled, Party leaders could embrace consumption as one of the fruits of socialism attained. Freed of its petty bourgeois associations, consumption became integral to the Soviet system and material well-being became central to the vision of life under socialism. It was this vision, articulated by Stalin himself, that came to be projected in official Soviet culture of the mid-1930s.

At the First Congress of Collective Farm Shock Workers in February 1933, Stalin stated that since collectivization had been accomplished, it was now time to proceed to the next step, which was "to make all the collective farm peasants prosperous. Yes, comrades, prosperous." He went on to argue that within two to three years, through conscientious work and better use of land and equipment, all peasants could be raised "to the level of people enjoying an abundance of produce and leading a fully cultured life."[29] At a time when the country was in the midst of a famine and millions of peasants were starving to death, Stalin's goal was unrealistic, even ludicrous. Yet his pronouncement marked a new emphasis on consumption in both official culture and Party policies, even if the reality was still extreme material deprivation.

At the Seventeenth Party Congress in early 1934, Stalin sharply repudiated a course of rapid industrialization at the expense of consumption, warning that this approach had "upset the country's economic life." He denounced "ultraleftist chatter" among officials who looked upon trade as "a secondary, worthless matter" and wished to abolish money in favor of direct exchange. Calling these people "as far from Marxism as the sky is from the ground," he said that money would continue for a long time, right up until "the first stage of communism." Stalin also stressed that "socialism means not poverty and deprivation but the elimination of poverty and deprivation and the organization of a rich and cultured life for all members of society." He concluded that "Marxist socialism means not the reduction of personal needs . . . but the comprehensive fulfillment of all the needs of culturally developing laboring people."[30]

Stalin continued to herald the shift from revolutionary asceticism to socialist abundance in speeches the following year. At the Second All-Union Congress of Collective Farm Shock Workers in February 1935, he directed that collectivized peasants be allowed to retain up to three cows as personal property (and more in regions such as Central Asia, where herding was prevalent). When one congress delegate advocated common ownership of all animals, Stalin intervened to say that this would take time. "A person is a person," he cautioned. "He wants to have something of his own. . . . He wants to have his own cow. There is nothing criminal in this." Stalin concluded that it would take a long time "to reshape human psychology," and that in the meantime it would be necessary "to develop peasants' consciousness" and to increase the availability of food products "to raise people's living standard."[31]

At the First All-Union Conference of Stakhanovites in November 1935, Stalin made his famous pronouncement "Life has become better, comrades. Life has become more joyous." He emphasized the population's material needs and noted that without adequate food, housing, and manufactured goods, little could be accomplished. Concluding that it was difficult to live "on freedom alone," he argued, "In order to live well and happily, the benefits of political freedom have to be supplemented by material benefits. A characteristic feature of our revolution consists in the fact that it gave the people not only freedom but also material benefits and the opportunity for a rich and cultured life."[32]

Stalin himself, then, trumpeted the new prominence of materialism and consumption in the Soviet system. His speeches reflected acknowledgment of human desires for personal ownership and material goods and a tacit admission that the Party had tried to proceed too quickly toward communism during the First Five-Year Plan. In this sense, the new course can be seen as a concession to human nature and the need for material incentives. But equally apparent was Stalin's new conviction that socialism required not only basic food and housing for the population but also a vision of future prosperity and abundance. The fact that Stalin felt the need to criticize "leftists" and insist that Marxist socialism meant "not the reduction of personal needs" but their fulfillment reveals that the struggle to define Soviet socialism was not over yet. Revolutionary asceticism, as practiced during the Civil War and again during the First Five-Year Plan, exerted a strong influence on some Party members. But when Stalin took a stand against it in the mid-1930s, the emphasis in official Soviet culture tilted heavily toward consumerism, not only as an incentive but as a vision of what socialism should be—happiness and plenty rather than suffering and poverty.

"Life Has Become More Joyous"

In conjunction with Stalin's slogan, the Politburo took some concrete measures to raise the standard of living: it allocated more resources to housing and consumer goods and ended rationing. While these measures raised the standard of living slightly, they did not lift the general population out of poverty. In fact, a harvest failure in 1936 created new food shortages at the very moment when living standards were supposed to be improving. Lacking real-life prosperity, the Soviet government instead created images of abundant food and copious consumer wares. It also sought to promote happiness through publicity of material rewards, symbols of prosperity, cheerful holiday celebrations, and even Soviet musical films to provide entertainment for the masses. These joyful images, while they raised people's spirits and hopes for a more prosperous future, accentuated the poverty in which most of the population lived.

Images of prosperity and happiness were transmitted through a variety of means. Model stores and economic exhibitions showcased a wide range of Soviet manufactured goods—sewing machines, washing machines, radios, cameras, automobiles, motorcycles. Newsreels showed stores stocked with champagne, smoked fish, and other delicacies.[33] Virtually none of

"Send the best agricultural achievements to the All-Union Agricultural Exhibition!" 1937. (Poster identification number RU/SU 1608, Poster Collection, Hoover Institution Archives.)

these items were actually for sale; if they were available at all, they were sold at model stores for prices far beyond the average citizen's earnings. The presence and publicity of these goods, then, was to create an image of plenty and an incentive for Soviet workers to work harder in the hope that they might one day be able to acquire such items.

The Soviet press also circulated images of abundance. A lead article in *Pravda*, titled "Live and Work in a Cultured Manner," declared that the country was "becoming richer." It explained that the Soviet people wished "to live in well-built cities and towns, and in beautiful homes. They want to dress cleanly and well."[34] An article on young women workers in Leningrad described the many pretty clothes they owned—dresses, blouses, stockings, and nice shoes. It concluded, "The new life we are building . . . becomes more and more rich, cultured, and happy every day."[35] Pamphlets and highly publicized conferences heralded improved living standards for peasants as well. The Second All-Union Congress of Collective Farm Shock Workers in 1935 stressed the peasantry's material benefits—new cultural facilities, saunas, well-equipped beauty salons, and so forth. Party officials followed up the conference with a pamphlet titled "Our Collectivized Peasants Live Prosperously," in which they claimed that peasants gathered large harvests and lived well.[36]

Holiday celebrations also served to convey a spirit of happiness and prosperity. In contrast to the militaristic marches of the First Five-Year Plan, holiday parades of the mid-1930s were occasions for fun and merrymaking. The 1935 May Day parade had 5,000 actors in costumes to represent popular heroes of literature and opera, and on Constitution Day later that year, the government organized fireworks, Ferris wheels, jazz bands, and ballroom dancing in Gorky Park.[37] New Year's received special attention as a festive holiday. Newspapers and journals were filled with images of sumptuous banquets and lavish balls, accompanied by stories about the happiness in people's lives.[38] Dancing, which had been frowned upon earlier, received special attention as a New Year's Eve activity, and Western dances such as the fox-trot and tango were once again permitted.[39] Kosarev even stressed dancing, along with "neat clothing, flowers, [and] love," as essential to young people's enjoyment of life.[40]

The Soviet government also sought to make New Year's a special holiday for children. One means of doing so was to revive the tradition of decorated fir trees, now reinvented as a secular symbol of New Year's instead of a religious symbol of Christmas. Pavel Postyshev, the second secretary of the Ukrainian Communist Party, argued that Soviet children should not be denied fir trees just because some "left deviationists" considered it a "bourgeois undertaking." He claimed that before the Revolution working-class children "looked with envy at [rich children's] fir trees sparkling with multicolored lights." So that all children might enjoy this pleasure under the Soviet government, he proposed that "collective" fir trees be placed in schools, orphanages, and children's clubs.[41] A trade union decree in December 1937 stated that "Soviet children love fir trees," and called for the installation of more trees as part of "a celebration of a joyous and happy childhood."[42] Children's New Year's celebrations were enlivened by games, gifts, and songs, including one song with the refrain "Thank you, our beloved Stalin."[43]

In addition to holidays, the Soviet government's "Life Has Become More Joyous" campaign included new forms of entertainment such as musical films. In contrast to the production-oriented films of the First Five-Year Plan, these films were comedies and melodramas with entertaining songs and dances. The first such film, *Cheerful Fellows,* directed by Grigorii Aleksandrov, opens with a group of singers strolling through a prosperous collective farm and goes on to slapstick scenes of the hero trying to dance while tied to a cow. The film also has a romantic plot starring a Marlene Dietrich look-alike, Liubov' Orlova. After falling in love, the hero and heroine travel to Moscow and perform at the Bolshoi Theater, where their humble clothes are transformed into a glamorous suit and gown.[44] Aleksandrov's later film *The Circus,* also starring Orlova, had entertaining songs and a romantic theme but it contained a serious plot as well. The heroine is an American woman with an African American child who finds acceptance among the Soviet circus performers and audience. In the final scene she joins a parade of all Soviet nationalities marching together in a symbolic gesture against racism.[45]

While some Soviet films of the mid-1930s still contained ideological messages, the fact that some did not marked an important departure from the films of the First Five-Year Plan. Moreover, Soviet musical films bore a striking resemblance to Western musicals and comedies of the same era, and reflected the influence of Western culture. As in Western Europe and the United States in those Depression years, the primary value of musical films was escapist entertainment. When Soviet audiences watched these films, they could temporarily forget about the food shortages, overcrowded housing, and dangerous working conditions that characterized their lives. For the moment they could share in the prosperity and happiness of the film characters in their imaginary carefree world of joy and optimism. The Soviet government actively encouraged people to partake of this world by attending movies and the theater as a means to live "culturally and cheerfully."[46]

There is no question that the emphasis on a joyous and prosperous life resonated deeply with the population's desires. After the grinding poverty and self-sacrificing asceticism of the First Five-Year Plan, people longed for improved material conditions and some entertainment and frivolity in their lives. But for the vast majority, the sumptuous foods, fashionable clothing, automobiles, and imported goods publicized by the Soviet media remained far out of reach. Most of them struggled to obtain the bare necessities of food and clothing throughout the Second Five-Year Plan. Given this continued hardship, we might ask whether official images of happiness and material wealth gave people any incentive to work harder, or whether they fueled envy and resentment instead. Did people accept the government's vision of future socialist prosperity, or did the contrast between ideal and reality only highlight what they lacked?

Memoirs and archival materials indicate that the "Life Has Become More Joyous" campaign did raise the hopes of some people. Many certainly responded to the entertainment of musical films and the allure of material goods much more enthusiastically than to ascetic ideals and political exhortations. Some even wrote letters mimicking the new language of the regime, expressing gratitude for "the cultured, cheerful, and wealthy life" bestowed by the Soviet government.[47] But the majority of Soviet citizens felt resentment over the array of foods and material items that they now saw pictured everywhere but could not acquire themselves. And the fact that the new course actually raised people's hopes and heightened awareness that a select few possessed luxury items while most did not only generated disillusionment and envy.

After the Seventeenth Party Congress in 1934, when Stalin had defined socialism as "not poverty and deprivation but the elimination of poverty and deprivation," some workers at factory meetings complained, "The speeches are good but there's no bread."[48] At a conference accompanying an exhibition of children's wares in 1936, members of the audience jeered, "Now we've seen that at the exhibition there are all imaginable things, and that's all very well, but they aren't in the stores and you won't find them." Others wrote anonymous letters complaining that life was becoming better only for the rich.[49] Many workers expressed particular disillusionment regarding the slogan "Life Has Become More Joyous," explaining that they expected living standards to get better and instead they had gotten worse. Soon people began to use the slogan "Life Has Become More Joyous" ironically, spouting it when something went wrong or when someone was experiencing hardship.[50]

Soviet holidays and celebrations also aroused some popular resentment. One diarist described the anniversary of the October Revolution in Tiumen in 1936; he noted the festive atmosphere, posters, decorations, music, and a marionette show witnessed by large crowds. But he concluded that "it is all false and strained," and complained that enormous resources had been wasted on the celebration when the rest of the year there were food shortages. He also asked why, if life had become joyous, so many people were drunk on the holiday.[51] In her study of Stalinist celebrations, Karen Petrone similarly concludes that widespread drunkenness on Soviet holidays reflected people's tacit refusal to accept the official meaning of celebrations.[52] For many Soviet citizens, holidays represented a chance to avoid work and get drunk rather than celebrate Soviet accomplishments.

Socialist Trade

After the crisis of 1932–33, the Stalinist leadership turned its attention to the problems of the Soviet distribution network. Of course the fundamental cause of shortages was the planned economy and the channeling of resources into heavy industry rather than consumption. But because Soviet leaders were unwilling to abandon economic planning or the industrialization drive, their only hope of improving living standards was to modify the distribution of goods. To do so, they abolished rationing and promoted a new concept of Soviet trade as efficient and bountiful. This new concept, while it did not go so far as market relations, did include some capitalist retail practices. To distinguish socialist trade from capitalism, Soviet officials pointed out the ability of retail to promote culture and stressed that an increase in material goods symbolized the cultural progress of the Soviet people. The concept of socialist trade, while seemingly contradictory, proved central to the new official emphasis on consumption and material advance.

Soviet distribution during the First Five-Year Plan had been based on rationing and on a system of closed shops at the place of employment, where people received most of their food and goods. But severe shortages and unrest in 1932–33 prompted Soviet leaders to see this system as overly bureaucratic and inefficient. At the November 1934 Central Committee plenum, Stalin criticized the existing system as mechanical distribution, which took no account of people's tastes and needs.[53] In its place Soviet leaders sought to establish "commercial" state trade, based not on ration coupons but on free exchange of money for goods. With the exception of peasant markets, where collective farm members were allowed to sell surplus agricultural produce, this exchange was limited to state stores—it was not a return to the private enterprise of the New Economic Policy. But given the strong anticommercial sentiment in the Party, the promotion of commercial state trade was a significant step. Indeed, after years of discrediting trade as anti-Soviet, the government faced a formidable task in reestablishing the legitimacy of commercial trade and in distinguishing socialist trade from capitalism.[54]

Soviet leaders began by abolishing the rationing system.[55] Israel Veitser, the new commissar of domestic trade, had previously served as the Soviet trade representative in Berlin and had an appreciation of a market system. He touted the advantages of "free trade," by which he meant unrationed trade, and said that rationing had been only an interim stage in Soviet economic development. The Soviet government ended bread rationing at the beginning of 1935 and ended rationing of all other goods by that October. In order to ensure adequate supplies after rationing ended, the Soviet government opened over 13,000 new bread shops, increased bread deliveries, and expanded store hours. It also increased the production of clothing as part of the Second Five-Year Plan's greater (though still inadequate) emphasis on consumer goods.[56]

Soviet leaders envisioned state stores filled with an abundance of food and manufactured items as part of this new system of socialist trade. They began by taking a trade census in 1935, which enumerated the facilities in every store and shop throughout the entire country. What the census revealed, however, was an extremely poorly equipped, poorly stocked state system that would have required a tremendous infusion of resources even to approach a vision of socialist plenty. Lacking the money to remake every store, the Soviet trade administration instead created a handful of model stores in Moscow and other large cities. These grocery and department stores were nicely refurbished and stocked with high-quality goods, sold at extremely high prices that only the elite could afford.[57]

The ideal on which these stores was based came from the West, particularly from the United States. While Soviet trade officials disparaged British retail as a "realm of small shopkeepers," they greatly admired the modern, large-scale merchandising of American department stores. The trade commissariat dispatched several delegations on study trips to the United States between 1935 and 1937. Upon their return, these delegates published enthusiastic endorsements of American trade methods, with only brief caveats about capitalist retail. Two long articles on Macy's department store in New York extolled its infinite stock and variety of goods, as well as its technical innovations in organization and marketing.[58] One Soviet trade journal devoted half of every issue to merchandising in the West, including articles on American display windows, advertising, new products, and customer service.[59]

With such an emphasis not only on materialism but on Western commercialism as well, it is tempting to view Soviet trade policy as a retreat from revolutionary values and a return to capitalist methods. According to Timasheff, "The restoration of the freedom of consumption was a conspicuous item in The Great Retreat."[60] But as Amy Randall has argued, such a characterization would obscure the ways in which the Soviet trade policy sought "to extend the Soviet revolutionary project." As she points out, the Soviet government tried to reform trade to build a more modern economy and to develop and integrate people as Soviet citizens.[61] Soviet trade accordingly emphasized not only Western marketing but rationalization, technological innovation, didacticism, and material advancement for workers and peasants.

Innovative technology and the efficient distribution of goods were to distinguish new Soviet trade both from the bare shelves of the First Five-Year Plan and from the small shops and outmoded retail techniques of the NEP and prerevolutionary eras. In this way, socialist trade, even if it relied on Western marketing techniques, could be distinguished from the "petty bourgeois" capitalism of previous periods. Soviet trade officials criticized small, disorganized row shops as remnants of "old, merchant Moscow," and instead accentuated the importance of rationalization and new technology.[62] They called for the scientific organization of goods within stores, preweighing and prepackaging of products, the optimal division of labor among salesclerks, and the use of meat-slicing machines and conveyer belts to speed the preparation and distribution of items.[63] Trade journals carried inspectors' reports that praised well-organized stores and criticized disorganized ones. Inspector M. S. Shakhramon'iants decried inefficient bookkeeping, asymmetrical product displays, poor discipline among salesclerks, and unhygienic conditions at Moscow's Central Department Store. His article implied that rationalization of the store would eliminate shortages of goods.[64]

Soviet officials seemed to believe that greater efficiency in the trade system and harder work by salesclerks would compensate for insufficient production and would alleviate shortages of consumer products. Salespeople were supposed to gather information on customer preferences and convey this information to store managers and producers; this substitute for a market mechanism would allegedly allow supply to correlate more closely with demand. According to Soviet trade officials, the leading salespeople also mitigated shortages by negotiating with local industries and searching other stores to procure scarce products for their customers. They even modified manufactured goods in accordance with customers' wishes. In one store, Stakhanovite employees repainted beds that were not selling well in order to make them more attractive.[65] Of course terrible shortages continued to plague the Soviet system; greater efficiency in retail could not make up for underproduction of consumer goods. But by stressing rationalization and innovation, Soviet officials could both modernize trade and turn a blind eye to the continued need to devote more resources to consumption.

Another way Soviet trade officials distinguished socialist from capitalist trade was to portray Soviet consumption as more democratic; that is, it benefited not just the rich, as in capitalist countries, but workers and peasants as well. One 1935 journal article noted that while the Great Depression had left common people in capitalist countries destitute, the masses in the Soviet Union were experiencing rapid growth in their material welfare and a rise in their "cultural level" as well.[66] Indeed, material prosperity in the Soviet context was equated not with individual greed but with collective advance. All members of the society were to benefit from the alleged abundance of goods, and they were to grow more modern and civilized as a result. Soviet trade officials proclaimed that "backward" peasants and workers could be transformed by the acquisition of urban clothing, home furnishings, and modern appliances. Molotov argued in 1936 that collective farm members' demand for "iron beds, hanging clocks, silk dresses, and so on" demonstrated that they were "no longer former peasants" but rather cultured Soviet citizens. Trade Commissar Veitser likewise said that peasants' greater interest in household articles such as saucepans and coffeepots proved that cultural "backwardness" had been eliminated.[67]

The distribution of modern clothing and appliances among national minorities was supposed to have the same civilizing effect, though it had an added cultural dimension as well. A book on Soviet trade in Central Asia asserted that Uzbeks' "cultural growth" was reflected in their increased demand for manufactured goods, such as phonographs, radios, and bicycles.[68] But the acquisition of manufactured items usually meant the importation of nonindigenous materials and habits; phonographs and radios could significantly change native peoples' leisure time and worldview. European and specifically Russian goods and clothing could also erode native culture and dress. A 1936 article claimed that the peoples of the far north requested "nice shawls with tassels," "colored ribbons," and "small tea cups with pretty, colorful designs."[69] Many members of national minorities desired such manufactured goods and clothing because of the novelty and wealth they represented, but their acquisition of such items undercut the production and use of traditional handicrafts. Soviet officials viewed such developments as the civilization of savage peoples, but for national minorities it meant the loss of traditions and native culture.

In accordance with the civilizing mission that material progress was to play, Soviet retail was also supposed to be didactic. Soviet salespeople were assigned the task of educating customers about products and instructing them on what they should buy. According to the deputy trade commissar, Z. S. Bolotin, "Our consumer is not used to many goods. It is necessary to instruct him toward new tastes, to stimulate new needs." A trade official in Khar'kov added that salesclerks should "organize the taste of the customer."[70] Given the earlier dearth of consumer goods, officials believed that Soviet consumers were especially in need of instruction to help them develop a taste for new goods. Didacticism in trade also corresponded with the more general Soviet mission of uplifting and educating the masses.

Because Soviet trade practices were intended to educate customers rather than to entice them into buying things they did not need, Soviet advertising was also distinct from capitalist advertising. Soviet officials believed that capitalist advertisements manipulated images to stimulate irrational desires. They preferred product exhibitions, because they considered the concrete display of items less deceptive than print images. Soviet print advertisements were relatively few, and they tended to be dry, straightforward representations of products rather than glossy images designed to seduce consumers.[71] This difference in advertising reflected the absence of a profit motive in Soviet trade. Soviet stores did not seek to maximize their sales; their aim was to serve, educate, and uplift their customers. Material advancement of all citizens would move Soviet society toward the socialist prosperity that Party leaders had promised.

Soviet officials' new attention to state trade represented an important part of the turn toward materialism and consumerism in the mid-1930s. Their vision of attractive and efficient stores, well stocked with high-quality food products and manufactured goods, contrasted sharply with the barebones asceticism and rationing of the First Five-Year Plan. Yet it would be misleading to characterize this shift in trade policy as a retreat, because that would imply a return to an earlier period or policy. The commercialism espoused by Soviet officials in the mid-1930s differed fundamentally from the limited capitalism of the New Economic Policy and from prerevolutionary capitalism. This difference consisted most essentially in the fact that trade in the mid-1930s was entirely state-run. The Soviet government did not permit limited free enterprise or small-scale private ownership of the means of production, as during the New Economic Policy.

Soviet trade differed from NEP-era capitalism in other ways as well. While trade officials sought to employ the retail and merchandising techniques of American capitalism, they did so in order to create a modern socialist trade system that would supersede both the scarcity of the First Five-Year Plan and the small-scale capitalism of earlier eras. Large-scale, technologically advanced distribution offered a means to create the socialist abundance and prosperity that Stalin and other Party leaders had promised. This prosperity was to be shared by all, as socialist trade was to provide for all citizens—not only the wealthy, as in capitalist societies. Indeed, the acquisition of modern clothing and manufactured goods was seen as a means to modernize "backward" peasants and national minorities and transform them into Soviet citizens. Salesclerks were even supposed to educate their customers in order to facilitate this advance and aid in the process of building a modern socialist society.

The only problem with this vision was that state stores remained badly underfunded and undersupplied throughout the 1930s. While Party leaders devoted slightly more resources to consumption, they continued to invest huge sums in heavy industry during the mid-1930s, and increased such investment still further as war approached at the end of the decade. Contrary to the elaborate plans of trade officials, Soviet stores remained largely empty and consumers continued to lack basic necessities. Unable to supply every store and every customer, Soviet officials operated a handful of model stores, well stocked with expensive food products and luxury goods. Only a small number of Soviet citizens were able to obtain these items and partake in the officially heralded prosperity. Among them were

Stakhanovite workers and members of the Party elite—the vanguard of a new lifestyle that allegedly all citizens would ultimately enjoy.

Stakhanovism and Social Hierarchy

While the majority of the population found the disjunction between ideals of prosperity and the reality of hardship disillusioning, living standards did rise markedly for some people during the mid-1930s. Indeed, central to the Soviet government's campaign to portray life as joyous and prosperous was the creation of Stakhanovite hero-workers, who exemplified the best of Soviet society not only in their work but in their lifestyles as well. These workers, along with the Party elite, received the material benefits highlighted in the "Life Has Become More Joyous" campaign. Moreover, Stakhanovites' high living standards were widely publicized to show other workers how they too might live. The material wealth of Stakhanovites and Party officials, however, contributed not only to a greater emphasis on materialism but to an increasing sense of social hierarchy in Soviet society.

As we saw in Chapter 1, Party leaders launched the Stakhanovite movement as a way to spur productivity among industrial workers. Stakhanovites were not the first hero-workers in the Soviet Union, but they were distinguished from their predecessors in two ways. The most prominent labor heroes to precede them, shock workers, had set records working in brigades rather than as individuals. Publicity surrounding them sometimes did not even mention them by name, referring to them as the shock-work brigade at a given factory or construction site.[72] Second, shock workers were glorified only for their labor accomplishments, whereas Stakhanovites were held up as models for workers to emulate in their lifestyle as well as their work. Much of the publicity surrounding Stakhanovism described not only Stakhanovites' labor accomplishments but also their home lives. Indeed, Stakhanovites' fine clothes and well-appointed housing became a shining example of the country's material progress—living proof that indeed life had become more joyous.

At a highly publicized conference of leading Stakhanovites and Party leaders, one hero-worker after another spoke of the high wages and material rewards he or she had earned. G. I. Likhoradov bragged that he earned over 1,000 rubles a month, and claimed that he wanted to earn even more, "because our Soviet government gives us the opportunity to work well, to make good wages and to live in a cultured way. Why should I not wear a good serge suit, why should I not smoke good cigarettes?"[73] A later conference held for Stakhanovite combine drivers sounded similar themes. When Molotov asked a Stakhanovite named Kobzar' how much he earned, the man answered 3,100 rubles a month, and said that his family now owned a bicycle, phonograph, camera, rifle, and watches. Another Stakhanovite, Ponomarev, who earned 4,500 rubles, announced that he wished "to explain to my beloved leader, Comrade Stalin, how I spend my money." Stalin interjected, "It's your money, so it's your business. Spend it as you wish." Ponomarev nonetheless went on to describe the new clothing, bicycle, phonograph, and books he had bought, and concluded, "There you have our joyous and happy life!"[74]

The Soviet press also highlighted the material and cultural advances of Stakhanovites. Fine clothing received special attention as an indication of cultural maturity, particularly for female Stakhanovites. One article told how proud a mother was of her Stakhanovite daughter, who earned high wages and dressed so attractively in "stylish" dresses; another described the high and increasing percentage of female Stakhanovites who owned fancy dresses, new shoes, and nice winter coats.[75] The journal *Stakhanovite* even urged the use of perfume and cosmetics, formerly available only to the "parasitic classes" but now important indicators of the cultural and hygienic progress that workers had made.[76]

Stakhanovites' housing also received considerable publicity. In contrast to the horrendous overcrowding and substandard housing endured by most workers, Stakhanovites were shown to have new, spacious accommodations, which they kept meticulously clean and tastefully decorated. One Stakhanovite's apartment was described as having "clean, comfortable, warmly heated rooms," with nicely upholstered new furniture and portraits of Soviet leaders on the walls.[77] Stakhanovite autobiographies also highlighted their material progress by describing the transformation of their housing. One Stakhanovite moved from a makeshift wooden barracks to a "beautiful apartment . . . in a multi-story stone building, constructed according to the latest word in technology," while another acquired an apartment allegedly better than the one in which the factory director lived.[78]

Publicizing the fine clothing and housing of Stakhanovites provided an incentive for other workers to work harder to try to achieve these rewards themselves. But such publicity also served the larger purpose of providing an example of advanced, cultured workers for others to emulate. Stakhanovites' fine clothing and cultural activities symbolized their transformation into the New Soviet Person. They acted as living examples of the Soviet Union's progress toward a modern, prosperous socialist society. Not coincidentally, the first industrial Stakhanovites were of peasant origin, and their Stakhanovite autobiographies stressed their transformation from backward peasants into conscious workers, from uncouth country bumpkins into cultured urbanites.[79]

Stakhanovites' importance as cultural role models is reflected in official emphasis on their participation in intellectual and cultural activities. A Stakhanovite speaking at a trade union conference called upon officials "to give us culture" in order to replace uncivilized leisure activities such as drinking.[80] One article portrayed Stakhanovites as spending their leisure time reading newspapers and journals, playing chess, and drinking tea. It also described regular Stakhanovite excursions to lectures, films, and the theater.[81] In an article titled "I Want to Be a Highly Cultured Person," a model worker wrote that she took evening classes and had started a reading circle at her factory, where workers enthusiastically discussed the classics of Russian literature.[82]

The fact that Stakhanovites served as cultural role models helped to justify their high social status. Not only were they receiving material rewards for their job performance, but they were elevating the material level of all workers and peasants by providing examples for them to follow. In 1935 Stalin said that model collective farm workers helped to raise "all collective farm members, both former middle peasants and former poor peasants, to the level of prosperous peasants, to the level of people who enjoy the abundance of products and who lead a fully cultured life."[83] Iaroslavskii referred to the "leading role" of both Party members and Stakhanovites, and said that their "personal example . . . can attract the backward workers, can convert them into leading workers, and can reeducate them."[84] Material gains were not made through the exploitation of others, as in capitalist society, and the improved standard of living would ultimately be shared by all. In championing Komsomol members' desire for material goods, Kosarev said, "Our young people do not want to arrogate things . . . by exploiting someone else. They know they can achieve for themselves only by raising the living standards of the whole collective in which they live and work."[85]

Official publications also emphasized the egalitarian nature of Soviet consumption. *The Book of Tasty and Nutritious Food,* published in 1939, included lavish and sumptuous dishes far beyond the means of the average citizen. But the book's authors proclaimed that it was intended "for the very broadest public," reflecting an expectation that, with time, these delicacies would be available to all Soviet citizens. Etiquette manuals from the 1930s, though intended primarily for rising Party officials and Stakhanovites, also avoided any hint of elitism or social hierarchy. These manuals stressed respect for other members of the collective but never deference to social superiors or a sense of station in society. In contrast to etiquette guides in capitalist countries, Soviet guides promoted culturedness for all, without reference to social distinctions.[86]

In theory, then, the material privileges of Stakhanovites and Party officials were not supposed to create a sense of social hierarchy in Soviet society. As Sheila Fitzpatrick has argued, Stakhanovites and Party members provided a living version of socialist realist art in that they showed the new socialist world as it was becoming. In this sense they were not elitist but rather a vanguard, leading all Soviet society to a higher standard of living and a cultured life.[87] As we saw in Chapter 2, Stalin boasted about the creation of a new intelligentsia and claimed that in time all workers and peasants would be made cultured. Indeed, the fact that both Stakhanovite heroes and newly promoted Party officials came from the ranks of the working class seemed to confirm that the laboring masses were becoming more cultured and prosperous under Soviet socialism. And for those who were feted as heroes or promoted into positions of authority, the Soviet system had delivered on its promise to create a society where rank-and-file workers could enjoy a prosperous life and even share in the power of the Soviet state.

But the celebrity and material gains of Stakhanovite heroes did not mean the advancement of all workers and peasants. In reality, the vast majority of people remained impoverished, despite the "Life Has Become More Joyous" campaign. For them the publicity given to Stakhanovites' fine clothing and comfortable housing could not help fomenting a sense of injustice and inequality. It is important to remember that the Second Five-Year Plan produced only a slight improvement in living standards from the desperate poverty and starvation of the early 1930s. The vast majority of people continued to struggle for basic food and clothing, and lived in overcrowded communal apartments or barracks.[88]

Not surprisingly, resentment against Stakhanovites became widespread, and in some cases erupted into sabotage and violence. While Stakhanovites at one Moscow textile mill were attending a banquet in their honor, other workers slashed their warps.[89] In other cases workers insulted Stakhanovites, hid their tools, wrecked their equipment, or physically assaulted them.[90] Soviet officials implicitly acknowledged such resentments when they published the account of a Komsomol member who wished to expel a highly paid worker who wore a new suit and tie. In this account the Komsomol member overcomes his envy and aspires to dress well himself and become more "cultured," but in real life such resentments were not so easily overcome.[91] The Commissariat of Justice issued a special circular in January 1936 citing the need to protect Stakhanovites from hostile "class-alien elements" in the workforce. It cited approvingly the case of a worker sentenced to five years in prison for threatening a female Stakhanovite and derisively calling her "a Parisian lady" for the prizes and fine clothing she had won.[92]

An even greater source of resentment was the material benefits enjoyed by the Party elite. These benefits did not receive publicity, but most people nonetheless knew that Party officials enjoyed a much higher standard of living than they did. The special stores, housing, medical clinics, and vacation homes for the Party elite created a sense of social hierarchy in an allegedly egalitarian society. While it is true that most Party officials came from the ranks of the working class, once they had been promoted they often sought to distinguish themselves materially from the rest of the population. Some Party officials lived extravagant lifestyles that clearly violated the spirit of socialist egalitarianism. But even those who lived only moderately better, wearing suits and living in private apartments, could inspire the envy of peasants and workers.

The Party elite had always enjoyed higher living standards than average citizens. From the time of the Civil War, when they received special rations, Party officials had been privileged on the grounds that their needs should be met so they could continue their work. And during the 1920s some Party functionaries displayed a definite acquisitiveness, securing nice apartments and expensive furniture for themselves and their relatives.[93] But the "Life Has Become More Joyous" campaign of the mid-1930s sanctioned a far greater degree of materialism, and the Party elite with its connections and power was in the best position to benefit from it. Elena Osokina has described in detail the mechanisms of distribution that maintained a hierarchy of consumption in Soviet society. The Party elite, as well as secret police and military officers, had special supply networks, stores, and dining halls that ensured that they received the best food, clothing, and manufactured goods.[94]

Party officials increased their wealth partly out of material greed. When Party leaders redirected official culture to underscore prosperity rather than self-sacrifice, functionaries took advantage of this shift to enrich themselves. But material possessions also served to legitimate the elite. Partly because many officials were former workers recently promoted into positions of authority, the new elite were insecure in their status and sought material affirmation to buttress their position. These newly promoted officials sought to dress and live in a manner that distinguished them from the working masses they came from and whom they now governed. People's dress, home furnishings, and manners all serve to classify or distinguish them in the social order.[95] In the Soviet Union, as in all societies, fine clothing and material possessions served to distinguish the new elite from the masses. While newly promoted officials did not necessarily have a deep understanding of high culture, they eagerly seized upon the superficial behaviors and material symbols of elite status to bolster their authority.

Though material symbols of status serve to legitimate the elite in all societies, they posed a particular problem in the Soviet Union, because "bourgeois" concerns with status and materialism were ideologically unacceptable. The new elite therefore sought to bolster their status and enjoy material luxuries without being labeled bourgeois. "Cultured" served as a euphemism for "bourgeois," and allowed one to discuss bourgeois respectability without using the term. In the same way that "intelligentsia" applied to Soviet officials and bureaucrats served as a euphemism for "elite," culturedness both justified and disguised the new social hierarchies and the pursuit of material possessions and status.[96] Vera Dunham has emphasized the importance of culturedness as a concept that "helped to bestow on material possessions attributes of dignity and of virtue."[97] Because Party leaders heralded material possessions as symbols of progress and culture, the new elite could pursue their desire for goods and legitimation in a way that did not seem to be bourgeois.

Party functionaries were thus partly responsible for the increasing degree of social hierarchy in Soviet society. Their successful pursuit of material goods widened the gap between common people and the Party elite. But it would be a mistake to overemphasize Party bureaucrats' material ambitions as the cause of the shift away from asceticism in official Soviet culture. As we have seen, the new stress on materialism and prosperity was a conscious policy adopted by the Stalinist leadership for particular political and ideological reasons. After the purported attainment of socialism, Stalin and other Politburo members had chosen to reorient Soviet official culture away from asceticism and toward material well-being. Their policy was welcomed by most Party bureaucrats, who clearly benefited from it, but the bureaucrats themselves did not initiate this policy.

Party propaganda in fact encouraged officials to seek fine clothing and a neat, well-groomed appearance. A 1935 article called upon engineers and industrial officials to be well dressed, noting that outward appearance "is closely connected with cultural growth and development."[98] The Soviet government sanctioned even elegant dress when it began to publish the magazine *Mody* (*Fashions*) in 1936. *Mody* contained pictures of regal suits and dresses for the new elite. Its articles, such as "What's New This Season," described the latest fashions in Western Europe, distinguishing between British and French styles. The magazine also discussed the types of fine material the clothing was made of and provided advice on fashions that best lent themselves to different types of figures.[99] Party officials in the 1930s took fine clothing for professional and social gatherings very seriously, and in some instances excluded those who were not properly attired.[100]

While some sense of hierarchy had always existed in Soviet society, Party functionaries' pursuit of more lavish tastes in the mid-1930s compounded social disparities and concomitant social resentments. Some members of the new elite began to live extravagant lifestyles that clashed with the state's egalitarian ethos and workers' sensibilities. At expensive Moscow restaurants and cafés high-ranking officials, dressed in imported European clothing, socialized and danced to the music of jazz bands.[101] The Party elite vacationed at deluxe health resorts, with well-upholstered rooms and nicely maintained grounds, and Party leaders owned expensive dachas built with money allocated by the Politburo.[102] Some Party officials also used their positions to acquire expensive foreign goods and lavish apartments.[103]

In isolated cases high-ranking Party officials engaged in even more extreme abuses of their authority in pursuit of personal gain and grandeur. Several Central Committee members, including Ian Rudzutak, Nikolai Antipov, and Genrikh Iagoda, built themselves "grandiose dacha-palaces" of fifteen to twenty rooms, all lavishly furnished. A district Party leader in Voronezh assigned himself an office in the local Party headquarters that took up half the building. He also built a special platform on the roof of the building from which he hung posters of himself and delivered "incendiary speeches." Numerous similar cases make clear that some members of the new elite far overstepped the fine line between "cultured" and extravagant living.[104]

The fine clothing and lavish lifestyles of the elite naturally aroused the resentment of the population overall. It was not only a violation of the egalitarian ideals of the Communist state that aroused such indignation in peasants and workers, but the fact that their own food, clothing, and housing were so inadequate. Particularly during the First Five-Year Plan but throughout the rest of the 1930s as well, much of the population went hungry. Many people dressed in ragged clothing and lived in overcrowded barracks or mud huts. The Soviet government devoted virtually all resources to the industrialization drive and very little to basic consumer needs.[105]

Some workers and peasants complained about the inequities in Soviet society and about the Party elite's riches in particular. Most of them knew that Party officials were better dressed and better fed than they were, and they greatly resented the special shops with luxury goods for the Party elite. They also expressed indignation at the fact that the elite had automobiles; one citizen said, "A new bourgeois has appeared in our country, they travel around in cars."[106] Based on secret police reports on the popular mood in the 1930s, Sarah Davies has concluded that the disparity in wealth and lifestyle provoked a sense of social polarization between common people ("us") and the new elite ("them").[107]

Letters written by peasants and workers in the 1930s support Davies's conclusions. A report on anonymous letters sent to the Soviet government in 1932 emphasized the population's bitter feelings toward local authorities, who were believed to be well fed and to have no concern for the needs of the people. It quoted one letter as saying, "Now officials eat well while workers and peasants live on the brink of famine."[108] Letters to the newspaper *Krest'ianskaia gazeta* in 1936 also voiced resentment toward the elite. One peasant complained that a Party official on his collective farm earned a high salary and that he and his wife flaunted their wealth. "His wife goes about in a silk dress and a nice fur coat. She does not work anywhere and does not even do her own laundry." The letter went on to list several other officials who earned high salaries and whose wives and family members did not work. Another letter writer pointed out that officials' wives who did not work violated the Soviet principle "He who does not work does not eat." This slogan clearly applied only to peasants and workers, the writer added, not to Party officials.[109]

While these resentments were not the impetus for the Great Purges, which were instigated by the Stalinist leadership itself, they provided one justification for the arrest and execution of thousands of Party officials. The Soviet press reported the purge of officials in an anti-elitist tone, and while purge commentaries gave Trotskyism, spying, and wrecking as the reasons for purging, they also contained information about the luxurious lifestyles of "enemies of the people." One high-ranking purge victim was denounced not only for his alleged connections with spies and traitors but because of his opulent apartment and expensive furniture made of Karelian birch. Other purged officials were said to have wasted thousands of rubles of state money on foreign automobiles and private dachas, where they lavishly entertained their families and friends.[110]

The Stalinist leadership, then, played on popular resentment to justify the Great Purges. For their part, Party officials discovered the dangers of excessive materialism, and some paid with their lives. Those who were not purged learned to hide their wealth or at least not to flaunt it. As we saw in Chapter 2, official culture began to stress modesty as an essential characteristic of Party members. More modest behavior did less to generate popular resentment toward the Party elite, and it also served the Stalinist leadership's aim of ensuring a docile and loyal Party organization. After the Great Purges, the privileged lives of Party officials receded from public view.

The more general emphasis on prosperity in Soviet official culture did not continue for long either. With the rising threat from Nazi Germany in the late 1930s, Party leaders began once again to devote most resources to heavy industry and military production in preparation for war. The Third Five-Year Plan severely slighted consumption, and the military mobilization of 1938 diverted labor and other resources from consumer production to the military.[111] Severe shortages of manufactured goods in 1938 resulted in long lines outside of stores, and by 1939 enormous lines were forming for food items as well. The Soviet-Finnish War of 1939–40 only exacerbated the shortages, and citizens began to ask authorities to reinstate rationing so that they would at least be guaranteed a bare minimum of food.[112] The Politburo rebuffed these requests and prohibited the operation of informal ration systems that sprang up. Party leaders clung to their ideal of socialist abundance, preferring to blame shortages on local bureaucrats' inefficiency rather than on the planned economy and military mobilization. Finally, when the Nazis invaded in 1941, Party leaders began to ration food and clothing once again and to call on the population to sacrifice for the cause. Official Soviet culture came once more to stress asceticism over materialism, as self-sacrifice became a necessity for national survival.

The mid-1930s shift toward consumerism was nonetheless an important development in what we term Stalinism. It not only reflected a significant political decision by Party leaders at a moment of economic crisis and popular unrest but also demonstrated a different definition of Soviet socialism—one based not on asceticism and self-sacrifice but on prosperity and happiness. If indeed all Soviet citizens had been able to partake of this prosperity, rather than simply a vanguard of Party officials and Stakhanovite heroes, then perhaps the population would have more fully accepted Soviet ideology and official culture. Instead the disparity between the elite and the masses and between official images and reality only heightened popular resentment and discontent with the government. In the long run, too, the emphasis on consumerism heightened the population's dissatisfaction with the Soviet system. The planned economy responded poorly to consumer demand and never provided the quantity or range of goods that people desired. By the second half of the twentieth century, Party leaders' embrace of mass consumption proved to be a substantial liability for the Soviet system, particularly in its competition with the capitalist West.

CHAPTER FIVE

Social and Cultural Unity
under Soviet Socialism

Today marks one year from the enactment of the Stalin
Constitution of victorious socialism. The Soviet Union, which
is holding elections for the highest organ of power, greets this
momentous anniversary with a powerful demonstration of the
moral and political unity of its people.

— *Uchitel'skaia gazeta*, December 5, 1937

In our country—a country where the socialist order has
triumphed completely, where there is no unemployment, where
every citizen of the Soviet Union is presented with the complete
opportunity to work and live honorably, any criminal act by its
nature can be nothing other than a manifestation of class
struggle.

— GENRIKH IAGODA, 1935[1]

W
hen examining Soviet official culture of the 1930s, one is confronted by several paradoxes. After it had collectivized agriculture, with the intention of destroying traditional peasant ways,
the Soviet government began to incorporate elements of peasant folklore
into official culture. Despite its denunciation of the tsarist past, this government also began to champion tsarist patriotic heroes and Russian literary classics. And at the same time that it launched a new wave of state
violence against "anti-Soviet elements," the Soviet government unveiled a
more democratic constitution, held elections, and sought to create a closer
bond between the Soviet people and their leaders. Some scholars have ex-

plained these developments as part of a retreat from socialism, but as we have seen, Party leaders did not waver in their commitment to Soviet socialism. In fact, it was their claim to have achieved socialism that allowed them to use select traditions, which could now be divorced from the capitalist past. That Party leaders *could* use these traditions, however, does not explain why they did use them, and here it is noteworthy that political leaders across Europe in the interwar period resorted to folklore and invented traditions in order to unite the population behind a common heritage. To explicate the paradoxes of Soviet official culture more fully, then, we must place it in the broader context of political efforts to promote social and cultural unity.

A wide range of modern European thinkers had grappled with the problem of social unity. Industrialization and urbanization had destroyed the seeming organic unity of traditional societies and in its place left severe class divisions and antagonisms. In order to recover the mythical social harmony of the past and overcome the atomization and alienation of modern society, social thinkers of many stripes—socialists, fascists, Nietzscheans, even liberals—sought to transcend bourgeois individualism. Proponents of solidarism in France, for example, advocated the scientific deployment of social forces and an end to exploitation as a means to return society to its natural state of social harmony.[2] Fascist aesthetics employed naturalism, folklore, and classicism, as well as mass marches and spectacles, to create a sense of wholeness and unity.[3] Socialist thought also stressed social harmony and unity. Marx had foreseen violent revolution as the means to destroy capitalism and its class antagonisms. But this violence, and the dictatorship of the proletariat that was to follow, were only steps on the path to a conflict-free society, where class hatred and alienation would disappear and complete social harmony would reign.

Adding to the urgency with which governments pursued social unity were the rising international tensions of the mid-to-late 1930s. Since the time of the First World War, political and military leaders throughout Europe were acutely aware that mass warfare required millions of soldiers and the total mobilization of the population. Social unity and a common sense of purpose greatly facilitated total mobilization for war. In fact, governments used folkloric symbols and patriotic heroes to project the image of a unified people and galvanize their populations for war. The Soviet government also sought to unite its population behind the Party leadership. A series of highly publicized conferences in the mid-1930s showed top Party leaders meeting with factory workers and collective farm members. The meetings sought to convey the connectedness and concern of Party leaders and the gratitude and support of common citizens. The Stalin cult at this time swelled to enormous proportions, as Stalin was portrayed every-where as a wise and benevolent leader supported unanimously by the peo-ple.

Party leaders also employed state violence in their pursuit of Soviet so-cial unity. One year after the Soviet government issued a new constitution that deemphasized class and restored political rights to persons previously disenfranchised, it launched a series of coercive operations, not only against alleged Trotskyists within the Party but against diaspora national minorities and "anti-Soviet elements" as well. The simultaneous increase in symbolic democratization and state violence can be explained only as a consequence of the purported attainment of socialism and of Party lead-ers' drive to achieve complete social unity. With the exploiting classes and remnants of capitalism eliminated, Party leaders believed they could re-store political rights to all citizens. But in their minds, anyone who con-tinued to defy the Soviet order was an inveterate enemy who had to be eradicated both to defend Soviet power and to progress toward an entirely harmonious communist society.

The 1936 Constitution and the Deemphasis of Class

Even before the 1936 Constitution was issued, official Soviet ideology began to deemphasize the importance of class. Previously one's class ori-gin had by definition been an indicator of political allegiance—proletari-ans supported the Soviet state and the bourgeoisie opposed it. But the elimination of capitalist remnants in the economy and the liquidation of the exploiting classes had changed the situation. After agriculture was col-lectivized and the planned economy established, there was no further eco-nomic basis for exploitation or a bourgeois mentality. Moreover, kulaks and other exploiters had been removed from society through deportation to labor camps and special settlements where they were to be reformed. According to official ideology, only three classes remained in Soviet soci-ety: the peasantry, the proletariat, and the intelligentsia.

An important milestone in the deemphasis of class origin came at the 1935 All-Union Conference of Leading Combine Drivers. One delegate to the conference, Comrade Kil'ba from Bashkiria, openly admitted that he was the son of a kulak. He explained that his father had been dekulakized and deported to a special settlement. Kil'ba himself had broken ties with his relatives and thus avoided deportation. He remained in his village and became a combine driver, and eventually emerged as the best on his col-lective farm. Local authorities had not wanted to send him to the confer-ence because of his kulak origins, he said, but the conference organizers had invited him nonetheless. Kil'ba concluded his speech by promising, "Although I am the son of a kulak, I will honestly fight for the interests of workers and peasants and for the building of socialism." Stalin at that point interjected, "A son does not answer for his father, though a father does answer for his son."[4]

Kil'ba's speech was clearly staged as a symbol of reconciliation between the Soviet regime and the children of kulaks. Whereas people of petty bourgeois social origin had been discriminated against earlier, the case of Kil'ba demonstrated that those with tainted social origins could nonetheless support the Soviet system, and that by working well they could be rewarded by the system. The fact that Stalin himself spoke up to say that people would not be held accountable for their parents' class identity added impetus to the deemphasis of class in Soviet ideology.

While in practice those of alien social origin often remained suspect, the official Party line was not to hold class origin against people.[5] When a former Party member in Iaroslavl' wrote to Kalinin in December 1935 complaining that he and his brother had been expelled from the Party only because his father had been labeled a kulak, Kalinin ordered them reinstated provided there was nothing against them except their social origin.[6] A few months later *Komsomol'skaia Pravda* printed a story about a Komsomol secretary who forced a woman to leave her husband, the son of a man shot for counterrevolutionary activity in 1917. The newspaper editors criticized the Komsomol secretary for overvigilance, noting that the husband, as the product of Soviet schools, posed no threat despite his social origins.[7]

The deemphasis of class as a determinant of political loyalty meant not only greater leniency toward those of petty bourgeois origin but a less privileged place for proletarians. While industrial workers continued to receive greater opportunities for education and promotion, they were not granted such opportunities as automatically as in the past. In September 1935, Ezhov stated that it was wrong to assume that workers should be admitted to the Communist Party solely by virtue of their social class. He also questioned the blind promotion of workers, declaring, "The working class did not fall down from heaven." Because the Soviet government had created its own intelligentsia, he argued, these more qualified people should be sought out and promoted instead of workers from the bench.[8]

Soviet political art also reflected the deemphasis of class and the less privileged place of industrial workers in the social hierarchy. Whereas proletarians were the focus of political art during the First Five-Year Plan, the number of posters depicting exclusively workers declined in the mid-1930s. Citizenship replaced class as the most operative category, and all loyal Soviet citizens were portrayed as equal contributors to socialism. People in other social groups—peasants, students, athletes, soldiers—were increasingly pictured alongside industrial workers. Peasants, who had previously been shown as illiterate, superstitious, and politically unreliable, were now presented in a positive light, as educated, prosperous, and loyal.[9]

The new constitution was also justified by reference to the new economic and social structure of the country. In January 1935 the Politburo called a Central Committee meeting "to decide on the necessary changes to the Constitution of the USSR." The Central Committee then announced a commission to draft a new constitution that would reflect "the victories and achievements that Soviet workers had won."[10] After a draft of the 1936 Constitution had been written and circulated, Stalin explained that the country had been fundamentally transformed since the 1924 Constitution had been issued. A new constitution was necessary to take account of economic transformation, collectivization, and industrialization—what he summed up as "the complete victory of the socialist system in all spheres of the economy."[11] Commissar of Justice Krylenko and other Soviet jurists also explained the 1936 Constitution as necessitated by the attainment of socialism, the shift in economic relations, and the elimination of exploiting classes.[12] Privately as well as publicly Party leaders cited socialist transformation as their reason for issuing a new constitution. At a closed Party meeting in June 1936, Ia. Iakovlev said that because of the great economic and social changes that had taken place and the "new order of classes," it was now possible to create a new constitutional order.[13]

Soviet leaders had other motivations for issuing the 1936 Constitution as well. Peter Solomon has emphasized that Stalin used the Constitution to enhance the legitimacy of the Soviet system in the eyes of both domestic and foreign observers. Defining the structures of the state constitutionally added to its respectability and helped to centralize its power. In this sense the Constitution was part of Stalin's broader effort to restore the authority of legal procedures and to create reliable central agencies to carry out his orders. The Constitution, while it did not in fact place any limits on Party leaders' authoritarian rule, also made the Soviet Union appear more democratic. The rising threat of Nazi Germany in the mid-1930s prompted a reorientation of Soviet foreign policy to seek international alliances and to direct Communist parties in Europe to cooperate with other leftist parties in the formation of antifascist popular fronts. If the Soviet Union was to achieve these objectives, it had to project a less dictatorial and more democratic image.[14]

The Stalin Constitution, as it was called, was published in draft form in June 1936 and issued in its final version in early December. The 1918 and 1924 constitutions and other pre-1936 Soviet legislation had listed cate-

Photographs of Stalin and Soviet achievements "under the banner of the Stalin Constitution." (Poster identification number RU/SU 1902, Poster Collection, Hoover Institution Archives.)

gories of social aliens (the former nobility, bourgeoisie, and petty bourgeoisie), who were deprived of voting rights and discriminated against in access to education and state services.[15] The 1936 Constitution, by contrast, provided equal rights for all citizens, including the right to vote, to work, and to receive education and old age and disability pensions.[16] A series of articles in the Soviet press explained the reasons for granting equal rights to all citizens. One article pointed out that the new economic conditions meant that the exploiting classes had been eliminated and that classes were no longer so important. Another article argued that the proletariat would continue to have a leading role in Soviet society, but that it would work to unite all citizens rather than to battle class enemies.[17] Molotov, in his speech on the 1936 Constitution at the Eighth All-Union Congress of Soviets, stressed that alien social origin no longer prevented people from loyally serving the Soviet government. Now not only workers but peasants, members of the intelligentsia, and even former nobles such as the writer Count Aleksei Tolstoi helped to build socialism.[18]

The 1936 Constitution delineated the three nonantagonistic classes in Soviet society—the proletariat, the peasantry, and the intelligentsia. While the allegiance of the intelligentsia had previously been suspect, under socialism a new and loyal intelligentsia had been created, according to Soviet leaders. Stalin stated in November 1936 that "our Soviet intelligentsia is a completely new intelligentsia, connected by all its roots to the working class and peasantry. It is now a full-fledged member of Soviet society, where together with workers and peasants, as one team, it builds the new classless socialist society."[19] A few years later at the Eighteenth Party Congress in 1939, Zhdanov cited the "withering of class boundaries" as the basis for the "moral-political unity of Soviet society."[20] Party leaders, then, saw the achievement of socialism as ushering in a new era of social unity, thereby resolving the class antagonisms of capitalist society. Just as Marx had predicted, violent revolution and the elimination of the exploiting classes had, in their eyes, created a new type of society, with social harmony and the cooperation of all members under the leadership of the Communist Party.

Mass Politics and the Stalin Cult

One of the interesting features of the 1936 Constitution was the fact that Soviet leaders allowed public discussion of the draft version before it was issued. They also encouraged citizens' feedback on another central piece of legislation in 1936, the decree outlawing abortion. While the Stalinist leadership did not give the population any real input into policy-making, it did promote a nondemocratic yet participatory form of politics. Involvement of the population stemmed from more general phenomena of the modern era—the rise of mass politics and mass warfare. As the ideal of popular sovereignty spread after the French Revolution, the entire population needed to be involved to legitimate governmental policies and military campaigns. And as the First World War had demonstrated so clearly, national defense now depended on governments' ability to mobilize their entire populations for war.[21] The Soviet government used a range of techniques, from public discussions and mass demonstrations to single-candidate elections and the Stalin cult, to involve the population in politics, albeit in a controlled, nondemocratic fashion.[22]

Just before public discussion of the draft constitution, the Soviet government permitted controlled feedback from the population on a draft of the decree banning abortion. In May 1936 the draft decree was published, and people were invited to discuss it and send in their comments. One article explained that because the decree would affect every Soviet citizen, "the government did not think it possible to promulgate such a law without a preliminary, widespread and thorough popular discussion." While the Soviet press published primarily letters endorsing the decree, it also published some dissenting letters arguing that abortion should not be outlawed. Thus, while the discussion did not affect the final form of the decree, it had the appearance of a genuine public debate. The press trumpeted this public discussion as evidence of "the enormous trust and love of the people toward their government." It also claimed this discussion demonstrated "the unity of the people cemented by the Party and government in the struggle for a socialist society and . . . the increasing civic consciousness among Soviet citizens."[23]

A draft of the new constitution was published in June 1936, and all citizens were encouraged to read and discuss it. Special meetings were held where people could provide their feedback regarding the draft and even propose amendments to it. The comments and suggestions put forth at these meetings were recorded and summarized for Party leaders. In addition, citizens were invited to send written responses to the draft, and many did so. While the final version of the Constitution, promulgated in December, did include a number of changes, there is no indication that they were based on popular opinion. In fact, the many complaints and negative comments received were not recognized in any way. Instead the Soviet press reported that all citizens, and especially rank-and-file workers, enthusiastically participated in the discussion and expressed their gratitude to Stalin.[24] Far from providing genuine democratic input, discussion of the draft constitution was an exercise in controlled participatory politics. By involving the population in the political process, Soviet leaders hoped to build support for their policies. Such participation, for example, allowed Molotov to claim in his speech heralding the new constitution that "the laborers express their complete solidarity with the Bolshevik policies of our Party and with its goal of achieving full communism."[25]

The responses to the draft constitution indicated that, contrary to Party leaders' proclamations, Soviet society was not at all harmonious. The liquidation of the "exploiting classes," far from resolving social conflicts, had left a deep legacy of animosity and distrust. This distrust emanated both from victims of dekulakization and from its perpetrators, who feared the return of former kulaks and the restoration of their rights. Many letters regarding the draft constitution complained of unfair deportations and incarcerations. One peasant cited the case of friends unjustly imprisoned and wrote that he was ashamed to live in an allegedly free country with so many prisoners. Others disparaged the draft constitution, expressing doubts about the rights it guaranteed and objecting that those rights meant little to people who were hungry.[26]

While the victims of Stalinism claimed the draft constitution did not do enough, many local officials and activists objected that it was too conciliatory. Some protested that not everyone should be given the right to vote and warned that former kulaks might be elected to local office and take revenge on those who had dekulakized them. Literally hundreds of participants in public meetings to discuss the draft constitution demanded that former kulaks, bourgeois exploiters, and white guards not have their rights restored. Others argued that former merchants, kulaks, and priests should receive rights only after they had first proved they could work honestly for several years. Some activists also felt that the draft constitution should contain stronger language and punishments for theft of state property and unwillingness to perform socially useful labor.[27] Even after the 1936 Constitution was issued, local officials frequently denied rights to formerly disenfranchised people and their children, in direct contradiction of the law and Party policy.[28]

Social tensions also affected Soviet leaders' plans to hold elections. As another form of participatory politics, the Soviet government replaced indirect with direct elections to the soviets, and announced in early 1937 that it would hold elections to the Supreme Soviet later in the year. At the February–March 1937 Plenum, Zhdanov told Central Committee members that these elections would be contested elections with universal, equal, and direct suffrage. He added that candidates could run without Communist Party approval. But Party and secret police reports later in the year informed Party leaders that many priests and religious leaders were planning to run for office and had strong support among the peasantry. These reports also revealed widespread peasant animosity toward Party officials and plans to vote them out of office. The Central Committee therefore canceled plans for multicandidate elections and instead held single-candidate elections at the end of 1937, with candidates chosen by the Communist Party.[29]

These elections became an exercise in civic participation and mass mobilization. Despite the fact that voters had no choice and nothing was being decided, government officials went to great lengths to ensure that every eligible person voted. In fact, mobilization efforts went far beyond the usual campaigns in factories and schools, and reached pensioners and housewives as well as workers.[30] Party officials in turn heralded overwhelming voter participation as an indication of the population's support of their policies. At the Eighteenth Party Congress, for example, Stalin boasted that 99.4 percent of eligible voters participated in the 1938 Supreme Soviet elections and gave their support to Communist Party candidates. "This means," he concluded, "that in the case of war, our front and home front will be stronger than in any other country, due to our uniformity and internal unity." He added that the Party should continue "to strengthen the moral-political unity of Soviet society and the friendly cooperation of workers, peasants, and the intelligentsia; and to do the utmost to strengthen the friendship of the peoples of the USSR, and to develop and cultivate Soviet patriotism."[31]

The Stalin cult was another important means to mobilize the population's support and build a link between the people and the Party leadership. Presenting Stalin as the personification of the Soviet system provided a tangible symbol to which people could attach their loyalty. When the writer Avdeenko concluded a speech with the words, "I thank you, Soviet power," Lev Mekhlis, a chief architect of the Stalin cult, chided him for not thanking Stalin instead, claiming that "Soviet power is above all Stalin." Similarly, Molotov presented Stalin as the incarnation of the "moral-political unity of the people."[32] In a vast country riddled with social antagonisms and presided over by an impersonal and brutal bureaucracy, the Stalin cult offered a rallying point and symbol of unity. And because it portrayed Stalin as a wise and benevolent leader, the cult gave the system not only a human face but one that appeared to care about people's welfare.

The Party built up the cult as part of a deliberate policy to promote loyalty to Stalin and the other leaders. A 1936 local Party report gave the following instructions:

> During agitation and propaganda in the press there must be more popularization of the leaders, and love for them must be fostered and inculcated in the masses, and unlimited loyalty, especially to cultivate the utmost love for

comrade Stalin and the other leaders amongst children and young people, inculcating Soviet patriotism, bringing them to fanaticism in love and defense of comrade Stalin and our socialist motherland.[33]

Cultivating love and loyalty toward Stalin, then, was explicitly intended to build patriotism and willingness to defend the country.

The Stalin cult is often dated from 1929, when on Stalin's fiftieth birthday he received a great deal of adulation in the press. But at that time the overall emphasis remained on the collective leadership, and Stalin was depicted as a strong but distant leader. It was only in 1934 that Stalin began to be presented in more personal terms as a warm, paternalistic figure, and it was only then that exaltation of his genius, wisdom, and caring became common in the press.[34] The Stalin cult stressed not only his tremendous abilities but also people's love and appreciation of him. The lyrics of one official song went as follows:

> Now at last we do live well,
> Comrade Stalin, we all agree
> That you have lifted us from hell
> And freed us from our poverty.[35]

In this way the Stalin cult expressed and sought to inculcate what Jeffrey Brooks has termed "an official core Soviet value: the idea that the citizens are immeasurably beholden to the leader, the Party, and the state."[36]

As part of the campaign to create a connection between the Stalinist leadership and the people, a series of highly publicized meetings was held where Stalin and other Party leaders met with exemplary workers and peasants. At Stakhanovite conferences at the Kremlin, workers met Party leaders and expressed their appreciation for the opportunity to work and live under the Soviet system.[37] Stalin, Molotov, Kliment Voroshilov, and other leaders attended the 1935 Conference of Leading Combine Drivers and gave the delegates words of encouragement and approval. One delegate, Comrade Petrova, became flustered as she delivered her prepared speech and said she was too scared to continue. Stalin encouraged her to proceed, saying, "We here are your family."[38] Similarly, a pilot invited to a 1937 Kremlin reception became nervous and forgot what to say, but then Stalin "looked at him with a smile . . . of such fatherly warmth" that his fear vanished.[39]

As the examples indicate, the Stalin cult sought not only to bring together the people and Party leaders but to create a symbolic family where Stalin was the father figure for the population. Official propaganda pre-

In *Unforgettable Meeting,* a painting by V. P. Efanov, Stalin honors a woman at a Kremlin reception: " . . . we must welcome the growing social activity of the working women and their promotion to leading posts as an indubitable indication of the growth of our culture." (Poster identification number RU/SU 563, Poster Collection, Hoover Institution Archives.)

sented Stalin as the paternal champion of women's rights and welfare benefits.[40] The Soviet press in 1934 began to refer to Stalin as "father" and frequently pictured him surrounded by children, smiling paternalistically. One frequently reproduced photograph showed Stalin with a Tajik girl, who wrote an accompanying article titled "Father Stalin."[41] Other Party leaders, including Molotov, Khrushchev, Anastas Mikoian, and Voroshilov, were also pictured with groups of children, and when the founder of the secret police, Feliks Dzerzhinskii, died in 1936, one of the memorial articles in *Pravda* was "F. E. Dzerzhinskii and Children." Soviet propaganda, then, sought to create a concerned, fatherly image for the entire leadership, not just Stalin alone.[42]

The Stalin cult is often assumed to be a continuation of the cult of the tsars, who were also presented as paternalistic, caring leaders. Indeed, the myth of the tsar as the "little father" of his people perhaps did prepare some Soviet citizens to think the same way about Stalin. But the use of paternalistic images and familial metaphors was not limited to the Soviet

Union. As one scholar has written about twentieth-century Britain, "The unifying ideology of the family itself provides a very important unifying image of the nation state." This image presented the king as the father of his people, the country as the motherland, and compatriots as brothers.[43] The fact that familial imagery could be used to promote social and political unity was another reason, in addition to pro-natalism, that the family was stressed in official Soviet culture. Indeed, the corollary to Stalin as a father figure was the Soviet Union as the motherland. In the early 1930s, official propaganda still referred to the socialist fatherland, but in the mid-1930s the Soviet press more often called the Soviet Union the motherland, in implicit union with Stalin as the country's father.[44]

In an interesting parallel to public discussion of the 1936 Constitution, the production of the Stalin cult elicited input from the population. Paintings of Stalin, for example, were exhibited and viewers were encouraged to write their comments in "opinion books." The comments would then be used selectively by Soviet cultural officials to praise or condemn painters. This practice allowed the controlled participation of the masses in cultural production and served both to inform officials of popular opinion and to involve people in cultural politics. At the same time that viewers gave their input, art criticism in the press and the exhibitions themselves sought to school people in the proper response to paintings. The mechanics of cultural production were thus multidirectional.[45] Soviet authorities involved the masses, but in a controlled way that sought to shape their understandings and inculcate official values. A similar process took place in literature and film, where a range of practices such as reader and viewer surveys, discussion groups, and letters to the press gave the population a voice, albeit highly censored, in cultural production.[46]

What were people's responses to the Stalin cult? Evidence indicates that beneficiaries of the Soviet system—those promoted in the Party and industrial bureaucracy, Stakhanovite workers, and some members of the military—held a genuine reverence for Stalin. In private letters opened and read by Soviet surveillance organs, some soldiers, for example, expressed their gratitude and loyalty to Stalin.[47] More common were people who adopted the official image of Stalin as a benefactor in order to make appeals for material aid. One woman who stood to receive a 2,000 ruble bonus because she had seven children wrote to local government officials expressing her "enormous thankfulness to our dear, beloved father and friend and teacher, Iosif Vissarionovich [Stalin]."[48] But people also bitterly criticized Stalin and the Stalin cult. Much of the population viewed Stalin and the other leaders as oppressors rather than benefactors, and far from feeling a bond with them, spoke of them as the elite who lived well while the common people suffered. Also common was subversive ridicule, as in peasant songs that described Party leaders without their clothes on.[49] The enormous propaganda effort to build up people's love for Stalin, then, was of limited success. Only with victory in the Second World War did a greater proportion of the Soviet population internalize the official image of Stalin as their great leader and protector.

The Cultural Canon and Political Legitimation

Literature, art, and architecture also had an important role to play in promoting the cultural unity of the population and strengthening the bond between leaders and people. Through the creation of a cultural canon, Soviet leaders sought to provide a set of shared values and a common cultural heritage that would bring people together. They also used culture as a tool of political legitimation. Whereas the avant-garde culture of the 1920s had a strong iconoclastic bent, Stalinist culture of the mid-1930s repudiated iconoclasm and replaced it with neoclassicism and socialist realism. Iconoclasm was no longer needed to destroy bourgeois culture after capitalist remnants had been eliminated. And now that socialism had been achieved, Soviet leaders advanced monumentalist architecture that legitimated the existing order and socialist realist literature that emphasized purity and decorum.

The search for a common, unifying culture actually predated the Revolution. A range of social thinkers throughout Europe in the late nineteenth century saw culture as a possible means to bridge class antagonisms and overcome the alienation of modern society.[50] These sentiments were particularly strong among the prerevolutionary Russian intelligentsia, many of whom believed culture could uplift the masses and bridge the gulf between the intelligentsia and the people. They conceived of a cultural order in which the lower classes would share in Russian high culture, created by educated Russians but made accessible to all. In literature, for example, the creation of an all-people's culture required a didactic popularization of the Russian classics. Such a popularization would allow this unified culture to be based on high Russian culture and its values rather than on "corrupt" commercialized culture, which the intelligentsia despised.[51]

In an extremely authoritarian manner, the Stalinist leadership achieved the prerevolutionary intelligentsia's goal by creating one unified culture for the entire population. With the attainment of socialism and the deemphasis of class, it made sense that all citizens share a common culture. No longer was it necessary for workers to maintain a separate proletarian culture or for cultural radicals to attack bourgeois culture. The elimination of the bourgeois classes had resolved the struggle against bourgeois culture, and with the end of class antagonisms, all citizens could embrace a common culture. Rather than being based on revolutionary, avant-garde culture, this common culture relied on traditional, even neoclassical forms, though with a socialist content.

The avant-garde was repudiated in part because it had been an iconoclastic culture that sought to destroy existing bourgeois culture and replace it with something new. Once socialism had been achieved, the new purpose of Soviet culture was perpetuation and legitimation rather than destruction. Whereas Soviet architecture of the 1920s had used unconventional forms to symbolize a break with the past, Stalinist architecture of the 1930s was neoclassical. The grandiose and symmetrical designs of Stalinist architecture also served to legitimate and hence to buttress the socialist order. Soviet officials explicitly put forward the architecture of ancient Rome as an appropriate model for socialist architecture, arguing that construction on such a grand scale showcased Soviet technical achievements. Neoclassical design linked Soviet culture to a universal, timeless tradition. It was to be an eternal culture that appealed to all people, and neoclassicism expressed this ambition as no other form could do.[52]

The other reason that Stalinist culture had no place for the avant-garde was the fact that its forms, from abstract art to discordant music, clashed with the goal of social harmony and unity. As Sheila Fitzpatrick has pointed out, formalist art was denounced as unacceptable and morally degenerate in the 1930s. In its place Soviet officials put forward classicism, which captured and promoted natural harmony and beauty. In other words, the social harmony of socialism was supposed to be reflected in harmonious cultural and artistic forms.[53] Like the Preservationists, who had initiated a neoclassical revival in early twentieth-century Russia, Stalinist cultural officials favored pure, harmonious forms as part of the well-ordered society they sought to create.[54]

Socialist realism itself was a form of classicism, in that it emphasized purity, restraint, and decorum.[55] As the only officially acceptable art and literary form after 1932, socialist realism replaced the avant-garde and proletarian art forms that predominated during the 1920s and the First Five-Year Plan. Boris Groys has shown that the avant-garde and socialist realism actually shared several traits: the desire to transform rather than merely to represent life; the belief in a totalistic, all-encompassing artistic vision; contempt for commercialized culture; and the desire to erase distinctions between high and low art.[56] As we have seen, the difference between socialist realism and the avant-garde lay in socialist realism's rejection of abstract, iconoclastic forms in favor of realist ones.

Some scholars have analyzed the contradictions of socialist realism, pointing out the impossibility of representing a socialist utopia in realist forms. Socialist realism, they argue, could not depict a nonexistent future through representations of current reality.[57] But Soviet leaders believed that they were already achieving socialism. As Stalin stated in 1932, "The artist ought to show life truthfully. And if he shows it truthfully, he cannot fail to show it moving to socialism. This is and will be socialist realism."[58] Of course socialist realist paintings of prosperous peasants working contentedly on collective farms did not at all correspond to the Soviet reality of widespread discontent, hardship, and starvation in the countryside. Socialist realism was instead a "realist" depiction of how life was supposed to be—an attempt by the Soviet cultural establishment to construct a reality that did not really exist. And although socialist realist art and literature were completely contradicted by material reality, they were consistent with the official ideological premise that socialism had been achieved and that hardship and social conflict would soon be eliminated.

The reliance on classical and traditional forms to express socialist culture led to a selective rediscovery of Russian classics in literature. Aleksandr Pushkin in particular assumed an extremely prominent place in the Soviet literary canon. In December 1935 the Soviet government announced plans to commemorate the hundredth anniversary of Pushkin's death in 1937 and formed the All-Union Pushkin Committee to coordinate the celebration. The committee ordered that every school throughout the country incorporate Pushkin in the curriculum, obligated every theater to perform Pushkin's plays, and arranged for 19 million copies of Pushkin's works to be published. It also held contests for the design of Pushkin statues, organized Pushkin evenings where his works were read, and even mandated the sale of Pushkin cakes.[59]

The glorification of Pushkin reversed avant-garde criticism of him as a symbol of cultural conservatism. A Futurist manifesto in 1912 had urged the intelligentsia to "cast Pushkin off the steamship of modernity," and after the Revolution, Vladimir Mayakovsky had declared, "We are shooting the old generals! Why not Pushkin?"[60] In fact, it was true that as a former aristocrat and serf owner, Pushkin was a somewhat unlikely emblem of revolutionary socialist culture. But Soviet official culture of the 1930s remade Pushkin into a "people's poet" who was neglected by his noble parents and raised by a serf nanny, who gave him a love for the common people. The Soviet press and textbooks also presented Pushkin as a fervent revolutionary, emphasizing his connections with the Decembrists and the radical poems of his youth. Neglecting to mention that near the end of his life he held an official position at the tsar's court, the Soviet portrayal presented

Pushkin as a fervent revolutionary who fought to liberate the people from tsarism.[61]

The politics of cultural production by which this particular version of Pushkin was formulated were fairly complex. The Pushkin Committee mandated publications on certain themes while Soviet censors and literary critics worked to refine the official image of Pushkin. Soviet depictions of Pushkin had to tread a fine line between presenting him as a rebel and at the same time making clear his respectability and lofty standing. An article titled "Mistakes of Pushkin Scholars" by M. Zagorskii faulted those who claimed that not all of Pushkin's works were successes in his day. Zagorskii stated that one play was subjected to tsarist censorship and could not be performed, but that Pushkin's other works had been worldwide successes.[62] One Party report noted that some articles described Pushkin as "rather carelessly dressed," presumably as a way to differentiate him from his aristocratic milieu. But according to the report, it was entirely unacceptable to present a writer of such stature in this way.[63]

Pushkin was also heralded as an essential precursor to socialist realism, whose idealism and critical realism made the creation of socialist realism possible.[64] Pushkin's writings, while presented as populist and anti-aristocratic, were not permitted to be too rebellious. As Katerina Clark has noted, the official Pushkin of the 1937 celebration was "the bard of Lenten rule and a Neoclassical tradition, not the Pushkin noted by others as an irreverent, irrepressible, and even bawdy poet."[65] Thus, while Pushkin was to have been a rebel against the tsarist establishment, he was also a highly venerated and respectable writer—one who had world-historical standing and who both created the Russian literary language and paved the way for socialist realism.

At the same time that Soviet propaganda stressed Pushkin's eminence, it also emphasized his accessibility to all readers, including the former lower classes and national minorities. An article titled "Pushkin for Construction Workers" told of special readings and discussions of Pushkin held at construction workers' clubs.[66] Another article claimed that tsarist censors had hidden the true Pushkin from the laboring masses, but that under the Soviet government "the genuine Pushkin" had been made available for workers and peasants to understand. It also cited the Soviet people's appreciation of Pushkin as evidence of their "cultural advance" and their "enormous attraction to art and literature."[67] National minorities within the Soviet Union were also supposed to read Pushkin, and the Soviet government ordered translations of his works into all the major Soviet languages.[68] The promotion of Pushkin as a cultural icon for all Soviet citizens thus fulfilled both the long-standing intelligentsia dream of bringing Russian high culture to the masses and the Soviet goal of creating a common culture to be shared by all members of the population.

The Soviet literary canon also incorporated some other prerevolutionary writers, though none received nearly the prominence of Pushkin. A series of articles presented Leo Tolstoy, for example, as part of Soviet cultural heritage. One article, "Lenin and Tolstoy," quoted Lenin as proclaiming that Tolstoy's great works deserved the widest possible attention. The tsarist government had suppressed Tolstoy's writings, it claimed, but the Soviet government made them available to everyone.[69] Somewhat paradoxically, Mayakovsky, who had virulently attacked the Russian classics, was also enshrined in the Soviet literary canon. It was possible to honor Mayakovsky, in part because he had committed suicide in 1930 and hence was no longer present to run afoul of the Party line. Many other contemporary Soviet writers were arrested during the Great Purges, and in such politically dangerous times it was impossible to know who might be next. Of the 101 writers selected to lead the Union of Soviet Writers in 1934, thirty had been arrested by 1938.[70]

In other cultural fields as well, leading figures of the past were rehabilitated in the mid-1930s and made part of the Soviet cultural canon. In music, for example, Mikhail Glinka was heralded as the first Russian national composer and his works began to be performed more regularly. To bolster his standing, one article pointed out that Glinka was a friend of Pushkin and that he used Pushkin's verses in his opera *Ruslan and Ludmila*. The article also heralded other classical composers of the prerevolutionary era, particularly the "Russian Five" (Mily Balakirev, César Cui, Modest Mussorgsky, Aleksandr Borodin, Nikolai Rimsky-Korsakov), famous for their efforts to compose Russian classical music.[71] The reliance on prerevolutionary cultural heroes allowed the Stalinist leadership not only to create an allegedly universal Soviet culture but to attach it to a timeless heritage.

In the same way that Party leaders selectively incorporated past cultural heroes into official culture, they also rehabilitated certain political and military leaders from the tsarist past. Historical heroes similarly provided a common heritage with which to unite the population and inspire collective toil and sacrifice for the Soviet state. Before the mid-1930s, Party leaders had denigrated the tsarist past and muted forms of Russian national expression. As we shall see, this suppression of Russian nationalism was an essential component of Soviet nationality policy—a means to overcome national minorities' resentment of past Russian imperialism. In 1935 Stalin declared that this resentment and mistrust had been overcome and replaced by mutual friendship among Soviet peoples.[72] Party leaders con-

cluded that in view of this friendship, they could now extol Russian national heroes without fear of antagonizing national minorities. The revival
of tsarist heroes was also conditioned by patriotic and military needs. With
rising international tensions in the mid-1930s, and in particular with the
national security threat posed by Nazi Germany and imperial Japan, Soviet
leaders increasingly focused on inculcating patriotism and preparing the
population for war. Tsarist heroes who had defeated foreign foes in the
past served as rallying points and examples for Soviet citizens to follow.

The glorification of tsarist heroes involved the partial repudiation of
existing Soviet historiography. In the mid-1930s the writings of Mikhail
Pokrovskii fell into disfavor because they presented an overly materialist
and negative version of prerevolutionary Russian history, one that neglected the positive accomplishments of tsarist leaders.[73] A 1934 Politburo
commission criticized the teaching of history in Soviet schools as too sociological and called for more political history. A subsequent Central Committee resolution, "On the Teaching of Civil History in the Schools of the
USSR," stressed the importance of historical figures and dates. Work soon
began on the writing of new history textbooks, though it was not until 1937
that the authoritative textbook, A. V. Shestakov's *Short Course on the History
of the USSR*, was approved and published. This text rehabilitated and extolled state-building tsars such as Yaroslav the Wise and Ivan the Great.[74]

Also in 1937 the first part of the film *Peter I* was released; it glorified Peter for making Russia into a great power and glossed over his repression of
common people. The next year the Politburo approved the making of several other historical films, including the second part of *Peter I, Alexander
Nevsky,* and *Minin and Pozharsky*—all traditional national heroes who previously received little attention in Soviet culture.[75] Stalin is said to have
explained the importance of honoring the tsars in a 1937 toast. He acknowledged that the tsars had "enslaved the people" but he praised them
because "they put together an enormous state [stretching] out to Kam-
chatka." And he proclaimed, "We Bolsheviks were the first to put together
and strengthen this state not in the interests of the landowners and capitalists but for the toilers and for all the great peoples who make up this
state."[76]

With the approach of the Second World War, Soviet authorities even
more explicitly advocated the promotion of historical figures to foster patriotism and prepare the population for war. In 1936 officials of the Commissariat of Education acknowledged "German fascism" and "Japanese
imperialism" as imminent national security threats that required teachers
to teach children to defend the motherland.[77] A 1939 Komsomol report
stated that "patriots of our motherland" built character among the young

generation, and that films such as *Alexander Nevsky* were particularly effective at preparing children to fight for their country.[78] In an April 1941 speech, Iaroslavskii said it was wrong to present an entirely negative view of the Russian past. Students should learn about Russia's great leaders and writers, he argued, because that heroic past helped inspire in youth "a love for this past and a love for their motherland."[79]

Soviet appeals to patriotism did not necessarily negate a commitment to socialist ideology. There was a logic to Stalin's argument, first stated in his February 4, 1931 speech, that the Revolution had for the first time given working people a fatherland, and that defense of it was necessary to protect socialism. In 1934 the Soviet press stated repeatedly that every Soviet citizen should love his fatherland or motherland (the word "motherland" becoming more common over the course of that year) and be prepared to die defending it.[80] By the end of the decade, Party leaders were providing justifications for patriotism in the Soviet context. Kalinin said that communist education should inculcate "love for the motherland, for the socialist motherland, and Soviet patriotism."[81] He thus included love for the *socialist* motherland as an essential part of communist education. In the same vein, Iaroslavskii recalled the declaration of Marx and Engels that the proletariat had no fatherland, and he conceded this was true of capitalist states, which allowed workers to starve. But the Soviet state was different: it provided its people with a bright future that inspired patriotism. He also contended that Soviet patriotism was indistinguishable from internationalism in that it embodied "a feeling of deep, brotherly international solidarity." Because the Soviet state sought "to build a new human society," it served the interests of all people, and not just its own citizens.[82]

Had Soviet leaders limited patriotic appeals to defense of the socialist motherland, they might have avoided some of the tensions that arose within Soviet ideology and nationality policy. But tsarist heroes such as Peter the Great were specifically Russian heroes, who had in fact conquered some of the national minorities in the Soviet empire. Invoking these heroes promoted Russian nationalism rather than Soviet patriotism or internationalism. A few Party leaders protested the Russocentric nature of the new history textbooks published in the late 1930s.[83] But overall, Stalinist culture in the years leading up to the Second World War assumed an increasingly nationalistic tone and came to equate Russian nationalistic appeals with Soviet patriotism.

In 1938 the journal *Bolshevik* published an article titled "The Magnificent Russian People," which proclaimed, "The history of the Great Russian people is the history of its heroic battles for independence and freedom against innumerable enemies, conquerors and interventionists, including

'German elements.'" The article went on to invoke the memory of Alexander Nevsky, and to describe the Russian people as "immortal."[84] This propaganda was designed to inspire pride and heroism among the population, and such nationalistic appeals undoubtedly had great emotional pull for some ethnic Russians. Nationalism attached people to a heroic past and to a timeless, immortal legacy. But in the Soviet context, Russian nationalism created certain ideological tensions and problems. The glorification of the Russian people and of tsarist heroes who had established the Russian empire placed national minorities in a subordinate position. While Party leaders hoped to unify all the nationalities of the Soviet Union, these attempts, as we will see, were undercut by this strain of Russian nationalism in Stalinist culture.

Nationalities and Folk Culture

The multi-ethnic character of the Soviet population posed a special problem for Soviet leaders in their quest to create a united and militarily strong society. According to Soviet ideology, ethnic and national identity would be superseded over time as people developed a socialist consciousness. But Lenin and Stalin had been careful to avoid any suppression of national minority sentiment, judging that such suppression under the tsarist autocracy had only exacerbated nationalist separatism within the empire. Instead, the Soviet Union was to be a federal union of nationalities who belonged to it voluntarily. In an effort to disarm nationalist separation, Party leaders actually fostered the development of national minority cultures. They also believed the furthering of national minority cultures would push ethnic groups along a historical time line toward socialism. Drawing on Marxism and Enlightenment thought, Soviet authorities saw all peoples as progressing from clans and tribes to ethnic groups, then to nationalities, and ultimately to socialism. Ethnic groups that had not yet achieved national consciousness, officials believed, had to be helped to evolve into nations, so that they would then progress toward socialism.[85]

As a number of scholars have pointed out, in reality Soviet nationality policy inadvertently contributed to the nationalist separatism that eventually broke up the Soviet Union. The federal structure of the country required people to identify themselves by their nationality. Moreover, the existence of governmental bodies, flags, emblems, and so forth for each national republic reinforced such national identifications rather than paving the way for them to be superseded by socialist consciousness.[86] But the Party leadership did not recognize national identifications in themselves as a problem. As long as such nationalist sentiments existed within

the Soviet framework—a union of nationalities under the aegis of a socialist government—they appeared to pose no threat. It was only bourgeois
nationalism and the nationalism of diaspora nationalities that Party leaders recognized as a danger. Stalin and his fellow leaders employed a combination of propaganda and coercion to direct nationalist sentiments
among national minorities. Soviet propaganda portrayed all nationalities
as united and harmonious, and promoted folklore—a depoliticized form
of national expression. Soviet leaders also carried out large-scale arrests
and deportations, particularly in the late 1930s, to incarcerate those suspected of fomenting bourgeois nationalism, and to remove forcibly some
members of diaspora nationalities from border regions.

A milestone in Soviet nationality policy occurred in December 1935. At
a highly publicized Kremlin reception for Tajik and Turkmen collective
farm peasants, Stalin proclaimed that socialism had made possible in-
terethnic cooperation and harmony. Recapitulating the thinking behind
Soviet nationality policy, Stalin condemned the tsarist government for its
Russian chauvinism and repression of national minorities. But he went on
to claim that eighteen years of Soviet rule had overcome the harmful tsarist
legacy and national minorities' distrust of Russians. According to Stalin,
this distrust had been replaced by "complete mutual trust." "The friendship between the peoples of the USSR" was "a great and serious achievement," he said, adding that while this friendship existed, "the peoples of
our country will be free and unconquerable."[87] For their part, the Tajik
and Turkmen peasants at the reception were dressed in native costumes
and spoke in their native languages; the account in *Pravda* thus showed
them preserving their national identity and using it to express their loyalty
to the Soviet government. Over the next four months Party leaders held a
series of similar receptions for representatives of other national minorities.
During the following two years they also sponsored festivals in Moscow to
showcase the national cultures of various national minorities. Propaganda
surrounding all of these events stressed the "friendship of peoples."[88]

In tandem with its new celebration of Russian history and culture, the
Soviet government trumpeted the accomplishments of national minorities
as well. It not only showcased national minorities' art and folk music, it
crowned a people's poet for each nationality—Taras Shevchenko for
Ukraine, Shota Rustaveli for Georgia, and Ianka Kupala for Belorussia.
The Soviet government also created research institutes to study and develop the cultures of national minorities.[89] In a sense these steps represented a continuation of the government's ostentatious promotion of
national consciousness among ethnic minorities. But the mid-1930s emphasis on national minority cultures served two other purposes as well—

to demonstrate that under Soviet rule ethnicities had achieved nationhood and to ensure that the national narratives of minorities dovetailed with the Russian national narrative.

Party leaders considered the development of national cultures to be an important sign of nationhood and progress toward socialism. In the 1930s, Soviet leaders shifted from a policy of ethnic proliferation to one of national consolidation, thereby decreasing the number of recognized nationalities and reducing the number of ethnically based territorial units within the country.[90] Soviet propaganda simultaneously heralded the consolidation of ethnic groups; it claimed, for example, that "the consolidation of the Kazakh people into a nation represents one of the remarkable victories of socialism in the USSR."[91] As Terry Martin concludes, Soviet commentators thus heralded the success of a policy that had transformed backward feudal tribes into socialist nations.[92] According to official ideology, then, the country as a whole had progressed to socialism, and ethnic groups had progressed to nationhood—not the nationhood of bourgeois exploitation and imperial domination but the nationhood of an advanced and conscious people voluntarily united with other nationalities under Soviet socialism.

To prove their nationhood, every nationality needed a clearly defined heritage, including its own language, costumes, folk songs, literature, heroes, and national narrative. With the revival of Russian history and culture and the official emphasis on the friendship of peoples, Party functionaries and intellectuals in national minority republics were required to write national narratives that stressed the historical cooperation and friendship of their nationality with the Russian people. Party leaders did not dictate these narratives; they issued general signals regarding their orientation, leaving local officials and historians to debate and formulate the narratives themselves. When a 1937 Politburo commission faulted manuscripts in a textbook competition for presenting an overly negative picture of Russian imperial domination, some Ukrainian writers and historians began for the first time to portray historic Russian-Ukrainian cooperation. While other historians criticized these accounts, Party officials rewarded authors who developed the story of Russian-Ukrainian cooperation, in particular Oleksandr Korniichuk, whose play *Bohdan Khmel'nyts'kyi* won the Stalin Prize.[93] The Cossack leader Bohdan Khmel'nyts'kyi served as an ideal hero for a Ukrainian historical narrative linked with Russia. He could be portrayed both as a heroic Ukrainian leader who fought for independence from Poland and as a partner of Russia because of his 1654 union with Muscovy.[94] Alongside past Russian national leaders, then, Soviet official culture glorified national minority heroes who symbolized the historic alliance between Russians and non-Russians.

In other ways, too, Soviet official culture began to present national minorities in an allied yet subordinate position to ethnic Russians. The Soviet press in the mid-1930s portrayed national minorities in a way that stressed their loyalty to the Soviet government. *Pravda* published letters of homage and gratitude from members of national minorities to Soviet leaders. The press also quoted non-Russian delegates to the 1934 Congress of Soviet writers who expressed their deference to Russian culture and their loyalty to Moscow. Moreover, a 1936 *Pravda* article titled "The Friendship of the USSR's Peoples Is Alive and Flourishing" stated that "the Great Russian People, first among equal participants of this brotherly union of peoples, provided enormous help to the weaker nations in the years of heroic struggle."[95]

Such familial metaphors were a central rhetorical device in Soviet propaganda to bolster unity among ethnic groups. This rhetoric was explicitly linked with familial metaphors of the Stalin cult, as Stalin was referred to as "the father of all Soviet peoples." The Kremlin receptions where Stalin received delegations of various national minorities served to reinforce this paternalistic image.[96] Other propaganda referred to "the brotherly union" of nationalities, or spoke of the Soviet republics as "eleven sisters" in the Soviet family.[97] A major flaw in these efforts, however, was a persistent strain of Russian chauvinism that contradicted appeals for unity and equality. References to the Russian people as "the elder brother" of other nationalities or as "first among equals" only confirmed suspicions in the minds of many national minorities that Soviet unity was based not on equality and self-determination but on Russian domination and assimilation.

Another practice to integrate nationalities and the Soviet population as a whole was the organization of mass parades and spectacles, where thousands of citizens could march together and shout in unison in a symbolic demonstration of their unity. Parades on Red Square were organized so that columns coming from different districts of Moscow would, in the words of Kaganovich, "all pour into Red Square at the same time." As Karen Petrone has discussed, these parades symbolically unified Soviet citizens of different classes and nationalities. Marchers would proceed past Lenin's mausoleum, where Stalin and other Party leaders stood, thereby demonstrating the allegiance of the population to the Stalinist leadership. The national minorities who took part in these parades were often identified by symbols of their economic or military contribution to the country. In one such parade, delegates from Uzbekistan carried banners proclaiming their cotton harvest, while Armenian and Ukrainian delegates touted their roles in defending the country's borders.[98]

In the summer of 1937 the Politburo ordered a physical culture parade to be held on Red Square with over 40,000 participants, including a dele-

Soviet nationalities march with banners that read "Greetings to the great Stalin." "Long live the brotherly union and great friendship of the peoples of the USSR!" (Poster identification number RU/SU 1842, Poster Collection, Hoover Institution Archives.)

gation from each republic and record holders in a variety of sports.[99] An article about this event, titled "The Parade of the Powerful Stalin Breed," stressed the unity of all the nationalities of the Soviet Union.

> The living poem created on Red Square by Russian, Ukrainian, Belorussian, Georgian, Armenian, Azerbaijani, Kazakh, Uzbek, Turkmen, Tajik, and Kirghiz physical culture participants proclaims in a loud, sonorous voice, which echoes around the entire world, the blood brotherhood and indissoluble friendship of the peoples that populate the broad expanse of the country of Soviets; . . . and [declares] that the brave, strong Soviet youth are an inexhaustible reserve for our powerful Red Army.[100]

Clearly physical culture parades were more than just a display of discipline and potential military strength. Parades symbolized the unity of Soviet society. In them all nationalities and social groups were symbolically united as they marched and performed synchronized exercises in perfect unison. In this sense physical culture parades were a type of mass spectacle characteristic of modern mass politics. In an age of popular sovereignty and mass warfare, the participation of thousands of citizens in theatrical rituals of unity and strength were important mobilizational mechanisms.

One curious aspect of Soviet official culture in the 1930s was its emphasis on folklore. While Proletkult leaders in the 1920s had condemned folklore and called for its elimination, at the First Congress of Soviet Writers in 1934 Gorky championed folklore as a genuine expression of people's optimism and aspirations. Gorky's statement marked the beginning of an official campaign to promote folklore. The Soviet government sponsored village expeditions to gather folkloric materials, which were then edited and polished before publication and performance. Official institutions were also established to oversee and showcase folklore. The Soviet government created the All-Union House of Folk Art in Moscow as well as institutes of national culture all across the country. It also sponsored folk singing competitions and festivals of national art featuring works produced by various Soviet nationalities.[101]

Soviet leaders promoted folklore for specific political purposes. Folk culture, like historical heroes, held strong emotional appeal and attached the Soviet people to an eternal past and future. The particular moment when the Soviet government employed these appeals—the mid-1930s—is explained not only by rising international tensions and preparation for war but also by the achievement of socialism and the deemphasis of class. Once class antagonisms had been overcome, it became possible to conceive of a people united and organically whole. Folk culture was the ideal medium to express this (fictitious) organic unity, because it was allegedly created by the people as a spontaneous form of self-expression.

It seems strange that the Soviet state, with its emphasis on economic modernization and progress, would resort to traditional folk culture and symbols. But the Soviet government in this sense was by no means unique. Other twentieth-century governments also employed folklore and traditional symbols for modern political mobilization. The Nazi government, for example, used folklore and folk costumes to conjure the image of a premodern, organically unified people. One of its slogans, "One empire, one people, one leader," presented the population as monolithic in order to unite the German population behind Hitler. It is one of the ironies of modernity that at the very moment when modern rationalism destroyed traditional culture, the demands of mass politics spurred the creation of invented traditions.[102]

The invented traditions of Soviet folk culture did not signal a return to traditional customs. For one thing, folk expressions in official culture were merged with symbols of progress and modernity; at the 1939 All-Union Agricultural Exhibition, Uzbekistan's exhibit juxtaposed ancient minarets with displays on mechanized cotton production.[103] For another, the Soviet folk songs and costumes produced by cultural officials were not authentic folk culture. Officially sponsored folklore publications and festivals presented only a certain version of traditional folk culture, which of course itself never existed in any pure form but rather was constantly evolving and interacting with elements of urban and official culture.[104] Soviet folklore promoted only those themes and forms that expressed national identity in a way that did not foment nationalist separatism or undermine socialism's ideological or acculturating mission. Some folklore was deemed culturally and ideologically unacceptable, such as "hooligan songs" and "cruel romances of the bourgeois type," and these forms were censored.[105] Soviet authorities also used traditional epic songs and folktales to glorify the Soviet Union and Party leaders. Folk singers, for example, were recruited to compose and perform folkloric panegyrics to Stalin.[106]

Soviet folklore was also exoticized in the sense that it reflected nationalities' cultures not as they existed in everyday life but rather as colorful, aestheticized, and superficial cultural forms. Thus national minorities were pictured in bright national costumes, singing apolitical songs. Soviet Georgia, for example, was invariably called "sunny socialist Georgia," and described as having fine weather that explained the "joyful" folk art produced there.[107] But no presentation of different values, social systems, or traditional economic and kinship relations was permitted. Soviet nationality policy, because it both permitted national self-expression and sought ultimately to supersede it, promoted controlled and depoliticized forms of nationalities' cultures. Folklore represented a cultural medium by which nationalities could express an identity in a way that did not threaten Soviet unity.

Soviet folklore was thus very much in keeping with Soviet nationality policy and with Stalin's formulation regarding cultures: "national in form, socialist in content." Soviet leaders since the Revolution had sought to depoliticize nationality and to disarm nationalist separatism by showing respect for national minorities and their cultures. They believed that by allowing and even encouraging national self-expression, they could demonstrate the superiority of socialism without provoking a nationalist backlash. Gradually national identities would disappear as people adopted a socialist consciousness. This approach, however, inadvertently reinforced national identities, as the peoples of the Soviet Union were constantly made to think in terms of ethnicity and nationality. Not only folkloric expressions but all aspects of public life—identification in passports, recruitment and hiring quotas, native-language education—became based on one's nationality.[108]

Over time officials as well as the population came to attach more rather than less significance to nationality. First during collectivization, then increasingly in the late 1930s, Party leaders themselves began to identify disloyal groups within the population in national terms. The worst peasant uprisings of collectivization occurred on the Polish-Ukrainian border and were accompanied by large-scale flight of Soviet peasants of Polish origin across the border into Poland. In response, the Politburo authorized the deportation of thousands of additional kulak families, stipulating that those of Polish nationality should be the first removed. They also referred to "Polish-kulak counterrevolutionary and spying elements," thereby merging the category of nationality with those of class enemy and spy.[109]

Once Party leaders considered socialism built and began to deemphasize class, nationality assumed an even greater place in their thinking about potential enemies. As Amir Weiner has argued, ethnic hostility replaced class antagonisms as the primary threat to social harmony. At the Seventeenth Party Congress in 1934, Stalin in fact warned that the survivals of capitalism were "much more tenacious in the sphere of the national problem . . . because they are able to disguise themselves in national costume."[110] A 1935 deportation order called for the removal of "counterrevolutionary nationalist (Polish and German) and anti-Soviet elements," thus replacing a hyphenated national-class enemy with a purely national one. In fact, roughly half the Polish and German populations living in the

Ukrainian border region were deported during operations in 1935–36. With the rising international tensions of the mid-to-late 1930s, the Party leadership became increasingly distrustful of the diaspora nationalities in the western borderlands and the Far East. Soviet authorities feared that these diaspora nationalities might not only be disloyal but be used by foreign aggressors. They therefore carried out massive deportations in 1937–38 of all Koreans from the Far East border region, and partial deportations of Poles, Latvians, Germans, Romanians, Estonians, Finns, Greeks, Iranians, and Chinese from their respective border regions. These operations referred, for example, to "the liquidation of the Polish Sabotage-Espionage Group" and "the destruction of espionage and sabotage contingents" of various diaspora nationalities.[111]

These ethnic deportations at least superficially resembled those carried out by the tsarist government during the First World War. At the turn of the century and particularly after 1905, tsarist officials were already focusing on nationality as the preeminent category of military statistics by which they determined the quality and reliability of the population.[112] When the Soviet government initially employed similar practices of statistically classifying the population, it did so not on an ethnic axis but on the basis of class—enumerating and ultimately deporting kulaks. But with the deemphasis of class in the mid-1930s and the rising threat from hostile nation-states on their borders, Soviet leaders came to see diaspora nationalities as a vulnerability or even a threat, which they dealt with through a series of coercive deportations. Soviet leaders' targeting of certain national groups stemmed not from a biological concept of nationality but from a concern that other states had control over the histories and traditions that shaped the consciousness of diaspora nationalities. As long as national consciousness could be channeled according to Soviet doctrine—national in form, socialist in content—it posed no threat. But national minorities with a consciousness shaped by a foreign power did represent a threat to Soviet unity and security, and members of these minorities were deported from border regions.[113] During the Second World War, the ethnicization of categories of the enemy became complete, as entire nationalities were deported not just from border regions but from their homes anywhere in the country.[114]

The ethnic deportations of the late 1930s coincided with the widespread arrests and executions of the Great Terror, which itself had an important nationality component. Hiroaki Kuromiya has shown that national minorities in the Donbas (and in particular the diaspora nationalities—Germans, Poles, and Greeks) suffered disproportionately in the terror.[115] Terry Martin has calculated that secret police operations to apprehend national minorities suspected of espionage and sabotage accounted for one-fifth of all arrests and one-third of all executions during the terror. In fact, secret police documents referred to these operations as directed against "nationalities of foreign governments," showing that police officials saw members of diaspora nationalities as loyal to the nation-state of their nationality, despite the fact that most of these people were Soviet citizens whose families had lived there for generations.[116] In this period the Soviet government also repressed so-called bourgeois nationalists—national minority political and cultural leaders suspected of promoting nationalist separatism. Soviet nationality policy permitted only the tightly controlled, depoliticized expressions of nationalism developed in Soviet official culture. Any other nationalist expression was seen as a violation of Soviet unity and a potential political threat to the integrity of the country.

Social Harmony through State Coercion

The Great Terror, of course, extended beyond national minorities and beyond purged Party members as well. In the late 1930s, hundreds of thousands of common people were incarcerated or executed as recidivist criminals, former kulaks, or "anti-Soviet elements." The so-called mass operations of 1937–38 coincided with the Great Purges and amounted to an effort to eliminate enemies not only within the Party and among diaspora nationalities but among the population as a whole. The terror overall, then, is best understood as state violence applied to "cleanse" society of any person who represented a potential threat to state security or of any dissenter to the socialist order. Dissent could take such seemingly innocuous forms as trading on the black market or engaging in "hooligan" behavior. In the eyes of Soviet authorities, such activity was far from innocuous; it constituted nonacceptance of socialism and a fundamental challenge to the utopia they were constructing.

Historians continue to debate the relative weight of national security considerations and ideological imperatives in the Stalinist leadership's decision to initiate the Great Terror. Oleg Khlevniuk has made a strong case that Stalin carried out the terror as a preemptive strike against potential fifth columnists. He argues that with war imminent, Stalin sought to eliminate all rivals and oppositionists, thus seeking to strengthen the country for the forthcoming struggle.[117] It is true that the threat to the Soviet Union from Germany and Japan was extreme by the late 1930s. Soviet leaders had no illusions about the inevitability of war or the ferocity of the impending battle. It is also true that all Soviet leaders and Stalin in particular believed they were surrounded by both external and internal enemies, and with the external enemies poised to attack, it became all the more imperative to deal mercilessly with the internal enemies.

At the same time, a case could be made that the primary impetus for the terror was ideological. To pursue their goal of a communist utopia, Soviet leaders were prepared to use violence to eliminate all opposition. Only the eradication of all enemies and dissenters would allow the creation of a pure and completely harmonious communist society.[118] While this argument too has merit, counterposing national security and ideology is something of a false dichotomy. In the minds of the Stalinist leadership, both national security concerns and ideological goals held tremendous weight, and in fact the two were inextricably intertwined. Soviet leaders could achieve communism only if they defended the Soviet motherland from the attack of capitalist countries. And from their point of view, they could defend the country only if they did progress toward communism by eliminating all dissent to the socialist order. A harmonious, unified society—to be achieved, paradoxically, through mass arrests and executions—both strengthened national security and moved the country toward communism.

Soviet leaders never believed that progress toward communism would proceed peacefully. Even after deporting overt class enemies (NEPmen and kulaks), Stalin and his fellow leaders continued to fixate on the enemies of Soviet socialism. As Stalin warned, the greater the power of the Soviet state, the more fiercely its opponents, both internal and external, would oppose it.[119] Such opposition required ever more extreme measures to eliminate those within the Soviet Union who still did not accept the socialist order and either openly or secretly tried to wreck it. And the growing threat from Nazi Germany in particular seemed to confirm that the capitalist countries were poised to intervene and destroy the socialist motherland if they could. The Second World War from this point of view was a battle fully expected by Soviet leaders. They anticipated it as their Armageddon—a life-and-death struggle to defend socialism from enemies. This battle not only was inevitable but had to be fought in order to vanquish the foes of socialism and allow further progress toward communism.[120]

To understand the logic and timing of the terror's mass operations, it is also important to consider how the achievement of socialism in the mid-1930s affected Party leaders' understanding of social problems and of continued resistance to their authority. Before collectivization, crime and other social problems could be blamed on the remnants of capitalism and the presence of class enemies. Kulaks and NEPmen were assumed to be opponents of the Soviet order and violators of socialist principles. But after dekulakization and the end of NEP, these class enemies were supposed to have been liquidated and a completely socialist economy created. According to the Soviet jurist A. Shliapochnikov, the establishment of socialism denied enemies their economic base and broke the power of organized class resistance. Commissar of Justice Krylenko and State Procurator Andrei Vyshinskii concurred, claiming that resistance to Soviet authorities no longer took place along class lines. But this meant that when crime did occur, repression could no longer be limited to class enemies. In 1935 Krylenko announced that punishments should now be applied universally. Whereas previously workers caught stealing were not considered dangerous criminals, now repression should be used, he argued, "to defend the socialist motherland not only from class enemies, but also from those, even among workers, who would destroy socialist discipline and socialist laws."[121]

After collectivization and dekulakization, crime could no longer be blamed on kulaks. Soviet crime reports began to focus on theft and hooliganism among workers and collectivized peasants. Statistics in a 1933 crime article showed that more than half of all crimes were committed by workers and collectivized peasants, and a 1937 report revealed that half of all those arrested for hooliganism were workers. The author of the crime article blamed the rise in crime among workers on the "penetration" of the working class by "declassified elements"—former kulaks and NEPmen who joined the working class and hid their class origins.[122] Stalin himself identified a new type of enemy in the era of socialism—the elusive or hidden enemy. Stalin began to develop this theme as early as 1933, when he noted that some of the last capitalist elements—private traders, kulaks, nobles, and priests—"have wormed their way into our factories and mills, into our institutions and trading organizations . . . some of them have even managed to worm their way into the Party."[123] At the Central Committee plenum in February–March 1937, Stalin declared that whereas the old enemies had been openly hostile, the new enemies were "people who formally are not [class] alien. Whereas the old vermin turned against our people, the new vermin, on the contrary, cringe before our people, extol our people, bow before them in order to win their trust."[124] While Stalin was warning primarily of enemies who had wormed their way into the Party and needed to be purged, his concept of the elusive and devious enemy was applied more broadly, as secret police officials increasingly sought to uncover hidden enemies throughout society.

The establishment of socialism prompted another important perceptual shift among Party leaders in regard to crime. Previously crime, particularly economic crime, had been understood as a remnant of capitalism. But with the creation of an entirely socialist economy where virtually all property was state-owned, the persistence of crime indicated political opposition to the socialist order. As David Shearer has argued, Soviet officials in the mid-1930s came to view criminals not just as social deviants but as opponents of socialism and enemies of the people and the state. This conflation of "criminal" with "enemy of the people" politicized crime and interpreted it as opposition to the Soviet order.[125] The very category "enemy of the people" was new at this time, and reflected Party leaders' belief that they had liquidated class enemies and the remnants of capitalism. Such progress made it possible to speak of "the people" as a united, monolithic entity, but it also meant that anyone who did not conform to the Soviet order was an inveterate adversary of the people and of Soviet socialism.

Soviet officials also came to perceive hooliganism as political opposition. A 1934 Komsomol report on technical institute students, for example, described hooligan behavior as "counterrevolutionary activity" that should be dealt with accordingly.[126] In a speech to regional secret police chiefs in 1935, Iagoda called the battle with counterrevolution their most honored duty, and then asked rhetorically, "But in today's situation, a hooligan, a bandit, a robber—isn't this the most genuine counter-revolutionary?"[127] The Commissariat of Justice instituted new measures to battle with hooliganism and in 1935 began to prosecute cases of hooliganism more vigorously, imposing prison sentences on roughly 40 percent of those convicted.[128] As with crime more generally, hooliganism was often blamed on "declassified elements"—former kulaks and NEPmen—who, deprived of the opportunity to exploit others economically, defied the Soviet order in other ways. One report stated that hooliganism reflected a new form of opposition by the class enemy, and attributed the rise of hooliganism among workers to people of "petty bourgeois origin." Another report claimed that "declassified elements" recruited homeless children into criminal gangs and were responsible for youth hooliganism in cities.[129] By 1940 a special Commissariat of Justice decree used the term "disorganizers of socialist society" to describe hooligans, and prescribed even harsher repressive measures.[130]

Soviet authorities devoted special attention to juvenile gangs. The large number of homeless children in urban areas had caused social problems since the Civil War. In the mid-1930s, however, police officials intensified their focus on the problem, and increasingly attributed anti-Soviet intent to youth hooliganism and crime.[131] To combat youth crime, the Soviet government decreed in 1935 that juveniles age twelve and over could be tried and sentenced as adults.[132] And after special conferences in Moscow, the police there enacted comprehensive and harsh measures to eradicate the problems of homeless children and youth hooliganism.[133]

The equation of crime and hooliganism with political opposition, then, led to both heightened attention and harsher punishments. Party officials were especially concerned with the sharp rise in crimes against the state, in particular the theft of state property.[134] Increased theft of state property was not surprising, given that the state assumed control of virtually all resources during collectivization and the First Five-Year Plan. As people struggled to survive during the extreme deprivation of the 1930s, many stole a bit of grain from their collective farm or materials from their factory to barter for food. Also widespread was black-marketeering, as people traded illegally to obtain the food and clothing that were not available in state stores. To Party leaders, such activity signaled opposition to the Soviet system and was a crime against the Soviet state. At the January 1933 Central Committee plenum, Stalin stated that to permit the theft of state or collective farm property "is to contribute to the undermining of the Soviet system."[135] At the very moment, then, that petty theft and black-market trading became a necessity for many Soviet citizens, it came to represent political opposition to Soviet officials.

In a similar manner, industrial accidents were also politicized. As early as the First Five-Year Plan, Party leaders had held show trials of "bourgeois specialists" whom they accused of sabotaging Soviet industry.[136] By 1937, virtually all accidents, defective goods, and broken machinery were labeled "wrecking," including incidents previously considered criminal negligence but not political crimes.[137] The increased politicization of accidents was of course connected with the Great Purges and the virulent propaganda campaign against Trotskyists, spies, and wreckers that accompanied them. But it also stemmed from officials' expectation that problems would not occur under socialism; if they did, they must have been perpetrated by people who deliberately sought to attack the socialist system. Criticism of Soviet policies and leaders similarly became even less tolerable than before. Beginning in 1935, the number of cases brought against people for "anti-Soviet agitation" greatly increased. Those overheard criticizing the Soviet government were subject to prosecution and imprisonment, usually for three to five years.[138] With the achievement of socialism in 1934, Party leaders viewed any further questioning or criticism of their policies as political opposition.

It is important to understand not only why the number of arrests multiplied in the second half of the 1930s but why the punishments imposed by the Soviet government became more severe. The Party purges and the mass operations of 1936–38 involved the incarceration and execution of millions of people. During previous operations such as dekulakization, Soviet authorities had also employed massive state coercion, but had not killed most of their victims. They had instead deported "kulaks" to labor camps and special settlements, where they were to be reformed through forced labor. While Party leaders believed it was necessary to remove these people from society physically, they assumed that the majority of them would ultimately reenter Soviet society after they had gained the proper consciousness. By contrast, a high percentage of those arrested in the Great Purges and mass operations were simply killed, without any effort to reform or rehabilitate them.

Extreme international tensions did play a central role in the decision to execute "Trotskyists" and "anti-Soviet elements." With war imminent, it seemed imperative to eliminate internal enemies in order to ensure that the socialist motherland could be defended. But here again it is important to remember that, according to official ideology, socialism had been achieved. During the 1920s, anti-Soviet behavior could be attributed to environmental factors—the remnants of capitalism and the petty bourgeois milieu of NEPmen and kulaks. Once these class enemies and harmful influences had been eliminated, individuals who continued to engage in crime, black-marketeering, or other anti-Soviet activities were viewed as fundamentally flawed. Because they could not be reformed or brought to accept the socialist order, they were eliminated completely.

The ideal of a pure socialist society contaminated by irredeemable "elements" that needed to be eliminated was therefore central to the thinking behind the purges and mass operations of the latter 1930s. With class enemies defeated, the entire population was to be united in its support of socialism. Molotov in 1937 cited the "unprecedented inner moral and political unity of the people," forged through the victorious struggle against the exploiting classes.[139] Because the people were united behind socialism, anyone who refused to accept socialism was "an enemy of the people." The Soviet press presented enemies as "scum" or "vermin" to be eradicated in order to purify society.[140] And the *Short Course* history of the Communist Party extolled the physical annihilation of elusive enemies as necessary for the purification of society.[141]

An important step toward the mass execution of criminals and other "anti-Soviet elements" was taken as early as 1933, when the Politburo authorized the secret police to execute people engaged in banditry in western Siberia. The same year the Politburo instructed the secret police to expel from Moscow all individuals who had two prior arrests for property crimes or hooliganism, and ordered "beggars and declassified elements" to be exiled or sent to labor camps.[142] In fact, throughout the mid-1930s the secret police arrested and deported a huge number of people from urban areas. Some 266,000 "socially harmful elements" were expelled from cities of the RSFSR in 1935; of those about 85,000 were charged by secret police tribunals, and the rest were simply deported as violators of the internal passport regime. A joint NKVD-Procuracy decree in April 1935 listed the following categories of "socially harmful elements": persons with criminal convictions and "continuing uncorrected ties" to the criminal world; persons with no definite place of work, including "professional" beggars; persons without urban residence permits; and children over the age of twelve engaged in criminal acts. All of these people were subject to extrajudicial sentencing by the secret police. Indeed, Iagoda used not only this decree but also the passport system and administrative fiat to remove persons deemed socially dangerous from the rest of the population.[143]

As Paul Hagenloh has argued, the mass operations of 1937–38 represented a radicalization of the Soviet government's policy toward "socially harmful elements." Throughout the mid-1930s, central officials believed they could completely eliminate crime in urban areas through strict implementation of the passport regime and the deportation of all socially marginal people.[144] This ideal of a pure society, uncontaminated by any criminals, former kulaks, or other suspect individuals, was pursued by even more deadly means beginning in 1937. On July 11 the Politburo's decree "On Anti-Soviet Elements" set execution and deportation quotas for dekulakized peasants and ex-convicts, specifying that 259,450 people be arrested and of those 72,950 be shot.[145] In January 1938 the Politburo approved additional execution and deportation quotas for former kulaks, criminals, and "actively anti-Soviet elements."[146] These mass operations resulted in the killing of hundreds of thousands of people, including not only former kulaks and criminals but former White officers, small-time traders, beggars, priests, and members of religious sects. The goal of the mass operations was thus to purge the body social of "alien" and "harmful" groups that did not fit into the new Soviet order.[147]

Of course the goal of creating a pure society did not necessarily entail the massive application of state violence. One could certainly imagine a utopian social enterprise that emphasized education and gradualism instead of deportations and executions. Even a regime that relied on state violence could have applied it in a more limited fashion; it might have arrested overt oppositionists without setting deportation and execution quotas for entire segments of the population. The mass operations reflected not only the fanaticism of the Stalinist leadership's drive to eliminate enemies but also the deployment of modern concepts and technologies of population management. Governments throughout history have used coercion in dealing with their people, but only in the twentieth century have they "scientifically" categorized their populations and targeted specific categories in large-scale excisionary operations. The idea of extracting "elements" from the population was predicated on a science of society and on the definition of a social field to which this science could be applied. Social statistics and social cataloguing provided a statistical representation of the population and hence a conceptual framework from which to refashion that population. Modern bureaucratic procedures, extensive police networks, and concentration camps provided the means to remove those deemed socially harmful.

Throughout the 1920s and 1930s the Soviet government compiled a vast human archive. Through censuses, questionnaires, and an internal passport system, Soviet officials sought to know their society and every person in it. This archive of the population identified those individuals who, by virtue of their social origins or anti-Soviet activity, were slated for excision. Officials even categorized "anti-Soviet elements" as more or less harmful, with the more harmful targeted for execution and the less harmful for deportation to labor camps where they would be reformed. During the Great Terror, when Stalin and the Politburo ordered mass executions and deportations, the Soviet secret police relied on these archival records of the population to know whom to arrest. The use of state violence to shape the population was thus predicated on a particular mapping of the politico-social body.[148]

Of course it is important to maintain a sense of human agency and to acknowledge that social statistics and interventionist technologies did not themselves cause the Great Terror—Stalin and his fellow leaders clearly bear responsibility for the deportations and executions they ordered. Their decision to launch the purges and mass operations reflected an unfettered ambition to achieve social unity and a communist utopia. For them, progress toward communism and indeed their own survival depended on the ruthless elimination of enemies. The mentality of Stalin and other leading Communists had been shaped by the Revolution and Civil War, when vanquishing their opponents had been a matter of life and death. With the rising threat from Nazi Germany in the late 1930s, Party leaders strove to eliminate both potential rivals within their ranks and alleged enemies among the general population. Social cataloguing and excisionary technologies contributed to the terror only insofar as Party leaders attached these modes of social intervention to their claims of history making and their drive to eradicate all opposition.[149]

Moreover, to say that the mass operations were predicated on social cataloguing and a science of society is not to say that these operations were conducted in a scientific, rational manner. While the secret police drew on its card files listing "anti-Soviet elements," it carried out the mass opera-

tions (and indeed the Great Terror as a whole) in a frenzy of denuncia-
tions, arrests, and executions. Secret police officials, afraid that they themselves might be criticized for a lack of vigilance, overfulfilled the arrest and
execution quotas dictated to them by the Politburo.[150] Even apart from
these excesses, the mass operations involved the arrest and execution of a
vast number of innocent people in an atmosphere of intense fear, suspicion, even hysteria. In this sense the Great Terror appears to have been the
antithesis of rational population management. Yet to conceive of and
launch a mass excisionary operation required not only a murderous determination to eliminate the enemies of Soviet socialism but a conceptual
framework based on social cataloguing and the technologies of modern
state violence. Modern concepts and technologies thus provided a necessary though not sufficient condition for the mass operations. Stalinist
terror was not simply a product of Russian backwardness or Stalin's vin-
dictiveness—it was not analogous to Ivan the Terrible's medieval *oprichnina*. Instead it reflected a modern conception of society as an artifact to
be sculpted through state intervention.

While it is important to examine the thinking behind the mass operations, it is also necessary to point out the incongruities and contradictions.
Party leaders sought to purify and strengthen their society by eliminating
those they deemed socially harmful. And they believed that the deportations and executions they carried out would make for a more harmonious,
more unified society. This unity, they believed, would also strengthen the
country and prepare it for war, by eliminating any potential internal opposition. Yet the effect of deporting and executing millions of people was
only to heighten social tensions and distrust. Far from promoting harmony
and social unity, state coercion left a legacy of fear and hatred, which affected
not only the relatives and friends of victims but other Soviet citizens as well.

While some people may have partially believed Soviet rhetoric about purifying society and eliminating enemies, many others came to distrust and
fear the government even more than they had done before. The terror
proved extremely detrimental to people's sense of security and to normal
social and economic functioning. In the wake of the purges and mass operations, labor productivity slipped, economic production fell, culture
stagnated, and military strength declined. The Soviet project suffered
from a fundamental contradiction between means and ends. Social unity
and a utopian society could not be achieved by massive state coercion. The
deportation and execution of people instead sowed disharmony and mistrust. Indeed, the Stalinist legacy—millions of innocent victims—would
haunt the Soviet Union for the remainder of its existence and contribute
greatly to its ultimate demise.

Conclusion

This examination of Soviet official culture and values has shown that Stalinism was neither a conscious retreat from Soviet socialism nor a return to prerevolutionary Russian conservatism. The Stalinist leadership did selectively use traditional symbols and institutions, but it did so for modern mobilizational purposes. Soviet leaders never abandoned their ideological goals of creating the New Soviet Person and achieving communism. The values they propagated through official culture were intended to further these goals and to transform the population into a modern, efficient socialist society. Values and culture in this sense were not neutral and did not mark a continuation of past Russian ways. Instead they were part of Soviet leaders' political program and reflected their quintessentially modern ambition to remake society.

The new values Soviet leaders sought to inculcate in the population included cleanliness, efficient labor, edifying leisure, and sobriety. These norms of "cultured" living reflected both the instrumental objective of ensuring the health and physical capacity of the population and a benevolent, aesthetic impulse to uplift the masses and create a more beautiful world. The Stalinist leadership established particularly stringent behavioral norms for Party members. Control commissions monitored the professional and personal conduct of Communists and carried out periodic purges of those deemed unfit for Party membership. In the process, these commissions produced an unwritten code of morality for Communists to follow, as well as norms of efficiency, decorum, and ideological purity.

The Soviet government also propagated norms of sexual behavior as it sought to manage reproduction and child raising through the institution of the family. Governments throughout Europe and around the world in the interwar period began to bolster the family as a means to increase the birth rate and safeguard the upbringing of children. In the Soviet case, the state's use of the family became plausible after it had eliminated capitalist remnants—only then could the family be trusted to instill socialist rather than bourgeois values. Legislation and propaganda to bolster the family did not signal a return to traditional ways or the creation of a private sphere free from government interference. On the contrary, Soviet leaders used the family as an instrument of the state—as a means to pursue the state's need for a high birth rate and social discipline.

Soviet leaders also set values concerning consumption. Within Soviet culture, as in other modern societies, asceticism had long been in tension with consumerism. Industrial production could be channeled either into satisfying consumer demand or into building up state economic and military power. The Soviet Union went through periods of extreme asceticism during the Civil War and the First Five-Year Plan, when citizens were forced to sacrifice their material needs for the "higher" goals of strengthening the state's military preparedness and building socialism. After socialism was purportedly attained in 1934, Stalin and his fellow leaders reoriented official culture to stress abundance and happiness in the Soviet Union. Consumerist values came to the fore, at least in theory, during the mid-1930s, before the Second World War triggered another period of asceticism and sacrifice.

The approach of the Second World War also prompted intensified efforts by the Stalinist leadership to enhance cultural and social unity. These efforts were part of a more general aspiration to overcome the alienation of modern society and create a world of complete social harmony. Soviet leaders felt they had taken an enormous step in this direction by eliminating class enemies, and the 1936 Constitution reflected this progress by restoring voting rights to all citizens. But the rising international threat increased the impetus to unite the Soviet population, and the Party leadership employed the Stalin cult, a common cultural canon, patriotic heroes, and folklore to do so. Party leaders also resorted to massive state coercion to eliminate "anti-Soviet elements" from society. The forms this coercion took were predicated on modern conceptions of the social field and modern technologies of social cataloguing and excision. Of course Stalin and his fellow leaders bear responsibility for the incarceration and execution of millions of people—it was when they attached these conceptions and technologies of social intervention to their agenda of violent revolutionary transformation that Stalinist terror resulted.

What, then, was Soviet socialism? How are we to explain it and characterize it? Most historical interpretations have explained the Soviet system in terms of factors unique to the Soviet Union—Russian autocratic traditions, social and economic underdevelopment, or Marxist ideology.[1] But the Soviet system is best understood as one particular response to the ambitions and challenges of the modern era. In countries throughout modern Europe, political leaders and social reformers aspired to solve social problems and rationalize everyday life through the inculcation of new cultural norms. Soviet norms of efficiency, hygiene, sobriety, and literacy all reflected this more general ambition to establish a rationalized and aestheticized social order. Soviet norms with respect to reproduction and the family similarly reflected the need of modern states to foster large, healthy populations for industrial labor and mass warfare. Soviet official culture also resembled the culture of other European states in the interwar period in its use of folklore and traditional symbols to promote social unity.

The purpose of placing Soviet socialism in the broader context of European modernity is not to deny or level the differences between the Soviet Union and other modern European states. Indeed, such a perspective helps to highlight what was in fact distinct about the Soviet system. While Soviet officials sought to inculcate behavioral norms common to other European reformers, they also promoted collectivist values quite different from the individualism of liberal democratic systems. In the sphere of elite values, the Communist Party not only dictated norms of neat dress and polite decorum but also enforced standards of ideological and moral purity through control commissions and purging. Soviet reproductive norms were distinguished by their rejection of eugenics and their emphasis on Lamarckism—an emphasis derived not only from Marxist ideology but from prerevolutionary Russian disciplinary culture, which stressed environmental over hereditary determinants of human traits. The Soviet economic system sought to satisfy the demands of mass consumption in a noncapitalist, nonexploitative manner, through which all members of society would allegedly benefit equally from their collective labor. And finally, the Soviet system offered a distinct solution to the problem of class stratification and social alienation in modern industrial societies. Through violent proletarian revolution and the elimination of "class enemies" and "enemies of the people," the Soviet regime was to create a completely unified, harmonious society. That it was a revolutionary regime formed at a moment of total war substantially lessened traditional constraints on state power and greatly heightened the willingness of Party leaders to deploy massive coercion in their bid to move history forward to communism.

The results of the Stalinist drive to refashion society were decidedly mixed. Soviet authorities did eliminate capitalism, establish a completely state-run planned economy, and industrialize the country extremely rapidly. They also markedly improved hygiene, eliminated epidemic diseases, reduced infant mortality, and vastly increased literacy. However fervently many Russians today wish to forget the entire Soviet experiment, it did permanently transform the country and much of everyday life. In addition, Party leaders established the ideal of the New Soviet Person—a productive, cultured citizen, free of selfish individualism and dedicated to the collective and to socialism. Some members of society, particularly those who aspired to rise within the system, internalized this ideal and strove to live up to it. Others, even while they did not abide by official norms, learned what cultured behavior was supposed to be.[2] The majority of the population learned to live within the system without accepting its collectivist values. Soviet citizens continued to place their own interests and needs first, and some engaged in passive resistance to Soviet policies. Traditional social networks aided people in their efforts both to obtain scarce goods and to resist adverse government policies.[3] In this sense, traditional networks and personal connections played a large role in daily life under Stalinism. But Stalinist culture and the Soviet system as Party leaders crafted it were not based on these networks and indeed sought to supplant them with an allegiance to the Soviet state. To describe Stalinism as a return to traditional Russian ways is to mischaracterize it in a fundamental way.

The intentions of Party leaders were not in themselves bad. They did aspire to fashion a better, more just world, in which alienation and class conflict would be replaced by a spirit of collectivism and social harmony. Their vision was a particular Marxian incarnation of more general Enlightenment and Romantic impulses to improve the world through reason and to recover the organic wholeness of humanity. The result of their attempt to build a communist utopia, however, was a brutally repressive system with millions of innocent victims. Unlike conservative, Burkean critiques of the Enlightenment, my study of Stalinist culture is not directed against the impulse to rationalize and improve society. The Enlightenment and social science deserve credit for enormous improvements in people's health and well-being. Social programs and attempts to rationalize social behavior do not in themselves pose a hazard; it is rather the normative assumptions and hierarchies often embedded in these allegedly objective undertakings that impinge on people's lives and freedom. When Soviet officials examined the lifestyles of workers, peasants, or national minorities, they looked through the lens of their own values and norms. Such norms, when imposed in a coercive way and when tied to claims of history making and utopianism, led to the extremes of Stalinist intervention and violence. My intention therefore is not to criticize progressive social programs but rather to provide a cautionary tale regarding the uncritical application of purportedly scientific social reform.

The other major lesson to be drawn from Stalinism is the danger of applying coercion to reshape society. Soviet leaders' attempts to change people's lifestyles and values through coercion and violence proved both deadly and largely ineffectual. Social change must be gradual and consensual if it is to succeed. Violent, directed social transformation only sparks resistance, either passive or overt. Even if violence achieves superficial change, it does not permanently transform the way people think and act. Moreover, in the Soviet case the means and ends were themselves in contradiction. State coercion by its very nature could not create social harmony. The arrest and execution of millions of people only sowed hatred, mistrust, and disharmony in Soviet society. And when Stalinist terror was finally allowed to be fully discussed in the Soviet Union under Gorbachev, it served to discredit the entire Soviet system and contributed greatly to its rapid demise.

The collapse of Soviet socialism also reflected the changing world of the late twentieth century. While the Soviet system responded to many of the ambitions and challenges of European modernity, it was not well suited to the postmodern era. The Soviet command economy possessed certain advantages in the modern industrial age, with its ability to mobilize labor and resources for large-scale mining operations and metallurgical plants, but it performed sluggishly in the postindustrial age, when growth shifted to the technology and service sectors. Trends throughout the world, from Thatcherism to Reaganism to privatization programs in developing countries, indicate that the downfall of the state-managed economy and authoritarian welfare policies of the Soviet Union reflected a more general turn away from the faith in rational government management of society that characterized the modern era. In part because of bureaucratic rigidity, especially apparent in the Soviet state planning agency's inability to adjust to the postindustrial economy, people came to see government management as inefficient or even as the source of economic and social problems.

Other phenomena, too, have eroded political leaders' and social thinkers' confidence in state management of society based on scientifically determined norms. Science and social science, while still central to European and American culture, have ceased to command people's unquestioning faith. Science, after all, provided both the justification (race science) and the means (Zyklon B gas) of the Holocaust. It supplied the theoretical postulates and practical knowledge for atomic weapons. Social

cataloguing and social engineering underlay many of the twentieth century's most brutal instances of state coercion, including Stalinist deportations and executions. Moreover, theorists and critics of science and social
science have pointed out that neither enterprise is purely objective, that
both employ interpretive frameworks riddled with biases.

At the same time that state intervention became increasingly discredited, it also appeared less necessary. In the modern era, government leaders needed to foster large and healthy populations for the demands of
industrial labor and mass warfare, but in the postmodern era, industrial
production has declined and robotic production has increasingly superseded manual labor.[4] In the realm of warfare, the development of com-
puter-guided missile systems and other high-tech weaponry has obviated
the need for mass armies of physically fit soldiers. Whereas in the first half
of the twentieth century a broad range of political leaders, military planners, industrialists, and social reformers actively sought to improve the
health and hygiene of the working poor, such is not the case today. Governments no longer prioritize the bodily health and well-being of their
populations, as evidenced by the decline in social welfare programs and
socialized medicine, not only in the former Soviet Union but throughout
the world.

The world also underwent considerable political and ideological change
in the second half of the twentieth century. The Soviet Union gained enormous prestige by defeating Nazi Germany, but in doing so it lost its role as
a bulwark against fascism. When the countries of Western Europe grudgingly gave up their overseas empires in the postwar era, Soviet anti-impe-
rialist ideology no longer held such appeal, and indeed the Soviet Union
itself appeared tainted as one of the few remaining world empires. Finally,
with the turnaround of the United States' economy, from the depression
of the 1930s to the postwar economic boom, the American model of liberal democratic capitalism came to outshine the model of Soviet socialism.
While Soviet official culture in the mid-1930s and again under Khrushchev
trumpeted the abundance of Soviet economic production, the Soviet
economy in fact proved ill suited for mass consumption, particularly in
comparison with the American economy, which exerted enormous worldwide allure in the realm of consumerism and popular culture.[5]

The Soviet system responded to many of the aspirations and challenges
of the modern era. It exemplified the modern ambition to refashion society through the propagation of new cultural norms and the exercise of
state coercion. It introduced government and expert intervention in people's lives as part of a utopian attempt to solve all problems and achieve
complete social harmony. And like other modern states, it strove to cate-

gorize, reshape, and mobilize its population to meet the needs of industrial labor and mass warfare. But those needs shifted in the postmodern era, when technology replaced manual labor as the source of economic and military power. Simultaneously people lost faith in rational government management of society and in social engineering projects, partly as a result of the Soviet Union's own brutal history. The Soviet system had displaced and killed millions of people as part of an effort to eliminate social strife and achieve a communist utopia. But it never delivered on its promises of social harmony or material abundance. And by the late twentieth century the Soviet system had little left to offer, save its own tainted legacy of coercion in the name of unattained ideals.

Abbreviations

d., dd.	delo, dela (file, files)
f.	fond (collection)
GARF	Gosudarstvennyi Arkhiv Rossiiskoi Federatsii (State Archive of the Russian Federation)
l., ll.	list, listy (page, pages)
op.	opis′ (inventory)
PRO	Public Record Office, U.K.
RGAE	Rossiiskii Gosudarstvennyi Arkhiv Ekonomiki (Russian State Archive of Economics)
RGASPI	Rossiiskii Gosudarstvennyi Arkhiv Sotsial′noi i Politicheskoi Istorii (Russian State Archive of Social and Political History)
TsGAODM	Tsentral′nyi Gosudarstvennyi Arkhiv Obshchestvennykh Dvizhenii Moskvy (Central State Archive of Social Movements of Moscow)
TsKhDMO	Tsentr Khraneniia Dokumentov Molodezhnykh Organizatsii (Center for the Preservation of Documents of Youth Organizations)
TsKhSD	Tsentr Khraneniia Sovremmenoi Dokumentatsii (Center for the Preservation of Contemporary Documentation)
TsMAM	Tsentral′nyi Munitsipal′nyi Arkhiv Moskvy (Central Municipal Archive of Moscow)

Notes

Introduction

1. Leon Trotsky, *The Revolution Betrayed: What Is the Soviet Union and Where Is It Going?* trans. Max Eastman, 5th ed. (New York, 1972), 105, 157, 248–49. Trotsky did not believe the Soviet Union in the mid–1930s had completely reverted to capitalism. He characterized the country as "a contradictory society halfway between capitalism and socialism," and he held out the hope that the workers would overthrow the bureaucracy and renew the advance toward socialism (255).

2. Nicholas S. Timasheff, *The Great Retreat: The Growth and Decline of Communism in Russia* (New York, 1946), chaps. 7–10.

3. Robert C. Tucker, "Stalinism as Revolution from Above," in *Stalinism: Essays in Historical Interpretation,* ed. Tucker (New York, 1977), 95–99.

4. Moshe Lewin, *The Making of the Soviet System: Essays in the Social History of Interwar Russia* (New York, 1985), 274. Other scholars, without making an explicit argument about the abandonment of socialism, also use the term "Great Retreat" to describe and periodize the mid-1930s.

5. Stephen Kotkin, *Magnetic Mountain: Stalinism as a Civilization* (Berkeley, 1995), 6. See also Igal Halfin, *From Darkness to Light: Class, Consciousness, and Salvation in Revolutionary Russia* (Pittsburgh, 2000), 17–27.

6. I. V. Stalin, "Otchetnyi doklad XVII s"ezdu partii o rabote TsK VKP(b)" (January 26, 1934), in his *Sochineniia* (Moscow, 1946–52), 13:308–9.

7. That is not to say that socialist thinkers before the Revolution had not debated some of these issues. On questions of the family and gender roles, for example, Karl Marx, Friedrich Engels, August Bebel, Clara Zetkin, and a number of Russian socialists had formulated ideas that influenced Soviet family policy; see Wendy Z. Goldman, *Women, the State, and Revolution: Soviet Family Policy and Social Life, 1917–1936* (New York, 1993), chap. 1.

8. On the complexity of the Soviet state, with its parallel Party and government bureaucratic hierarchies and its statized professions, see Lynne Viola, "Introduction," in *Contending with Stalinism: Soviet Power and Popular Resistance in the 1930s,* ed. Viola (Ithaca, 2002), 9–13.

9. As Serhy Yekelchyk concludes in his study of official Soviet culture and history writing in Ukraine, "The local bureaucrats and intellectuals who interpreted the vague yet powerful signals from Moscow emerge as major players shaping Stalinist historical imagination": "Stalinist Patriotism as Imperial Discourse: Reconciling the Ukrainian and Russian 'Heroic Pasts,' 1939–1945," *Kritika* 3, no. 1 (2002): 52.

10. Katerina Clark, *Petersburg, Crucible of Cultural Revolution* (Cambridge, Mass., 1995), ix–x. Clark's focus is on literature and high culture, but her metaphor of an ecosystem also applies to the values and behavioral norms of Soviet official culture.

11. In each chapter I briefly discuss the popular response to cultural norms, though my focus remains on official culture itself. There is now a rich literature on the reception of Soviet official culture and the ways in which the population adapted to or resisted Stalinist policies. See, for example, Sheila Fitzpatrick, *Everyday Stalinism: Ordinary Life in Extraordinary Times: Soviet Russia in the 1930s* (New York, 1999); Sarah Davies, *Popular Opinion in Stalin's Russia: Terror, Propaganda, and Dissent, 1934–1941* (New York, 1997); Jochen Hellbeck, "Working, Struggling, Becoming: Stalin-Era Autobiographical Texts," *The Russian Review* 60, no. 3 (2001); Viola, *Contending with Stalinism;* David L. Hoffmann, *Peasant Metropolis: Social Identities in Moscow, 1929–1941* (Ithaca, 1994).

12. Definitions of modernity that emphasize liberal democracy and industrial capitalism derive in part from the ascendancy of the United States and the development of modernization theory in the post–World War II era. Modernization theory stressed allegedly universal processes of industrialization and democratization, and offered a two-stage model of historical evolution (traditional–modern) to counter the three-stage model of Marxism (feudalism–capitalism–socialism). See Stephen Kotkin, "Modern Times: The Soviet Union and the Interwar Conjuncture," *Kritika* 2, no. 1 (2001): 157.

13. Anthony Giddens, *The Consequences of Modernity* (Stanford, 1990), 53, 83.

14. James C. Scott, *Seeing Like a State: How Certain Schemes to Improve the Human Condition Have Failed* (New Haven, 1998), 4. Scott uses the term "high modernism" to refer to the modern ethos of social intervention that I am describing.

15. Zygmunt Bauman, *Modernity and the Holocaust* (Ithaca, 1991), 12–18.

16. Michel Foucault dates what he calls "anatomo-politics of the human body" from seventeenth-century efforts to extract maximum labor from workers and eighteenth-century state programs to increase the population by reducing infant mortality. See Michel Foucault, *The History of Sexuality*, trans. Robert Hurley (New York, 1980), 139–40.

17. For further discussion, see David L. Hoffmann, "European Modernity and Soviet Socialism," in *Russian Modernity: Politics, Knowledge, Practices*, ed. Hoffmann and Yanni Kotsonis (New York, 2000).

18. Eric Hobsbawm and Terence Ranger, eds., *The Invention of Tradition* (Cambridge, 1983).

19. The paradigm of neo-traditionalism has been counterposed to an understanding of Stalinism as exemplifying elements of modernity. But these two historiographical approaches are not necessarily mutually exclusive. Neo-traditionalism involved the use of traditions for modern mobilizational purposes; it was only after industrialization and urbanization largely destroyed traditional folk culture that political leaders invented traditions to galvanize popular support in the age of mass politics and mass warfare. For more on neo-traditionalism, see Terry Martin, "Modernization or Neo-traditionalism? Ascribed Nationality and Soviet Primordialism," in Hoffmann and Kotsonis, *Russian Modernity.*

20. Thinkers as disparate as Marx, Richard Wagner, and Friedrich Nietzsche all contemplated means to restore social unity. See Clark, *Petersburg*, 80. Clark also places Marxist thought in its broader intellectual context of "romantic anticapitalism"—a term she uses to describe the ideas of a variety of thinkers, including Max Weber and members

of his Heidelberg circle, who criticized capitalist society for its alienation, individualism, and commodification of culture; see 15–17.

21. As discussed in Chapter 5, Aleksandr Pushkin was enshrined in the Soviet literary canon but was portrayed as a revolutionary and a precursor to socialist realism.

22. Boris Groys, *The Total Art of Stalinism: Avant-Garde, Aesthetic Dictatorship, and Beyond*, trans. Charles Rougle (Princeton, 1992).

23. This book focuses on the cultural norms of Soviet modernity. For a complementary analysis of the state institutions and practices of Soviet modernity, see David L. Hoffmann and Peter Holquist, *Cultivating the Masses: The Modern Social State in Russia, 1914–1939* (Ithaca, forthcoming).

Chapter 1. Acculturating the Masses

1. Richard Stites, *Revolutionary Dreams: Utopian Vision and Experimental Life in the Russian Revolution* (New York, 1989).

2. Because Russian intellectuals blamed the wretched state of the lower classes not on the peasants and workers themselves but on political oppression and economic exploitation under the tsarist autocracy, they believed in environmental and cultural (not biological) solutions to social problems. See Laura Engelstein, *The Keys to Happiness: Sex and the Search for Modernity in Fin-de-Siècle Russia* (Ithaca, 1992); Daniel Todes, *Darwin without Malthus: The Struggle for Existence in Russian Evolutionary Thought* (Oxford, 1990).

3. Steve Smith, "The Soviet Meaning of Swearing: Workers and Bad Language in Early Soviet Russia," *Past and Present*, August 1998, 177–78.

4. Sheila Fitzpatrick, "'Middle-Class Values' and Social Life in the 1930's," in *Soviet Culture and Society*, ed. Richard Sheldon and Tony L. Thompson (Boulder, Colo., 1989), 21. See also Vera Dunham, *In Stalin's Time: Middleclass Values in Soviet Fiction* (New York, 1976), which focuses more on the use of *kul'turnost'* to validate the material acquisitiveness of Soviet bureaucrats in the postwar era.

5. Norbert Elias, *The Civilizing Process: Sociogenetic and Psychogenetic Investigations*, trans. Edmund Jephcott, rev. ed. (Malden, Mass., 2000), 366–67.

6. Vadim Volkov, "The Concept of *Kul'turnost'*: Notes on the Stalinist Civilizing Process," in *Stalinism: New Directions*, ed. Sheila Fitzpatrick (New York, 2000).

7. Elias, *Civilizing Process*, 34–41, 430–31.

8. Louis Chevalier, *Laboring Classes and Dangerous Classes in Paris during the First Half of the Nineteenth Century*, trans. Frank Jellinek (New York, 1973), 359–61.

9. Paul Weindling, "German-Soviet Cooperation in Science: The Case of the Laboratory for Racial Research," *Nuncius*, 1986, no. 1, 226–27.

10. *Za zdorovyi kul'turnyi byt: Sbornik statei* (Moscow/Leningrad, 1931), 39; M. S. Malinovskii and E. M. Shvartzman, *Gigiena zhenshchiny*, 3d ed. (Moscow/Leningrad, 1935), 3–4, 12–13, 34–35; A. V. Mol'kov, ed., *Shkol'naia gigiena* (Moscow/Leningrad, 1937), 22, 163.

11. *Gigiena i zdorov'e*, 1936, no. 20, 12–13.

12. *Klub*, 1929, no. 10, 39–40. For further discussion of dental hygiene, see Tricia Ann Starks, "The Body Soviet: Health, Hygiene, and the Path to a New Life in the Soviet Union in the 1920s" (dissertation, Ohio State University, 2000), chap. 2.

13. GARF, f. 7952, op. 3, d. 387, ll. 3–9. My thanks go to Tricia Starks for bringing this questionnaire to my attention.

14. N. Semashko, *Iskusstvo odevat'sia* (Moscow/Leningrad, 1927), 17.

15. A. Makarenko, *Problems of Soviet School Education*, trans. O. Shartse (Moscow, 1965), 149–51. (Collection of Makarenko's writings and lectures from the 1930s.)

16. *Partrabotnik* (Sverdlovsk), 1935, no. 1, 10; A. K. Toporkov, *Kak stat' kul'turnym* (Moscow, 1929), 122.

17. These ideas originated in Western Europe and were adopted by Soviet health officials. David S. Barnes, *The Making of a Social Disease: Tuberculosis in Nineteenth-Century France* (Berkeley, 1995), 114–15; *Gigiena i zdorov'e rabochei i krest'ianskoi sem'i*, 1926, no. 18, 6; no. 21, 13; no. 21, 13; *Gigiena i zdorov'e*, 1938, no. 5, 4–5.

18. Barnes, *Making of a Social Disease*, 112–22.

19. *Gigiena i sotsialisticheskoe zdravookhranenie*, 1932, no. 4/5, 58.

20. *Za zdorovyi kul'turnyi byt: Sbornik statei*, 23.

21. Yuri Slezkine, *Arctic Mirrors: Russia and the Small Peoples of the North* (Ithaca, 1994), 150–63.

22. Paula Michaels, "Medical Propaganda and Cultural Revolution in Soviet Kazakhstan, 1928–41," *The Russian Review*, 2000, no. 2.

23. Starks, "Body Soviet," chap. 2.

24. GARF, f. 9226, op. 1, d. 6, ll. 3–4, 16.

25. GARF, f. 8009, op. 3, d. 4, ll. 2–4; f. 4085, op. 12, d. 385, l. 104. On inspections, see also TsMAM, f. 552, op. 1, d. 72, ll. 45–46, 67; GARF, f. 9226, op. 1, d. 6, l. 19.

26. RGASPI, f. 112, op. 5, d. 563, l. 74; GARF, f. A-2306, op. 39, d. 48, l. 29; f. 7709, op. 4, d. 6, l. 6.

27. Michael David-Fox, *Revolution of the Mind: Higher Learning among the Bolsheviks, 1918–1929* (Ithaca, 1997), 172–73. See also Julie Cassidy, *The Enemy on Trial: Early Soviet Courts on Stage and Screen* (De Kalb, Ill., 2000); Elizabeth Wood, "The Trial of Lenin: Legitimating the Revolution through Political Theater, 1920–1923," *The Russian Review*, 2002, no. 2.

28. Toporkov, *Kak stat' kul'turnym*, 133.

29. *Gigiena i zdorov'e*, 1936, no. 20, 12–13.

30. *Partorganizator* (Leningrad), 1935, no. 4, 20.

31. See, for example, *Gigiena i sotsialisticheskoe zdravookhranenie*, 1932, no. 2/3, 40.

32. *Za zdorovoi kul'turnyi byt: Sbornik statei*, 37; *Partrabotnik* (Sverdlovsk), 1935, no.3, 16; S. Lapitskaia, *Byt rabochikh Trekhgornoi manufaktury* (Moscow, 1935) 161–63.

33. Starks, "Body Soviet," chap. 2.

34. *Vsesoiuznoe soveshchanie zhen khoziaistvennikov i inzhenerno-tekhnicheskikh rabotnikov tiazheloi promyshlennosti: Stenograficheskii otchet* (Moscow, 1936), 8. On the founding of the movement, see also RGASPI, f. 17, op. 120, d. 255, ll. 14–16; GARF, f. 7709, op. 6, d. 2, ll. 126–29; Mary Buckley, "The Untold Story of *Obshchestvennitsa* in the 1930's: A Research Note" (paper presented at the World Slavic Congress, 1995), 3.

35. See Robert Maier, "Die Hausfrau als Kul'turtreger im Sozialismus: Zur Geschichte der Ehefrauen-Bewegung in den 30er Jahren," in *Kultur im Stalinismus*, ed. Gabriele Gorzka (Bremen, 1994).

36. GARF, f. 5451, op. 20, d. 22, l. 2; RGASPI, f. 17, op. 120, d. 255, ll. 2–3.

37. GARF, f. 9226, op. 1, d. 6, ll. 39–40.

38. David Horn, *Social Bodies: Science, Reproduction, and Italian Modernity* (Princeton, 1994), 116–18; Barnes, *Making of a Social Disease*, 131; Claudia Koonz, *Mothers in the Fatherland: Women, the Family, and Nazi Politics* (New York, 1987), 79; Sheldon G. Garon, *Molding Japanese Minds: The State in Everyday Life* (Princeton, 1997), 129–32.

39. *Vsesoiuznoe soveshchanie zhen*, 19.

40. See Rebecca Balmas Neary, "Mothering Socialist Society: The Wife-Activists' Movement and the Soviet Culture of Daily Life, 1934–1941," *The Russian Review*, 1999, no. 3, 397.

41. GARF, f. 5451, op. 20, d. 201, l. 1; *Gigiena i zdorov'e*, 1938, no. 4, 3.

42. *Obshchestvennitsa,* 1937, no. 3, 12; Buckley, "Untold Story," 12.

43. RGASPI, f. 17, op. 120, d. 255, ll. 2–3; *Zheny inzhenerov i tekhnikov* (Moscow, 1936), 2.

44. V. Shveitser and A. Ul'rikh, *Zheny komandirov tiazheloi promyshlennosti* (Moscow, 1936), 43; *Udarnitsa Urala,* 1936, no. 1, 8, as quoted in Buckley, "Untold Story," 7.

45. For further discussion, see Sheila Fitzpatrick, "Becoming Cultured: Socialist Realism and the Representation of Privilege and Taste," in *The Cultural Front: Power and Culture in Revolutionary Russia* (Ithaca, 1992), 234.

46. *Rabotnitsa i krest'ianka,* 1936, no. 10, 2–3.

47. Sarah Davies, *Popular Opinion in Stalin's Russia: Terror, Propaganda, and Dissent* (New York, 1997), 64.

48. David L. Hoffmann, *Peasant Metropolis: Social Identities in Moscow* (Ithaca, 1994), 136–41. While housing improved slightly during the Second Five-Year Plan, many workers remained in barracks and mud huts; see, for example, RGASPI, f. 17, op. 120, d. 339, l. 20.

49. GARF, f. 9226, op. 1, d. 6, l. 18.

50. RGASPI, f. 78, op. 1, d. 549, l. 123; d. 833, ll. 16–18.

51. Nataliia Kozlova, "Zalozhniki slova," *Sotsiologicheskie issledovania,* 1995, no. 9/10, 18–19. See also Catriona Kelly, *Refining Russia: Advice Literature, Polite Culture, and Gender from Catherine to Yeltsin* (New York, 2001), 303–4.

52. O. V. Khlevniuk, "Izmenenie kul'turnogo oblika gorodskikh rabochikh SSSR, 1926–1939" (dissertation, Institute of History, USSR, 1986), 128.

53. A. V. Mol'kov and N. A. Semashko, eds., *Sotsial'naia gigiena: Rukovodstvo dlia studentov-medikov* (Moscow/Leningrad, 1927), 250–51; S. I. Kaplun, *Obshchaia gigiena truda* (Moscow/Leningrad, 1940).

54. *Gigiena truda,* 1934, no. 1, 13; no. 5, 27–29.

55. Ibid., no. 3, 93.

56. A. B. Zalkind, ed., *Psikhonevrologicheskie nauki v SSSR: Materialy I Vsesoiuznogo s"ezda po izucheniiu povedeniia cheloveka* (Moscow, 1930), 5–8.

57. Anson Rabinbach, *The Human Motor: Energy, Fatigue, and the Origins of Modernity* (New York, 1990), 274–78.

58. Toby Clark, "The 'New Man's' Body: A Motif in Early Soviet Culture," in *Art of the Soviets: Painting, Sculpture, and Architecture in a One-Party State, 1917–1992,* ed. Matthew Cullerne Bown and Brandon Taylor (New York, 1993), 36.

59. Rabinbach, *Human Motor,* 2–8.

60. As quoted in Clark, "'New Man's' Body," 36.

61. Stites, *Revolutionary Dreams,* 152–54. On the ideas of Platon Kerzhentsev, a Soviet efficiency expert who sought to "introduce scientific principles not only into man's economic activity or production but into all organized activity or work," see ibid., 155–59

62. Lewis H. Siegelbaum, "*Okhrana truda:* Industrial Hygiene, Psychotechnics, and Industrialization in the USSR," in *Health and Society in Revolutionary Russia,* ed. Susan Gross Solomon and John F. Hutchinson (Bloomington, 1990), 226–27.

63. Kendall E. Bailes, *Technology and Society under Lenin and Stalin* (Princeton, 1978), 50–52.

64. Hoffmann, *Peasant Metropolis,* 78–79. Even during the First Five-Year Plan, Gastev's ideas remained controversial. As discussed below, some Party officials believed that Soviet workers could exceed the limits of rationalized labor, and they opposed Taylor's methods as overly technocratic.

65. E. Thompson, "Time, Work-Discipline, and Industrial Capitalism," *Past and Present,* 1967, no. 38, 60, 90.

66. *Voprosy profdvizheniia*, 1935, no. 2/3, 8; *Industrializatsiia SSSR: Dokumenty i materialy* (Moscow, 1971), 3:525; I. L. Kornakovskii, ed., *Iz istorii razvitiia metallurgicheskoi promyshlennosti Moskvy, 1883–1932 gg: Dokumenty i materialy* (Moscow, 1981), 186.

67. See Hiroaki Kuromiya, *Stalin's Industrial Revolution: Politics and Workers, 1928–1932* (New York, 1988), 115–23; O. V. Khlevniuk, *Udarniki pervoi piatiletki* (Moscow, 1989).

68. RGASPI, f. 85, op. 29, d. 640, ll. 3–7. For a full discussion of Stakhanov's record, see Lewis Siegelbaum, *Stakhanovism and the Politics of Productivity in the USSR, 1935–1941* (New York, 1988), 67–74.

69. TsMAM, f. 415, op. 2, d. 448, ll. 10–13.

70. RGAE, f. 7995, op. 1, d. 344, ll. 116–20; TsMAM, f. 176, op. 4, d. 4, l. 181.

71. See Stephen E. Hanson, *Time and Revolution: Marxism and the Design of Soviet Institutions* (Chapel Hill, 1997), 152–55.

72. *Sbornik vazhneishikh postanovlenii po trudu* (Moscow, 1935), 99; *Bol'shevik*, 1932, no. 21, 3.

73. O. V. Khlevniuk, "26 iiulia 1940 goda: Illiuzii i real'nosti administrirovaniia," *Kommunist*, 1989, no. 9, 87–89.

74. Hoffmann, *Peasant Metropolis*, 101–4.

75. For further discussion of Soviet labor policy, see Stephen Kotkin, *Magnetic Mountain: Stalinism as a Civilization* (Berkeley, 1995). The constitution of Weimar Germany also listed labor as both a right and an obligation, and the Nazi government placed people not gainfully employed in labor camps; H. W. V. Temperley, ed., *A History of the Peace Conference of Paris*, vol. 3 (London, 1920), 375–36; Lisa Pine, *Nazi Family Policy, 1933–1945* (New York, 1997), 118.

76. O. V. Khlevniuk, "Prinuditel'nyi trud v ekonomike SSSR, 1929–1941 gody," *Svobodnaia mysl'*, 1992, no. 13; James R. Harris, "The Growth of the Gulag: Forced Labor in the Urals Region, 1929–1931," *The Russian Review*, 1997, no. 2.

77. Laura L. Phillips, *Bolsheviks and the Bottle: Drink and Worker Culture in St. Petersburg, 1900–1929* (De Kalb, Ill., 2000), 22–23.

78. N. Bukharin, "Vospitanie smeny: Kak dolzhen vesti sebia komsomolets," in *Komsomol'skii byt: Sbornik*, ed. I. Razin (Moscow/Leningrad, 1927), 26; TsKhDMO, f. 1, op. 2, d. 109, ll. 66–67. For further discussion, see Kathy Transchel, "Under the Influence: Drinking, Temperance, and Cultural Revolution in Russia, 1900–1932" (dissertation, University of North Carolina, Chapel Hill, 1996).

79. RGASPI, f. 17, op. 21, d. 1370, l. 198.

80. *Komsomol'skaia pravda*, January 27, 1936, 4. See also Anne E. Gorsuch, *Youth in Revolutionary Russia: Enthusiasts, Bohemians, Delinquents* (Bloomington, 2000).

81. TsKhDMO, f. 1, op. 23, d. 1304, l. 107; *Smena*, 1938, no. 12, 19.

82. GARF, f. A-2306, op. 39, d. 17, l. 7; *Partrabotnik* (Sverdlovsk), 1937, no. 2, 27.

83. Lynn Mally, *Revolutionary Acts: Amateur Theater and the Soviet State, 1917–1938* (Ithaca, 2000), 205–6. As Mally notes, Soviet amateur theater was in a sense the fulfillment of prerevolutionary theater activists' dream of civilizing the people through theater.

84. RGASPI, f. 89, op. 9, d. 75, ll. 1–4; *Profsoiuznyi rabotnik*, 1937, no. 11, 15.

85. Lewis Siegelbaum, "Shaping of Soviet Workers' Leisure: Workers' Clubs and Palaces of Culture in the 1930s," *International Labor and Working Class History*, Fall 1999, 89.

86. S. Garshtein, *Za zdorovyi kul'turnyi byt* (Moscow, 1932), 3–4.

87. See, for example, N. A. Semashko, *Novyi byt i polovoi vopros* (Moscow/Leningrad, 1926), 15; GARF, f. A-482, op. 11, d. 58, l. 9.

88. K. Mechonoshin, "Fizicheskoe vospitanie trudiashchikhsia," *Fizicheskaia kul'tura*, 1923, no. 3/4, 2–3, as cited in Stefan Plaggenborg, *Revolutionskultur: Menschenbilder und*

kulturelle Praxis in Sowjetrussland zwischen Oktoberrevolution und Stalinismus (Cologne, 1996), 81.

89. *Gimnastika na predpriiatiak i proizvoditel'nost' truda* (Moscow, 1936), 5.

90. Plaggenborg, *Revolutionskultur*, 80.

91. Clark, "'New Man's' Body," 40.

92. Soviet musical films of the 1930s portrayed smiling peasants who sang while working in the fields and factory workers who swung their hammers in time to music; see the documentary *East Side Story*, dir. Dana Ranga (Germany, 1997).

93. Vsevolod Meierhold, "The Actor of the Future and Biomechanics," in *Meierhold on Theatre*, ed. Edward Brown (New York, 1969), 197–98, 200.

94. *Gimnastika na predpriiatiak*, 25. Studies on labor productivity showed that workers who did physical exercises at the start of the workday and during breaks were more productive than workers who did not; *Gigiena i sotsialisticheskoe zdravookhranenie*, 1932, no. 4/5, 27–30.

95. Kaplun, *Obshchaia gigiena truda*, 91–92.

96. Semashko, *Novyi byt*, 15.

97. GARF, f. A-482, op. 11, d. 19, l. 68; d. 58, l. 8. A 1934 report claimed that Germans spent weekends in the countryside absorbing fresh air and sunshine, and that these activities promoted good health; GARF, f. 7876, op. 2, d. 153, l. 5.

98. "Otdykh i son," *Gigiena i zdorov'e rabochei i krest'ianskoi sem'i*, 1926, no. 21, 2.

99. See Starks, "Body Soviet."

100. GARF, f. A-482, op. 11, d. 58, l. 8.

101. Ibid., d. 19, l. 77.

102. Ibid., d. 58, l. 8.

103. In the nineteenth century European thinkers had already stressed the moral benefits of physical exercise. See Harvey Green, *Fit for America: Health, Fitness, Sport, and American Society* (New York, 1986), 183.

104. K. Tsetkin, "Lenin o morale i voprosakh pola," in Razin, *Komsomol'skii byt*, 20.

105. James Riordan, "Sexual Minorities: The Status of Gays and Lesbians in Russian–Soviet-Russian Society," in *Women in Russia and Ukraine*, ed. Rosalind Marsh (New York, 1996), 107.

106. A. Gvozdev, "Postanovka 'D. Ye.' v 'Teatre imeni Vs. Meyerkhol'da,'" *Zhizn' isskustva*, no. 26 (June 24, 1924), 6, as cited in Katerina Clark, *Petersburg, Crucible of Cultural Revolution* (Cambridge, Mass., 1995), 162.

107. TsMAM, f. 1289, op. 1, d. 173, l. 1; *Klub*, 1929, no. 10, 41; *Molodoi bol'shevik*, 1932, no. 23/24, 16; *Pravda*, December 22, 1937, 2.

108. TsKhDMO, f. 1, op. 23, d. 1360, ll. 69–71; d. 1397, ll. 103–14.

109. Gorsuch, *Youth in Revolutionary Russia*, 120–25; RGASPI, f. 78, op. 1, d. 833, ll. 111–13.

110. A. Kosarev, ed., *Istoriia metro Moskvy: Rasskazy stroitelei metro* (Moscow, 1935), 270; TsMAM, f. 5301, op. 1, d. 68, l. 2; f. 214, op. 1, d. 125, l. 13.

111. RGASPI, f. 112, op. 5, d. 563, l. 110.

112. Clark, *Petersburg*, 66–67; Joan Neuberger, *Hooliganism: Crime, Culture, and Power in St. Petersburg, 1900–1914* (Berkeley, 1993), 254.

113. Lynn Mally, *Culture of the Future: The Proletkult Movement in Revolutionary Russia* (Berkeley, 1990), 15.

114. Ibid., xviii–xx, 43, 199. On the gradual demise of Proletkult, see 200–228.

115. Michael David-Fox, "What Is Cultural Revolution?" *The Russian Review*, 1999, no. 2, 188–93; and his *Revolution of the Mind*, 106.

116. See Sheila Fitzpatrick, ed., *Cultural Revolution in Russia, 1928–1931* (Bloomington, 1978).

117. Mally, *Revolutionary Acts,* 179.

118. David-Fox, "What Is Cultural Revolution?" 199–200.

119. Stalin, *Sochineniia* (Moscow, 1946–52), 13:69–73, 66–67.

120. Mally, *Revolutionary Acts,* 178–79.

121. Nicholas S. Timasheff, *The Great Retreat: The Growth and Decline of Communism in Russia* (New York, 1946), 208–11; Larry E. Holmes, *The Schoolhouse and the Kremlin: Reforming Education in Soviet Russia, 1917–1931* (Bloomington, 1991), 32–35.

122. E. Thomas Ewing, "Stalinism at Work: Teacher Certification (1936–39) and Soviet Power," *The Russian Review* 57, no. 2 (April 1998): 219.

123. Holmes, *Schoolhouse and the Kremlin,* 137; TsMAM, f. 528, op. 1, d. 247, ll. 17–18. Whereas Timasheff described 1930s educational reforms as part of the Great Retreat, E. Thomas Ewing concludes that these changes "were less of a 'retreat' than an accommodation to teachers' beliefs." He argues that Stalinist classroom practices "simultaneously repudiated and borrowed from the past": *The Teachers of Stalinism: Policy, Practices, and Power in Soviet Schools of the 1930s* (New York, 2002), 159.

124. TsMAM, f. 528, op. 1, d. 243, ll. 45–48.

125. RGASPI, f. 17, op. 120, d. 326, ll. 24–25; op. 126, d. 2, ll. 39–43. See also TsKhDMO, f. 1, op. 23, d. 1360, l. 1.

126. RGASPI, f. 17, op. 126, d. 2, ll. 20–37. On the militarization of education in the 1938–41 period, see ibid., op. 3, d. 998, ll. 78–79; op. 126, d. 4, ll. 1–2.

127. Makarenko, *Problems of Soviet School Education,* 55–59.

128. See the entry on Makarenko by Larry Holmes in *Modern Encyclopedia of Russian and Soviet History,* ed. Joseph L. Wieczynski, 60 vols. (Gulf Breeze, Fla.: Academic International Press, 1976–2000), 20:241–43.

129. Makarenko, *Problems of Soviet School Education,* 147–48.

130. A. S. Makarenko, *A Book for Parents,* trans. Robert Daglish (Moscow, n.d.), 303.

131. Ibid., 304–7.

132. Gorsuch, *Youth in Revolutionary Russia,* 90.

133. Smith, "Soviet Meaning of Swearing," 192–98.

134. F. Kulikov, "Za novogo cheloveka: Iz dnevnika kul'tarmeitsa," *Na rubezhe,* 1935, no. 10, 101.

135. *Sovetskoe iskusstvo,* August 11, 1935, 4.

136. GARF, f. 3316, op. 41, d. 85, ll. 41–42.

137. *Smena,* 1938, no. 12, 19; RGASPI, f. 78, op. 1, d. 833, l. 29.

138. L. Trotskii, *Voprosy byta: Epokha "kul'turnichestva" i ee zadachi,* 3d ed. (Moscow, 1925), 74.

139. Clark, *Petersburg,* 207–9, 285–86.

140. *Izmeneniia sotsial'noi struktury sovetskogo obshchestva, 1921–seredina '30-kh godov* (Moscow, 1979), 206; TsMAM, f. 1289, op. 1, d. 185, l. 2.

141. TsMAM, f. 2617, op. 1, d. 130, l. 15; *Novyi proletarii.*

142. D. Lekarenko and V. A. Nevskii, "Chitatel'skii spros rabochei molodezhi," *Krasnyi bibliotekar',* 1935, no. 6, 23; Khlevniuk, "Izmenenie," 84.

143. V. Vasilevskaia, "Kak chitaiut knigu malogramotnye," *Krasnyi bibliotekar',* 1931, no. 5/6, 90–96.

144. GARF, f. A-2306, op. 39, d. 78, l. 3.

145. See Jochen Hellbeck, "Self-Realization in the Stalinist System: Two Soviet Diaries of the 1930s," in Hoffmann and Kotsonis, *Russian Modernity.*

146. Kozlova, "Zalozhniki slova," 23–29.

147. GARF, f. 3316, op. 41, d. 197, l. 8; RGASPI, f. 78, op. 1, d. 833, ll. 25–31, 96, 115–28.

148. RGASPI, f. 112, op. 46, d. 5, l. 81; GARF, f. A-2306, op. 69, d. 2363, ll. 1–8.

149. TsMAM, f. 214, op. 1, d. 284, l. 4; f. 1289, op. 1, d. 173, l. 1; Hoffmann, *Peasant Metropolis,* 182–89, 205–9.

150. Jochen Hellbeck, "Working, Struggling, Becoming: Stalin-Era Autobiographical Texts," *The Russian Review,* 2001, no. 3.

151. Trotskii, *Voprosy byta,* 71.

152. Makarenko, *Problems of Soviet School Eduation,* 62, 139.

153. Oleg Kharkhordin, *The Collective and the Individual in Russia: A Study of Practices* (Berkeley, 1999), 204. On the emphasis on collectivism in Soviet literature and film, see Richard Stites, *Russian Popular Culture: Entertainment and Society since 1900* (New York, 1997), 6–7.

154. Makarenko, *Book for Parents,* 410.

155. Lewis Siegelbaum and Andrei Sokolov, *Stalinism as a Way of Life: A Narrative in Documents* (New Haven, 2000), 384.

156. *Pravda,* February 13, 1937, 1.

157. *Komsomol'skii rabotnik,* 1940, no. 8, 1–2.

158. Daniel Peris, *Storming the Heavens: The Soviet League of the Militant Godless* (Ithaca, 1998); William Husband, *"Godless Communists": Atheism and Society in Soviet Russia, 1917–1932* (De Kalb, Ill., 2000), 60–68; *Kirovets,* May 13, 1938, 3.

159. Garshtein, *Za zdorovyi kul'turnyi byt,* 5.

160. RGASPI, f. 17, op. 120, d. 138, ll. 36–37.

161. *XVII s'ezd,* 29–30.

162. Elena Osokina, *Ierarkhiia potrebleniia: O zhizni liudei v usloviiakh Stalinskogo snabzheniia, 1928–1935 gg.* (Moscow, 1993), 63–64; RGAE, f. 7622, op. 1, d. 251, ll. 3–5.

163. Kotkin, *Magnetic Mountain,* 109–20.

164. For further discussion, see Clark, *Petersburg,* 51.

165. S. Frederick Starr, "Visionary Town Planning during the Cultural Revolution," in Fitzpatrick, *Cultural Revolution,* 208–11; Anatole Kopp, *Town and Revolution: Soviet Architecture and City Planning, 1917–1935,* trans. Thomas E. Burton (New York, 1970). On the more general "high modernist" ethos of urban planners around the world, see James C. Scott, *Seeing Like a State: How Certain Schemes to Improve the Human Condition Have Failed* (New Haven, 1998).

166. See, for example, RGASPI, f. 17, op. 116, d. 30, l. 25.

167. A. B. Zalkind, "Etika, byt i molodezh," in Razin, *Komsomol'skii byt,* 79.

168. *Za kommunicheskie kadry* (Leningrad, 1931), 102–4.

169. David-Fox, *Revolution of the Mind,* 109–10; TsMAM, f. 5301, op. 4, d. 66, ll. 14–20; GARF, f. 5451, op. 14, d. 306, l. 5; *Aviamotor,* July 4, 1931, 3. Stalin's criticism of wage leveling in his 1931 "New Conditions" speech tended to undercut official support for communes.

170. RGASPI, f. 477, op. 1, d. 20, ll. 161–62; Regine Robin, "Stalinism and Popular Culture," in *The Culture of the Stalin Period,* ed. Hans Gunther (New York, 1990), 33; Christel Lane, *The Rites of Rulers* (New York, 1981), 207.

171. L. M. Zak and S. S. Zimina, eds., *Gor'kii i sozdanie istorii fabrik i zavodov: Sbornik dokumentov* (Moscow, 1959). For further discussion, see Kotkin, *Magnetic Mountain,* 215–17.

172. See Mark von Hagen, *Soldiers in the Proletarian Dictatorship: The Red Army and the Soviet Socialist State, 1917–1930* (Ithaca, 1990).

173. As quoted in Gorsuch, *Youth in Revolutionary Russia,* 15.

174. *Komsomol'skaia pravda,* January 29, 1936, 1; January 30, 1936, 3.

175. As quoted in Kharkhordin, *Collective and the Individual,* 94.

176. RGASPI, f. 17, op. 120, d. 326, ll. 15–16 (Young Pioneers' Rules of Behavior, issued in 1938). Young Pioneer membership grew from 6.7 million in 1934 to 11 million in 1939; TsKhDMO, f. 1, op. 23, d. 1361, l. 1.

177. See Gorsuch, *Youth in Revolutionary Russia*, 52.

178. *Pomoshch' samoobrazovaniiu*, 1923, no. 1, 4, as quoted in Kelly, *Refining Russia*, 268.

179. *Sputnik kommunista*, 1930, no. 2, 38–39.

180. Hellbeck, "Working, Struggling, Becoming," 342.

181. See, for example, the last page of *Ogonek*, 1936, nos. 1, 2/3, 10.

182. Igal Halfin, "From Darkness to Light: Student Communist Autobiography during NEP," *Jahrbücher für Geschichte Osteuropas* 45, no. 2 (1997).

183. Hellbeck, "Working, Struggling, Becoming," 351.

184. RGASPI, f. 17, op. 120, d. 146, l. 19.

185. Kotkin, *Magnetic Mountain*, 21–23; Hellbeck, "Self-Realization in the Stalinist System," 234–35.

186. Hellbeck, "Working, Struggling, Becoming," 350–51.

187. Ibid., 356–57.

188. TsKhDMO, f. 1, op. 23, d. 1088, l. 94.

189. RGASPI, f. 78, op. 1, d. 833, l. 11.

190. Fitzpatrick, *Everyday Stalinism*.

191. RGASPI, f. 78, op. 1, d. 833, ll. 1–2.

192. See, for example, GARF, f. 5451, op. 13, d. 76, l. 51; f. 7952, op. 3, d. 522, ll. 1–4; *Iunyi kommunist*, 1937, no. 5, 19; *Voprosy profdvizheniia*, 1937, no. 11, 11–13; Husband, "Godless Communists," 140–50.

193. Peris, *League of the Militant Godless*, 224; V. Zenzinov, *Vstrecha s Rossiei: Kak i chem zhivut v sovetskom soiuze: Pis'ma v krasnuiu armiiu 1939–40* (New York, 1944), 274–78.

194. Lynne Viola, *Peasant Rebels under Stalin: Collectivization and the Culture of Peasant Resistance* (New York, 1996), 133–54, 236–38.

195. Hoffmann, *Peasant Metropolis*, 62–63.

196. *Voprosy profdvizheniia*, 1933, no. 1/2, 26–27. On labor turnover, see Ia. Kats, "Tekuchest' rabochei sily v krupnoi promyshlennosti," *Plan*, 1937, no. 9, 21; *Industrializatsiia SSSR*, 3:421.

197. See Jeffrey J. Rossman, "The Teikovo Cotton Workers' Strike of April 1932: Class, Gender, and Identity Politics in Stalin's Russia," *The Russian Review*, 1997, no. 1; Donald Filtzer, *Soviet Workers and Stalinist Industrialization: The Formation of Modern Soviet Industrial Relations, 1928–1941* (New York, 1986), 81–85.

198. TsKhDMO, f. 1, op. 23, d. 1072, ll. 108–9.

199. Sarah Davies, "'Us against Them': Social Identity in Soviet Russia, 1934–41," *The Russian Review*, 1997, no. 1, 72, 79–82.

200. See the dozens of cases in TsMAM, f. 819, op. 2, d. 21. For a 1936 report on the persistence of "thief-bandit ways" among Tashkent schoolchildren, see TsKhDMO, f. 1, op. 23, d. 1188, l. 40.

201. Catriona Kelly, "*Kul'turnost'* in the Soviet Union: Ideal and Reality," in *Reinterpreting Russia*, ed. Geoffrey Hosking and Robert Service (London, 1999), 199. See also Kelly, *Refining Russia*, chap. 4.

Chapter 2. A Code of Behavior for Communists

1. See Pierre Bourdieu, *Outline of a Theory of Practice* (New York, 1977), 94.

2. Sheila Fitzpatrick, "On Power and Culture," in Fitzpatrick, *The Cultural Front: Power and Culture in Revolutionary Russia* (Ithaca, 1992), 12–13.

3. Richard Stites, *Revolutionary Dreams: Utopian Vision and Experimental Life in the Russian Revolution* (New York, 1989), 68.

4. See Richard T. De George, *Soviet Ethics and Morality* (Ann Arbor, 1969), 4–7.

5. William G. Rosenberg, ed., *Bolshevik Visions: First Phase of the Cultural Revolution in Soviet Russia* (Ann Arbor, 1990), 19, 29.

6. V. I. Lenin, "Zadachi Soiuzov Molodezhi," in *O kommunisticheskoi nravstvennosti* (Moscow, 1961), 216–18.

7. E. M. Iaroslavskii, "O partetike," in *Partiinaia etika: Dokumenty i materialy diskussii 20-kh godov*, ed. M. A. Makarevich (Moscow, 1989), 170–71. See also RGASPI, f. 89, op. 3, d. 144, l. 6.

8. N. Krupskaia, "What a Communist Ought to Be Like" (1922), in Rosenberg, *Bolshevik Visions*, 40.

9. M. Neznamov, "O zateriannoi tsennosti," in *Kakim dolzhen byt' kommunist: Sbornik*, ed. E. Iaroslavskii (Moscow/Leningrad, 1926), 112–13. E. A. Preobrazhenskii also took a position of ethical nihilism in his 1923 publication "On Morality and Class Norms." See Makarevich, *Partiinaia etika*, 10–11.

10. See Stites, *Revolutionary Dreams*, 117.

11. L. Trotskii, *Voprosy byta: Epokha "kul'turnichestva" i ee zadachi*, 3d ed. (Moscow, 1925). See also M. N. Liadov, *Voprosy byta* (Moscow, 1925).

12. L. Balabanov (L. Tol'm), "Zateriannaia tsennost'," in Iaroslavskii, *Kakim dolzhen byt' kommunist*, 111.

13. N. Bukharin, "Vospitanie smeny: Kak dolzhen vesti sebia komsomolets," in *Komsomol'skii byt: Sbornik*, ed. I. Razin (Moscow/Leningrad, 1927), 21–26.

14. RGASPI, f. 89, op. 3, d. 70, ll. 1–2.

15. A. Stratonitskii, *Voprosy byta v Komsomole* (Moscow, 1926), 104.

16. Makarevich, *Partiinaia etika*, 15–16.

17. Michael David-Fox, *Revolution of the Mind: Higher Learning among the Bolsheviks* (Ithaca, 1997), 101–4.

18. Leonard Schapiro, *The Communist Party of the Soviet Union*, 2d ed. (New York, 1971), 260; Makarevich, *Partiinaia etika*, 2d ed. (New York, 1971), 8–9. For more on the origins of the Central Control Commission, see Oleg Kharkhordin, *The Collective and the Individual in Russia: A Study of Practices* (Berkeley, 1999), 37–40.

19. Makarevich, *Partiinaia etika*, 140.

20. Schapiro, *Communist Party*, 261; Makarevich, *Partiinaia etika*, 147–48.

21. A. A. Sol'ts, "Iz otcheta tsentral'noi kontrol'noi komissii na XI s"ezde RKP(b)," in Makarevich, *Partiinaia etika*, 141–42.

22. Makarevich, *Partiinaia etika*, 153–62.

23. A. A. Sol'ts, "O partetike," ibid., 283–85.

24. RGASPI, f. 89, op. 8, d. 774, ll. 92–97; op. 9, d. 81, ll. 14–16. The Communist Party put its moral code in writing only in 1961, when it promulgated "The Moral Code of the Builder of Communism." See De George, *Soviet Ethics*, 83.

25. GARF, f. 7709, op. 4, d. 7, l. 178.

26. Han-Henning Schröder, "Upward Social Mobility and Mass Repression: The Communist Party and Soviet Society in the Thirties," in *Stalinism: Its Nature and Aftermath*, ed. Nick Lampert and Gábor Tamas Rittersporn (Armonk, N.Y., 1991), 162.

27. T. H. Rigby, *Communist Party Membership in the USSR, 1917–1967* (Princeton, 1968), 116.

28. Sheila Fitzpatrick, "Stalin and the Making of a New Elite," in her *Cultural Front*, 161–62.

29. I. V. Stalin, *Sochineniia* (Moscow, 1946–52), 13:67.

30. Fitzpatrick, "Stalin and the Making of a New Elite," in her *Cultural Front*, 149–82.

31. RGASPI, f. 112, op. 2, d. 573, l. 43.

32. RGASPI, f. 17, op. 120, d. 339, l. 57.

33. Ibid., ll. 1–2.

34. Ibid., l. 30.

35. Victor Kravchenko, *I Chose Freedom* (New York, 1946), 83–86.

36. RGASPI, f. 112, op. 58, d. 10, l. 609.

37. RGASPI, f. 17, op. 120, d. 339, l. 12.

38. GARF, f. 7709, op. 8, d. 7, ll. 22–23, 80.

39. See Catriona Kelly, *Refining Russia: Advice Literature, Polite Culture, and Gender from Catherine to Yeltsin* (New York, 2001), 261–78.

40. A. K. Toporkov, *Kak stat' kul'turnym* (Moscow, 1929), 70–71.

41. Ibid., 78–79.

42. GARF, f. A-353, op. 13, d. 4, ll. 5–12.

43. GARF, f. 8131 s. ch., op. 28, d. 4, l. 19.

44. GARF, f. A-353, op. 10, d. 54, l. 111.

45. Toporkov, *Kak stat' kul'turnym*, 82–84.

46. RGASPI, f. 112, op. 5, d. 563, l. 54.

47. Nicolas Werth, ed., *Etre Communist en URSS sous Staline* (Paris, 1981), 72–77. See also *Partorganizator* (Leningrad), 1935, no. 1–2, 41.

48. Nicolas Werth, "Alphabetisation et idéologie en Russe Soviétique," *Vingtieme siècle: Revue d'histoire*, 1986, no. 10, 33.

49. A. Kosarev, *Otchet TsK VLKSM desiatomy vsesoiuznomy s'ezdu Leninskogo Komsomola* (Moscow, 1936), 48. In Chapter 5 I discuss the reasons for a focus on classic works of literature.

50. Vadim Volkov, "The Concept of *Kul'turnost'*: Notes on the Stalinist Civilizing Process," in *Stalinism: New Directions*, ed. Sheila Fitzpatrick (New York, 2000), 227.

51. Toporkov, *Kak stat' kul'turnym*, 96–98.

52. Ibid., 67–68.

53. As quoted in Sheila Fitzpatrick, *Everyday Stalinism: Ordinary Life in Extraordinary Times: Soviet Russia in the 1930s* (New York, 1999), 82–83.

54. *Partrabotnik* (Sverdlovsk), 1935, no. 3, 20.

55. *Komsomol'skaia pravda*, January 4, 1936, 2.

56. RGASPI, f. 17, op. 127, d. 2, l. 16.

57. TsMAM, f. 459, op. 1, d. 100, l. 11.

58. *Sovetskaia iustitsiia*, 1936, no. 14, 7. For further discussion of Stalin and Vyshinskii's efforts to strengthen legal procedures as a way to centralize power, see Peter H. Solomon, *Soviet Criminal Justice under Stalin* (New York, 1996), 155, 169.

59. I. V. Stalin, "Po povodu smerti Lenina" (speech given January 26, 1924), in his *O Lenine* (Moscow, 1937).

60. Werth, *Etre Communist*, 28–36, 92–94.

61. *Partorganizator* (Leningrad), 1935, no. 10, 5–6.

62. On the rituals surrounding Party membership, see Stephen Kotkin, *Magnetic Mountain: Stalinism as a Civilization* (Berkeley, 1995), 295–96.

63. See Igal Halfin, "Looking into the Oppositionists' Souls: Inquisition Communist Style," *The Russian Review*, 2001, no. 3, 316, 323–24.

64. Werth, *Etre Communist*, 83–6.

65. Smolensk Party archive, WKP, 523, 3–10.

66. As quoted in Eric Naiman, *Sex in Public: The Incarnation of Early Soviet Ideology* (Princeton, 1997), 91–92.

67. RGASPI, f. 17, op. 120, d. 76, l. 1.

68. See Kharkhordin, *Collective and the Individual,* 270–71.

69. RGASPI, f. 89, op. 8, d. 780, ll. 7–9.

70. GARF, f. 3316, op. 41, d. 135, l. 46; RGASPI, f. 17, op. 127, d. 2, l. 29; f. 112, op. 46, d. 5, l. 19.

71. Toporkov, *Kak stat' kul'turnym,* 50–51, 71.

72. E. K. Pramnek, *Kak rabotat' i rukovodit' (iz opyta partraboty)* (Gorky, 1933), 185.

73. Werth, *Etre Commnist,* 69.

74. See Kharkhordin, *Collective and the Individual,* 164–67. Kharkhordin points out that the 1930s purges differed from those in the 1920s not only in their greater focus on individuals but in their emphasis on "revelation by deeds" rather than social origin as an indication of loyalty to the Party.

75. GARF, f. 3316 s. ch., op. 64, d. 1621, ll. 1–4.

76. GARF, f. A-353, op. 10, d. 65, ll. 106–7.

77. Werth, *Etre Communist,* 180.

78. Iv. Pindiur, "Kak my rastim i vospityvaem partiinye kadry," *Partrabotnik* (Gorky), 1936, no. 5–6, 21–22.

79. E. Shtakov, "O vospitanii kommunista," *Partrabonik* (Gorky), 1936, no. 1, 29.

80. *Pravda,* February 27, 1937, 1.

81. See Oleg Khlevnyuk, "The Objectives of the Great Terror, 1937–1938," in *Soviet History, 1917–1953: Essays in Honour of R. W. Davies* (London, 1995). For other interpretations of the purges, see J. Arch Getty, *The Origins of the Great Purges* (New York, 1985); Gábor Tamas Rittersporn, *Stalinist Simplifications and Soviet Complications: Social Tensions and Political Conflicts in the USSR* (Philadelphia, 1991).

82. Naiman, *Sex in Public,* 13.

83. See Gábor Tamas Rittersporn, "The Omnipresent Conspiracy: On Soviet Imagery of Politics and Social Relations in the 1930s," in *Stalinism: Its Nature and Aftermath: Essays in Honour of Moshe Lewin,* ed. Nick Lampert and Rittersporn (Armonk, N.Y., 1991).

84. Vladimir Brovkin, *Russia after Lenin: Politics, Culture, and Society, 1921–1929* (New York, 1998), 40–46.

85. Rigby, *Communist Party Membership,* 96–97, 127–28.

86. Makarevich, *Partiinaia etika,* 395–463. See also TsKhSD, f. 6, op. 6, d. 3, ll. 36–37, on a Party member purged in 1924 for beating his wife.

87. Werth, *Etre Communist,* 227–29.

88. Rigby, *Communist Party Membership,* 176–79.

89. Leonard Schapiro, *The Communist Party of the Soviet Union,* 2d ed. (New York, 1971), 439.

90. Ibid.

91. Rigby, *Communist Party Membership,* 201. See also Kharkhordin, *Collective and the Individual,* 179–80.

92. RGASPI, f. 17, op. 120, d. 100, ll. 11–12, 29, 53–54; f. 613, op. 1, d. 181, ll. 1–4, 13, 22; d. 182, ll. 1, 23–29; op. 2, d. 180, l. 5; d. 183, l. 10; d. 184, l. 18; GARF, f. 3316 s. ch., op. 65, d. 123, l. 4.

93. RGASPI, f. 89, op. 3, d. 110, ll. 35–36; d. 126, ll. 22–23.

94. Rigby, *Communist Party Membership,* 206–7.

95. RGASPI, f. 17, op. 120, d. 179, ll. 33, 100–116. The same was true of a January 1936 conference, presided over by Ezhov, on the results of document verification. See RGASPI, f. 17, op. 120, d. 240, ll. 1–20.

96. *Partrabotnik* (Gorky), 1936, no. 1, 12–14.

97. RGASPI, f. 112, op. 2, d. 362, l. 30; TsMAM, f. 459, op. 1, d. 74, ll. 13–14; *Partrabotnik* (Gorky), 1936, no. 1, 31.

98. For proceedings of the plenum including the speeches by Ezhov and Enukidze, see J. Arch Getty and Oleg V. Naumov, eds., *The Road to Terror: Stalin and the Self-Destruction of the Bolsheviks, 1932–1939* (New Haven, 1999), 160–77.

99. RGASPI, f. 17, op. 3, d. 965, l. 12.

100. TsAODM, f. 3, op. 17, d. 4, l. 96.

101. For further discussion of the ideological and political imperatives behind the Great Purges, see Graeme Gill, *The Origins of the Stalinist Political System* (New York, 1990), 311–12; Amir Weiner, "Nature, Nurture, and Memory in a Socialist Utopia: Delineating the Soviet Socio-Ethnic Body in the Age of Socialism," *American Historical Review,* 1999, no. 4, 1121; Stephen E. Hanson, *Time and Revolution: Marxism and the Design of Soviet Institutions* (Chapel Hill, 1997), 167–70.

102. RGASPI, f. 17, op. 7, d. 546, l. 1.

103. *Smena,* 1937, no. 8, 25–26; 1938, no. 112, 20.

104. RGASPI f. 17, op. 21, d. 754, ll. 145, 217–18.

105. See, for example, ibid., op. 85, d. 486, l. 12.

106. Smolensk Party Archive, WKP 523, 7.

107. TsKhSD, f. 6, op. 6, d. 2, l. 21; RGASPI, f. 17, op. 21, d. 754, l. 82; op. 3, d. 995, l. 6; op. 114, d. 467, l. 45.

108. RGASPI, f. 17, op. 21, d. 754, l. 46.

109. Ibid., op. 114, d. 467, l. 10; TsMAM, f. 819, op. 2, d. 15, ll. 206–8; GARF, f. 8131 s. ch., op. 28, d. 10, l. 18.

110. RGASPI, f. 17, op. 21, d. 754, l. 81. See also TsKhSD, f. 6, op. 6, d. 3, ll. 20–21, on a Party member purged in 1940 for frequenting a brothel abroad.

111. RGASPI, f. 17, op. 21, d. 1370, l. 27; d. 2626, l. 40.

112. Ibid., d. 2626, l. 61. See also TsMAM, f. 819, op. 2, d. 27, l. 140.

113. RGASPI, f. 17, op. 21, d. 754, l. 269.

114. Werth, *Etre Communist,* 87–90. See also TsKhSD, f. 6, op. 6, d. 1, l. 13.

115. RGASPI, f. 17, op. 21, d. 754, l. 248.

116. TsAODM, f. 459, op. 1, d. 84, l. 7.

117. *Partrabotnik* (Stalingrad), 1937, no. 8, 58.

118. *Za bol'shevistskii stil'* (Moscow, 1937), 12–14. See also Fitzpatrick, *Everyday Stalinism,* 196–97.

119. Getty and Naumov, *Road to Terror,* 495, 532–38.

120. RGASPI, f. 477, op. 1, d. 14, l. 25.

121. TsKhSD, f. 89, op. 73, dd. 4–7.

122. *Smena,* 1938, no. 12, 20.

123. RGASPI, f. 477, op. 1, d. 52, ll. 17–18.

124. TsKhDMO, f. 1, op. 23, d. 1424, l. 91; M. Kareva, *Sotsialisticheskoe pravo i sotsialisticheskaia nravstvennost'* (Moscow, 1940).

125. RGASPI, f. 17, op. 3, d. 995, l. 21.

126. Ibid., op. 127, d. 3, ll. 26–29.

127. Werth, *Etre Communist,* 94.

128. RGASPI, f. 17, op. 85, d. 486, l. 31.

129. Ibid., l. 68.

130. TsKhDMO, f. 1, op. 23, d. 1072, ll. 21–23.

131. See Volkov, "Concept of Kul'turnost'," 223.

132. M. Kitaev, "Sanatorii TsK VKP(b) im. Stalina v Zheleznovodske," in Nikolaevsky Collection, Hoover Institution Archives, box 274, folder 19, pp. 30, 18.

133. TsKhDMO, f. 1, op. 23, d. 1088, ll. 95–96.

134. Kitaev, "Sanatorii TsK VKP(b) im. Stalina," 16–17.

135. Ibid., 10, 32–33.

136. Ibid., 11–12.
137. *Komsomol'skaia pravda*, January 3, 1936, 3.
138. TsKhDMO, f. 1, op. 23, d. 1088, l. 98.
139. Makarevich, *Partiinaia etika*, 198.
140. Kitaev, "Sanatorii TsK VKP(b) im. Stalina," 19, 36. On "sexual dissoluteness" among Komsomol members in 1936, see TsKhDMO, f. 1, op. 23, d. 1188, l. 92.
141. RGASPI, f. 17, op. 21, d. 1370, ll. 27–29. See also Douglas Northrop, "Subaltern Dialogues: Subversion and Resistance in Soviet Uzbek Family Law," in *Contending with Stalinism: Soviet Power and Popular Resistance in the 1930s*, ed. Lynne Viola (Ithaca, 2002).
142. Jochen Hellbeck, "Self-Realization in the Stalinist System: Two Soviet Diaries of the 1930s," in *Russian Modernity: Politics, Knowledge, Practices*, ed. David Hoffmann and Yanni Kotsonis (New York, 2000), 232–33.
143. As quoted in Jochen Hellbeck, "Working, Struggling, Becoming: Stalin-Era Autobiographical Texts," *The Russian Review* 60, no. 3 (2001), 351. See also "Diary of Galina Vladimirovna Shtange," in *Intimacy and Terror: Soviet Diaries of the 1930s*, ed. Véronique Garros, Nataliia Korenevskaya, and Thomas Lahusen (New York, 1995).
144. Nataliia Kozlova, "Krest'ianskii syn," *Sotsiologicheskie issledovaniia*, 1994, no. 6, 114–20. On the internalization of official values, see also Larry E. Holmes, *Stalin's School: Moscow's Model School No. 25, 1931–1937* (Pittsburgh, 1999), 101–3.
145. TsKhDMO, f. 1, op. 23, d. 1088, ll. 94–95.
146. Kharkhordin, *Collective and the Individual*, 270–71.
147. James R. Harris, "The Purging of Local Cliques in the Urals Region, 1936–37," in Fitzpatrick, *Stalinism*, 263.
148. TsAODM, f. 262, op. 1, d. 115, l. 140; f. 432, op. 1, d. 165, ll. 188–90; d. 176, l. 31; Getty and Naumov, *Road to Terror*, 493.
149. Eugenia Semyonovna Ginzburg, *Journey into the Whirlwind*, trans. Paul Stevenson and Max Hayward (New York, 1967), 36.
150. See Rittersporn, "Omnipresent Conspiracy."
151. Sarah Davies, *Popular Opinion in Stalin's Russia: Terror, Propaganda, and Dissent* (New York, 1997), 131–32.
152. RGASPI, f. 477, op. 1, d. 57, l. 65.
153. Ibid., l. 17.
154. RGASPI, f. 17, op. 21, d. 754, ll. 58–59.
155. RGASPI, f. 613, op. 1, d. 181, l. 66. See also O. V. Khlevniuk, "1937 god: Protivodeistvie repressiiam," *Kommunist*, 1989, no. 18.
156. Andrei Arzhilovskii, "Dnevnik 36–37-ogo godov," *Ural*, 1992, no. 3, 152.
157. Ginzburg, *Journey into the Whirlwind*, 10.
158. *XVIII S"ezd vsesoiuznoi kommunisticheskoi partii (b): 10–21 marta 1939 g.: Stenograficheskii otchet* (Moscow, 1939), 25, 37.
159. RGASPI, f. 477, op. 1, d. 20, ll. 33–36. See also the opening speech of the congress by Viacheslav Molotov, d. 1, l. 6.
160. Ibid., d. 20, ll. 24–26.

Chapter 3. Stalinist Family Values

1. Nicholas S. Timasheff, *The Great Retreat: The Growth and Decline of Communism in Russia* (New York, 1946), 193–97.
2. Richard Stites, *The Women's Liberation Movement in Russia: Feminism, Nihilism, and Bolshevism, 1860–1930* (Princeton, 1977), 363–69.

3. Alexandra Kollontai, *Alexandra Kollontai: Selected Articles and Speeches*, ed. I. M. Dazhina et al., trans. Cynthia Carlile (Moscow, 1984), 109.

4. Aleksandra Kollontai, *Sem'ia i kommunisticheskoe gosudarstvo* (Moscow, 1918), 21–22. For further discussion of Kollontai's ideas on free love, see Barbara Evans Clements, *Bolshevik Feminist: The Life of Aleksandra Kollontai* (Bloomington, 1979), 227–28.

5. A. Kollontai, *Trud zhenshchiny v evoliutsii khoziaistva* (Moscow/Petrograd, 1923), 146, 161–62; Gans Piil'man, *Byt v kolkhozakh* (Moscow/Leningrad, 1931), 3–4, 17.

6. Kollontai, *Trud zhenshchiny*, 152.

7. S. Ia. Vol'fson, *Sotsiologiia braka i sem'i* (Minsk, 1929), as cited in Wendy Z. Goldman, *Women, the State, and Revolution: Soviet Family Policy and Social Life, 1917–1936* (New York, 1993), 1, 310.

8. Kollontai, *Sem'ia*, 18–19.

9. Elizabeth Waters, "The Modernization of Russian Motherhood, 1917–37," *Soviet Studies*, 1992, no. 1, 128.

10. Eric Naiman, *Sex in Public: The Incarnation of Early Soviet Ideology* (Princeton, 1997), 190.

11. Nicolas Werth, "Alphabetisation et idéologie en Russe Soviétique," *Vingtième siècle: Revue d'histoire*, 1986, no. 10, 85.

12. K. Tsetkin, "Lenin o morale i voprosakh," in *Komsomol'skii byt: Sbornik*, ed. O. Razin (Moscow/Leningrad, 1927), 18–21.

13. RGASPI, f. 89, op. 3, d. 70, l. 3; Naiman, *Sex in Public*, 18–19; M. A. Makarevich, ed., *Partiinaia etika: Dokumenty i materialy diskussii 20-kh godov* (Moscow, 1989), 168. The same ideas continued to be repeated in the 1930s; see K. N. Kovalev, *Voprosy pola, polovogo vospitaniia, braka i sem'i* (Moscow, 1931), 2.

14. Naiman, *Sex in Public*, 18–19, 144; William G. Rosenberg, ed., *Bolshevik Visions: First Phase of the Cultural Revolution in Soviet Russia* (Ann Arbor, 1990), 107.

15. A. B. Zalkind, *Polovoi vopros v usloviiakh sovetskoi obshchestvennosti: Sbornik statei* (Leningrad, 1926), 6–14, 47–59.

16. As quoted in Naiman, *Sex in Public*, 121.

17. E. A. Arkin, *Pis'ma o vospitanii detei*, izd. 3, vyp. 1 (Moscow, 1936), 92–94; M. S. Malinovskii and E. M. Shvartsman, *Gigiena zhenshchiny*, 3d ed. (Moscow/Leningrad, 1935), 192–93.

18. Naiman, *Sex in Public*, 137–39, 210.

19. Katerina Clark, *Petersburg, Crucible of Cultural Revolution* (Cambridge, Mass., 1995), 210–11.

20. See Sheila Fitzpatrick, "Sex and Revolution," in *The Cultural Front: Power and Culture in Revolutionary Russia* (Ithaca, 1992), 89–90.

21. As quoted in Elizabeth Wood, *The Baba and the Comrade: Gender and Politics in Revolutionary Russia* (Bloomington, 1997), 112.

22. N. B. Lebina and M. V. Shkarovskii, *Prostitutsiia v Peterburge (40-e gg. XIX v.–40-e gg. XX v.)* (Moscow, 1994), 94–95.

23. GARF, f. 4085, op. 12, d. 37, ll. 32–35.

24. Wood, *Baba and the Comrade*, 112; N. B. Lebina, *Povsednevnaia zhizn' sovetskogo goroda: Normy i anomalii, 1920–1930 gody* (St. Petersburg, 1999), 84.

25. Lebina, *Povsednevnaia zhizn'*, 93–97; Frances Lee Bernstein, "What Everyone Should Know about Sex: Gender, Sexual Enlightenment, and the Politics of Health in Revolutionary Russia, 1918–1931" (dissertation, Columbia University, 1997), 396–97.

26. Bernstein, "What Everyone Should Know," 58. Governments in other countries at this time also sought to control sexual behavior to prevent venereal disease. See, for example, the report of the 1923 British Committee of Inquiry on VD, which called for

more rigorous medical intervention and instruction: PRO, MH 55/191. See also Magnus Hirschfield, *The Sexual History of the World War* (New York, 1941).

27. GARF, f. A-482, op. 1, d. 27, ll. 1–4.

28. On 1920s research that forced Soviet sexologists to revise their view that syphilis among peasants was mostly nonvenereal, see Susan Gross Solomon, "Innocence and Sexuality in Soviet Medical Discourse," in *Women in Russia and Ukraine,* ed. Rosalind Marsh (New York, 1996).

29. GARF, f. A-482, op. 1, d. 27, l. 8; TsMAM, f. 552, op. 1, d. 50, ll. 57–58. On mock trials as a means to instill morals, see also Tricia Ann Starks, "The Body Soviet: Health, Hygiene, and the Path to a New Life in the Soviet Union in the 1920s" (dissertation, Ohio State University, 2000), chap. 2.

30. *Gigiena i zdorov'e rabochei i krest'ianskoi sem'i,* 1926, no. 18, 14.

31. TsMAM f. 552, op. 1, d. 50, ll. 74, 87; d. 26, ll. 3–6.

32. Bernstein, "What Everyone Should Know," 3–4, 389–97.

33. RGASPI, f. 78, op. 1, d. 549, l. 45; Goldman, *Women, the State, and Revolution,* 244–45. See also Sheila Fitzpatrick, *Everyday Stalinism: Ordinary Life in Extraordinary Times: Soviet Russia in the 1930s* (New York, 1999), 143–47; Rosenberg, *Bolshevik Visions,* 111–26.

34. Goldman, *Women, the State, and Revolution,* 341.

35. General Ludendorff, *The General Staff and Its Problems: The History of the Relations between the High Command and the German Imperial Government as Revealed by Official Documents,* trans. F. A. Holt, vol. 1 (New York, 1920), 203–14.

36. Maria Sophia Quine, *Population Politics in Twentieth-Century Europe: Fascist Dictatorships and Liberal Democracies* (New York, 1996), 17–18; PRO, MH 58/311. For further discussion, see David L. Hoffmann and Peter Holquist, *Cultivating the Masses: The Modern Social State in Russia, 1914–1939* (Ithaca, forthcoming).

37. Ansley Coale, Barbara Anderson, and Erna Harm, *Human Fertility in Russia since the Nineteenth Century* (Princeton, 1979), 16; Frank Lorimer, *The Population of the Soviet Union* (Geneva, 1946), 40–41.

38. RGAE, f. 1562 s. ch., op. 329, d. 21, ll. 125–27. The totals for all Ukraine in 1933 were 449,877 births and 1,908,907 deaths (l. 109).

39. S. G. Strumilin, "K probleme rozhdaemosti v rabochei srede," in *Problemy ekonomiki truda* (Moscow, 1957), 194–98.

40. Ibid., 201–4; V. Z. Drobizhev, *V istokov sovetskoi demografii* (Moscow, 1987), 22.

41. E. A. Sadvokasova, *Sotsial'no—gigienicheskie aspekty regulirovaniia razmerov sem'i* (Moscow, 1969), 28–29.

42. William H. Schneider, *Quality and Quantity: The Quest for Biological Regeneration in Twentieth-Century France* (New York, 1990), 120; Karen Offen, "Body Politics: Women, Work, and the Politics of Motherhood in France, 1900–1950," in *Maternity and Gender Policies: Women and the Rise of the European Welfare State, 1880s-1950s,* ed. Gisela Bock and Pat Thane (New York, 1991), 138; Victoria de Grazia, *How Fascism Ruled Women: Italy, 1922–1945* (Berkeley, 1992), 58; Lisa Pine, *Nazi Family Policy, 1933–1945* (New York, 1997), 19–20; Elisabeth Domansky, "Militarization and Reproduction in World War I Germany," in *Society, Culture and the State in Germany, 1870–1930,* ed. Geoff Eley (Ann Arbor, 1996), 450–51; Claudia Koonz, *Mothers in the Fatherland: Women, the Family, and Nazi Politics* (New York, 1987), 185–87.

43. Susan Gross Solomon, "The Demographic Argument in Soviet Debates over the Legalization of Abortion in the 1920s," *Cahiers du monde russe et soviétique* 33 (1992), no. 1, 66–67.

44. Peter H. Solomon Jr., *Soviet Criminal Justice under Stalin* (New York, 1996), 212.

45. See Goldman, *Women, the State, and Revolution,* 255–56.

46. Ibid., 288; A. E. Kanevskii, *Sud nad Annoi Gorbovoi, po obvineniiu v proizvodstve sebe vykidysha(aborta)* (Odessa, 1925), 7–8, as cited in Naiman, *Sex in Public*, 109.

47. RGAE, f. 1562 s. ch., op. 329, d. 407, l. 67; *Izvestiia,* July 12, 1936, as cited in Lorimer, *Population of the Soviet Union*, 127.

48. *Sobranie zakonov i rasporiazhenii,* July 21, 1936, 510–11; RGASPI, f. 17, op. 3, d. 976, l. 4; d. 980, l. 1; d. 982, ll. 126–30.

49. *Rabotnitsa i krest'ianka*, 1936, no. 11, 6; no. 12, 1; *Izvestiia,* June 5, 1935; *Pravda,* September 5, 1936, 4.

50. N. A. Semashko, "Zamechatel'nyi zakon (o zapreshchenii aborta)," *Front nauki i tekhniki*, 1936, no. 7, 38.

51. Paul Weindling, *Health, Race, and German Politics between National Unification and Nazism, 1870–1945* (New York, 1989), 252–53; Quine, *Population Politics*, 71, 79, 105–6; Cornelia Usborne, *The Politics of the Body in Weimar Germany: Women's Reproductive Rights and Duties* (London, 1992), 20–21; Susan Pedersen, *Family, Dependence, and the Origins of the Welfare State: Britain and France, 1914–1945* (Cambridge, 1993), 4; Carl Ipsen, *Dictating Demography: The Problem of Population in Fascist Italy* (New York, 1996), 73; David G. Horn, *Social Bodies: Science, Reproduction, and Italian Modernity* (Princeton, 1994), 89–90; Karen Offen, "Body Politics: Women, Work, and the Politics of Motherhood in France, 1900–1950," in Bock and Thane, *Maternity and Gender Policies*, 138, 150; Pine, *Nazi Family Policy*, 109.

52. *Sobranie zakonov i rasporiazhenii,* July 21, 1936, 511; GARF, f. 5446, op. 18a, d. 2753, l. 4. The Soviet government had to allot 35 million rubles in 1936 alone to pay such bonuses: GARF, f. 5446, op. 18a, d. 2753, l. 31.

53. *Resoliutsii III Vses. soveshchaniia po okhrane materinstva i mladenchestva* (1926), 2, 10; GARF, f. 5446, op. 18a, d. 2754, l. 32. For further discussion, see Hoffmann and Holquist, *Cultivating the Masses*, chap. 3.

54. See Francine Hirsch, "Race without the Practice of Racial Politics," *Slavic Review* 61, no. 1 (2002): 40–41.

55. Drobizhev, *V istokov sovetskoi demografii*, 109, 122; GARF, f. 5446, op. 18a, d. 2754, l. 45. See, for example, the draft of a pamphlet by Elena Stasova, "For Women in the USSR All Paths Are Open," in which she stresses the concern and material aid provided by the Soviet government to mothers: RGASPI, f. 17, op. 120, d. 202, l. 11.

56. GARF, f. 4085, op. 12, d. 320, l. 16; A. V. Mol'kov and N. A. Semashko, eds., *Sotsial'naia gigiena: Rukovodstvo dlia studentov-medikov* (Moscow/Leningrad, 1927), 318. For further discussion, see Melanie Ilic, *Women Workers in the Soviet Interwar Economy: From "Protection" to "Equality"* (New York, 1999), 57–66.

57. *Martenovka,* May 1, 1936, 5; *Rabotnitsa i krest'ianka*, 1936, no. 2, 20; no. 7, 20–21; no. 15, 5; *Gigiena i zdorov'e*, 1938, no. 4, 6.

58. Offen, "Body Politics," 138, 150; Pine, *Nazi Family Policy*, 96; Koonz, *Mothers in the Fatherland*, 185–86.

59. Quine, *Population Politics*, 55–58. Beginning in the nineteenth century and continuing through the interwar period, commentators contrasted the sterilizing effect of the city with the "natural" fertility of the countryside. See Horn, *Social Bodies*, 98–99.

60. Quine, *Population Politics*, 86; Mary Nash, "Pronatalism and Motherhood in Franco's Spain," in Bock and Thane, *Maternity and Gender Policies*, 160–66.

61. Koonz, *Mothers in the Fatherland*, 178; Gisela Bock, "Antinatalism, Maternity, and Paternity in National Sect Racism," in Bock and Thane, *Maternity and Gender Policies*, 243.

62. *Sobranie zakonov i rasporiazhenii,* July 21, 1936, 515.

63. Timasheff, *Great Retreat*, 200; *Pravda,* June 26, 1935, 1; *Rabotnitsa i krest'ianka*, 1936, no. 12, 2; *Komsomol'skii rabotnik*, 1940, no. 8, 3.

64. *Pravda*, June 26, 1935.

65. *Sotsialisticheskaia zakonnost'*, 1939, no. 2.

66. *Rabotnitsa i krest'ianka*, 1936, no. 12, 2; *Komsomol'skii rabotnik*, 1940, no. 8, 3.

67. Rudolf Schlesinger, ed., *Changing Attitudes in Soviet Russia: The Family in the USSR* (London, 1949), 307–8; I. Bachelis and S. Tregub, eds., *Za liubov' i schast'e v nashe sem'e* (Moscow, 1936), 11.

68. Robert Thurston, "The Soviet Family during the Great Terror, 1935–1941," *Soviet Studies*, 1991, no. 3, 559–60.

69. *Komsomol'skaia pravda*, October 27, 1935, 1.

70. *Gosudarstvennoe upravlenie: Kodifitsirovannyi sbornik zakonodatel'stva RSFSR na 1 ianvariia 1934 goda* (Moscow, 1934), 49.

71. *Sobranie zakonov i rasporiazhenii*, July 21, 1936, 515–16.

72. GARF, f. 9492 s. ch., op. 1, d. 2, l. 183; TsMAM, f. 819, op. 1, d. 3, l. 1; f. 2429, op. 7, d. 200, l. 34; d. 220, l. 4.

73. *Pravda*, June 9, 1936, 1; *Ogonek*, January 10, 1936, 4; Timasheff, *Great Retreat*, 197.

74. James van Geldern, "The Centre and the Periphery: Cultural and Social Geography in Mass Culture of the 1930s," in *New Directions in Soviet History*, ed. Stephen White (New York, 1992), 72; Jeffrey Brooks, "Public Identities in *Pravda* during the 1920s," ibid., 34–36; RGASPI, f. 78, op. 1, d. 833, l. 56; Bachelis and Tregub, *Za liubov' i schast'e*, 40–48.

75. As quoted in Goldman, *Women, the State, and Revolution*, 98. See also *Sbornik deistvuiushchikh uzakonenii i rasporiazhenii pravitel'stva soiuza SSSR i pravitel'stva RSFSR, postanovlenii detkomissii pri VTsIK i vedomstvennykh rasporiazhenii* (Moscow, 1929).

76. A. Makarenko, *A Book for Parents*, trans. Robert Daglish (Moscow, n.d.), 24, 117; Getts Khillig, "Kak A. S. Makarenko otkryl sem'iu: K istorii sozdaniia i vozdeistviia kniga dlia roditelei 1936–1939 gg.," *Cahiers du monde russe et soviétique* 33 (1992), no. 1, 84–85.

77. Goldman, *Women, the State, and Revolution*, 324–25.

78. *O rassledovanii i rassmotrenii del o nesovershennoletnikh* (Moscow, 1937), 25–32. At this time the Soviet government also lowered the age of criminal responsibility, allowing the police to send delinquent children twelve and over to labor camps. Alongside an emphasis on parental responsibility, then, Soviet authorities used coercion to deal with the problem of unsupervised children.

79. TsKhDMO f. 1, op. 23, d. 1074, ll. 98–99, 108; *Sotsialisticheskaia zakonnost'*, 1939, no. 2.

80. TsMAM, f. 528, op. 1, d. 775, l. 71; V. Svetlov, "Socialist Society and the Family," in Schlesinger, *Changing Attitudes*, 334. See also GARF, f. A-2306, op. 69, d. 2600, ll. 25–26.

81. Quoted in Pine, *Nazi Family Policy*, 15. See also Koonz, *Mothers in the Fatherland*, 14, 180.

82. Pine, *Nazi Family Policy*, 16–18.

83. *Komsomol'skii rabotnik*, 1940, no. 8, 21–22.

84. GARF, f. A-482, op. 11, d. 40, l. 6; d. 79, l. 33; f. 5528, op. 5, d. 39, l. 2; A. I. Aliakrinskii, *Brak, sem'ia i opeka: Prakticheskoe rukovodstvo dlia organov ZAGS* (Moscow, 1930), 124; TsMAM, f. 528, op. 1, d. 465, ll. 25–26; f. 819, op. 2, d. 9, ll. 92–93, 273–74. The Russian family code of 1882, which had been drafted but never implemented, also stressed parents' obligation to prepare children for productive citizenship and stipulated that abusive or neglectful parents could be deprived of custody. See William G. Wagner, *Marriage, Property, and Law in Late Imperial Russia* (New York, 1994), 166–67.

85. Jacques Donzelot, *The Policing of Families*, trans. Robert Hurley (New York, 1979), 89, 92.

86. Marriage had been established in Western culture as the only kind of sexual expression that befits civilization. See Isabel V. Hull, *Sexuality, State, and Civil Society in Germany, 1700–1815* (Ithaca, 1996), 294–96.

87. *Istochnik*, 1993, no. 5/6, 164–65.

88. Dan Healey, *Homosexual Desire in Revolutionary Russia: The Regulation of Sexual and Gender Dissent* (Chicago, 2001), 182–90. See also Laura Engelstein, "Soviet Policy toward Male Homosexuality: Its Origins and Historical Roots," *Journal of Homosexuality* 25, no. 3/4 (1994).

89. N. V. Krylenko, "Ob izmeneniiakh i dopolneniiakh kodeksov RSFSR," *Sovetskaia iustitsiia*, 1936, no. 7, as cited in Healey, *Homosexual Desire*, 196. See also James Riordan, "Sexual Minorities: The Status of Gays and Lesbians in Russian–Soviet-Russian Society," in Marsh, *Women in Russia and Ukraine*, 160; Igor Kon, "Sexual Minorities," in *Sex and Russian Society*, ed. Kon and James Riordan (Bloomington, 1993), 92.

90. On the prosecution of sodomy cases after 1933, see Healey, *Homosexual Desire*, chap. 8.

91. See Douglas Northrop, "Subaltern Dialogues: Subversion and Resistance in Soviet Uzbek Family Law," in *Contending with Stalinism: Soviet Power and Popular Resistance in the 1930s*, ed. Lynne Viola (Ithaca, 2002).

92. *Rabotnitsa*, 1936, no. 17, 5, as quoted in Lynne Attwood, *Creating the New Soviet Woman: Women's Magazines as Engineers of Female Identity, 1922–1953* (New York, 1999), 116; *Pravda*, May 28, 1936, 1.

93. Janet Hyer, "Managing the Female Organism: Doctors and the Medicalization of Women's Paid Work in Soviet Russia during the 1920s," in Marsh, *Women in Russia and Ukraine*, 113. Sex reform experts in Weimar Germany were also influenced by industrial rationalization and sought, in the words of one scholar, "the extension of assembly-line techniques into housework and the bedroom": Atina Grossmann, "The New Woman and the Rationalization of Sexuality in Weimar Germany," in *Powers of Desire: The Politics of Sexuality*, ed. Ann Snitow, Christine Stansell, and Sharon Thompson (New York, 1983), 163.

94. A. S. Gofshtein, "Ratsionalizatsiia materinstva," *Vrachebnoe delo*, 1927, no. 19, as cited in Hyer, "Managing the Female Organism," 113–18.

95. Hyer, "Managing the Female Organism," 115.

96. Ibid., 116–17; Thomas Schrand, "Industrialization and the Stalinist Gender System: Women Workers in the Soviet Economy, 1928–1941" (dissertation, University of Michigan, 1994), 159–60. See also GARF, f. 5528, op. 5, d. 44, ll. 4–5. For further discussion of restrictions on women's heavy labor and the degree to which these restrictions were followed in practice, see Ilic, *Women Workers*, 112–29.

97. *Resoliutsii III Vsesoiuznogo soveshchaniia po okhane materinstva i mladenchestva* (1926), 17–18; Malinovskii and Shvartsman, *Gigiena zhenshchiny*, 5–32.

98. Kathryn Helen Reisdorfer, "Seeing through the Screen: An Examination of Women in Soviet and German Popular Cinema in the Inter-War Years" (dissertation, University of Minnesota, 1993), 208, 218; *Traktoristy*, dir. Gleb Aleinikov and Igor' Aleinikov (1939). See also Victoria Bonnell, *Iconography of Power: Soviet Political Posters under Lenin and Stalin* (Berkeley, 1997). In some instances, Soviet women were portrayed as having positions of equality or even authority in the workplace; see Choi Chatterjee, *Celebrating Women: Gender, Festival Culture, and Bolshevik Ideology, 1910–1939* (Pittsburgh, 2002), 148–49.

99. RGASPI, f. 17, op. 3, d. 981, l. 69.

100. Offen, "Body Politics," 138.

101. Pine, *Nazi Family Policy*, 22.

102. Chatterjee, *Celebrating Women*, 143.

103. Karen Petrone, *Life Has Become More Joyous, Comrades: Celebrations in the Time of Stalin* (Bloomington, 2000), 59; Gail Warshofsky Lapidus, *Women in Soviet Society* (Berkeley, 1978), 103–15.

104. Anne E. Gorsuch, *Youth in Revolutionary Russia: Enthusiasts, Bohemians, Delinquents* (Bloomington, 2000), 100–102; Wood, *Baba and the Comrade*, 56, 67. See also Barbara Evans Clements, "The Effects of the Civil War on Women and Family Relations," in *Party, State, and Society in the Russian Civil War: Explorations in Social History*, ed. Diane Koenker et al. (Bloomington, 1989).

105. *Rabotnitsa*, 1938, no. 21, 10–11; 1939, no. 4, 8, as cited in Attwood, *Creating the New Soviet Woman*, 127.

106. *Komsomol'skii rabotnik*, 1940, no. 8, 29.

107. Petrone, *Life Has Become More Joyous*, 59–61.

108. GARF, f. 5446, op. 18a, d. 2753, ll. 15, 22, 26, 35. Evidence gathered during discussions of the 1936 constitution indicates that even before the increase in resources allocated for mothers, peasants in particular were requesting monetary support for large families: GARF, f. 3316, op. 40, d. 18, l. 117.

109. *Izvestiia*, May 29, 1936, 3–4; May 30, 1936, 3; June 2, 1936, 3. See also Thurston, "Soviet Family," 557; Sarah Davies, *Popular Opinion in Stalin's Russia: Terror, Propaganda, and Dissent* (New York, 1997), 66–67.

110. GARF, f. 5446, op. 18a, d. 2753, l. 85; RGAE, f. 1562 s. ch., op. 329, d. 407, ll. 22–25. Another 1937 report noted that the figure of 323,438 cases of incomplete abortions that had to be completed in hospitals in the RSFSR was clear evidence of a mass of underground abortions: GARF, f. A-482, op. 29, d. 5, l. 9.

111. *Sovetskaia iustitsiia*, 1936, no. 34, 16; RGAE, f. 1562, s. ch., op. 329, d. 407, l. 25; TsMAM, f. 819, op. 2, d. 27, ll. 12–15. Many persons who had performed multiple abortions were sentenced to four or more years' imprisonment.

112. From 1938 to 1940, prosecutions for abortion declined, and despite a rise in convictions in 1941, the criminalization of abortion overall proved to be, in the words of one leading scholar, "a particularly ineffective extension of the criminal law": Peter Solomon, *Soviet Criminal Justice*, 220–21.

113. David L. Ransel, *Village Mothers: Three Generations of Change in Russia and Tataria* (Bloomington, 2000), 71–72.

114. Nash, "Pronatalism and Motherhood," 174; Bock, "Antinatalism," 245; Pine, *Nazi Family Policy*, 181; Koonz, *Mothers in the Fatherland*, 187.

115. Lorimer, *Population of the Soviet Union*, 134; Coale et al., *Human Fertility*, 16. Fertility in the first quarter of 1938 was substantially below the 1937 level: RGAE, f. 1562 s. ch., op. 329, d. 186, l. 5. For further discussion, see Goldman, *Women, the State, and Revolution*, 294–95; Ransel, *Village Mothers*, 71.

116. GARF, f. 5446, op. 18a, d. 2753, l. 8.

117. Ibid., op. 17, d. 315, ll. 71–72; TsMAM, f. 1289, op. 1, d. 174, ll. 3–4; Ransel, *Village Mothers*, 74–76.

118. TsKhDMO, f. 1, op. 23, d. 1264, ll. 6, 29. See also Waters, "Modernization of Russian Motherhood," 131–34.

119. F. Panforov, *The Village Bruski* (Moscow, 1937), 4:132, as quoted in Xenia Gasiorowska, *Women in Soviet Fiction* (Madison, 1968), 53.

120. See Stalin's statement for the resolutions of the 1935 congress of collective farm shock workers, RGASPI, f. 17, op. 120, d. 138, l. 85.

121. In a few instances propaganda did urge men to help with child care and housework; see Chatterjee, *Celebrating Women*, 156.

122. Starks, "Body Soviet," chap. 3; Gasiorowska, *Women in Soviet Fiction*, 103.

123. Susan M. Kingsbury and Mildred Fairchild, *Factory, Family, and Woman in the So-

viet Union (New York, 1935), 249; *Trud v SSSR: Ekonomiko-statisticheskii spravochnik* (Moscow, 1932), 172.

124. *XVII s'ezd VKP(b), 26 ianvar' – 10 fevral' 1934 g.: Stenograficheskii otchet* (Moscow, 1934), 25.

125. Stalin, *Sochineniia,* vol. 1 (Stanford, 1967), 74–76.

126. Lapidus, *Women in Soviet Society,* 99; David L. Hoffmann, *Peasant Metropolis: Social Identities in Moscow, 1929–1941* (Ithaca, 1994), 120–22. See also Wendy Goldman, "Babas at the Bench: Gender Conflict in Soviet Industry in the 1930s," in *Women in the Stalin Era,* ed. Melanie Ilic (New York, 2001).

Chapter 4. Mass Consumption in a Socialist Society

1. See Stephen Kotkin, "Modern Times: The Soviet Union and the Interwar Conjuncture," *Kritika,* 2001, no. 1, 137.

2. See Victoria de Grazia, "Nationalizing Women: The Competition between Fascist and Commercial Cultural Models in Mussolini's Italy," in *The Sex of Things: Gender and Consumption in Historical Perspective,* ed. de Grazia and Ellen Furlough (Berkeley, 1996); Kotkin, "Modern Times."

3. As quoted in Daniel R. Brower, *Training the Nihilists: Education and Radicalism in Tsarist Russia* (Ithaca, 1975), 15.

4. Nikolai Chernyshevsky, *What Is to Be Done?* trans. Michael R. Katz (Ithaca, 1989), 278–83.

5. Anne E. Gorsuch, *Youth in Revolutionary Russia: Enthusiasts, Bohemians, Delinquents* (Bloomington, 2000), 92, 125.

6. As quoted ibid., 82.

7. Richard Stites, *Revolutionary Dreams: Utopian Vision and Experimental Life in the Russian Revolution* (New York, 1989), 118; Gorsuch, *Youth in Revolutionary Russia,* 89.

8. Vera S. Dunham, *In Stalin's Time: Middleclass Values in Soviet Fiction* (New York, 1976), 41.

9. Gorsuch, *Youth in Revolutionary Russia,* 54–55.

10. Eric Naiman, *Sex in Public: The Incarnation of Early Soviet Ideology* (Princeton, 1997), 183; Svetlana Boym, *Common Places: Mythologies of Everyday Life in Russia* (Cambridge, 1994), 8.

11. *Komsomol'skaia pravda,* November 4, 1928, 3.

12. Iulia Obertreis, "'Byvshee' i 'izlishnee': Izmenenie sotsial'nykh norm v zhilishchnoi sfere v 1920–1930-e gg.: Na materialakh Leningrada," in *Normy i tsennosti povsednevnoi zhizni: Stanovlenie sotsialisticheskogo obraza zhizni v Rossii 1920–30–e gody,* ed. Timo Vikhavainen (St. Petersburg, 2000), 90.

13. Gorsuch, *Youth in Revolutionary Russia,* 24–25, 126.

14. A. Stratonitskii, *Voprosy byta v Komsomole* (Leningrad, 1926), 19, as quoted ibid., 91.

15. Gorsuch, *Youth in Revolutionary Russia,* 124–25, 72–73.

16. L. A. Gordon and E. V. Klopov, *Chto eto bylo? Razmyshleniia o predposylkakh i itogakh togo, chto sluchilos' s nami v 30–40e gody* (Moscow, 1989), 52–68.

17. See A. A. Tverdokhleb, "Material'noe blagosostoianie rabochego klassa Moskvy v 1917–1937 gg." (dissertation, Moscow State University, 1970); *Pravda,* September 16, 1988, 3 (V. Danilov).

18. For a discussion of the rationing system, see Elena A. Osokina, *Ierarkhiia potrebleniia: O zhizni liudei v usloviiakh Stalinskogo snabzheniia, 1928–1935 gg.* (Moscow, 1993); R. W. Davies, *The Soviet Economy in Turmoil* (Cambridge, Mass., 1989), 289–98.

19. R. W. Davies, *Crisis and Progress in the Soviet Economy, 1931–1933* (London, 1996), 463.

20. Rosalinde Sartorti, "Stalinism and Carnival: Organization and Aesthetics of Political Holidays," in *The Culture of the Stalin Period*, ed. Hans Gunther (New York, 1990), 62–63.

21. Gorsuch, *Youth in Revolutionary Russia*, 185.

22. As quoted in O. V. Khlevniuk, "Izmenenie kul'turnogo oblika gorodskikh rabochikh SSSR, 1926–1939" (dissertation, Institute of History, Moscow, 1986), 119–20.

23. See, for example, Valentin Kataev, *Time, Forward*, trans. Charles Malamuth (Bloomington, 1976); Sergei Igonin, "My stroim," *Aviamotor,* June 27, 1930, 3.

24. Stalin, *Sochineniia* (Moscow, 1946–52), 13:56–61.

25. Ibid., 59–60.

26. Davies, *Crisis and Progress*, 213, 321, 355–56. See also Vadim Rogovin, *Stalinskii Neonep* (Moscow, 1992), 16–17.

27. O. V. Khlevniuk, *1937-i: Stalin, NKVD, i sovetskoe obshchestvo* (Moscow, 1992), 10–13. See also Jeffrey J. Rossman, "The Teikovo Cotton Workers' Strike of April 1932: Class, Gender, and Identity Politics in Stalin's Russia," *The Russian Review*, 1997, no. 1.

28. Reprinted in *The Road to Terror,* ed. J. Arch Getty and Oleg V. Naumov (New Haven, 1999), 54–58.

29. Stalin, *Sochineniia*, 13:254–56.

30. *XVII s'ezd VKP(b), 26 ianvar'–10 fevral' 1934 g.: Stenograficheskii otchet* (Moscow, 1934), 26, 30–31.

31. RGASPI, f. 17, op. 120, d. 138, ll. 78–80.

32. Stalin, *Sochineniia* (Stanford, 1967), 1 [XIV]: 89–90.

33. Julie Hessler, "Cultured Trade: The Stalinist Turn toward Consumerism," in *Stalinism: New Directions*, ed. Sheila Fitzpatrick (New York, 2000), 196; Karen Petrone, *Life Has Become More Joyous, Comrades: Celebrations in the Time of Stalin* (Bloomington, 2000), 99.

34. *Pravda*, May 6, 1936, 1.

35. *Gigiena i zdorov'e*, 1936, no. 20, 13.

36. RGASPI, f. 17, op. 120, d. 138, l. 7; d. 139, l. 35.

37. Sartorti, "Stalinism and Carnival," 65.

38. *Ogonek,* January 10, 1936, 14–15; *Komsomol'skaia pravda,* January 3, 1936, 4.

39. *Vecherniaia krasnaia gazeta*, December 21, 1933, 4; Gorsuch, *Youth in Revolutionary Russia*, 187.

40. TsKhDMO, f. 1, op. 23, d. 1074, l. 100.

41. Petrone, *Life Has Become More Joyous*, 85.

42. GARF, f. 7709, op. 7, d. 9, l. 392.

43. Petrone, *Life Has Become More Joyous*, 90–96.

44. *Veselye rebiata*, dir. Grigorii V. Aleksandrov (1934). See also Kathryn Helen Reisdorfer, "Seeing through the Screen: An Examination of Women in Soviet and German Popular Cinema in the Inter-War Years" (dissertation, University of Minnesota, 1993), 226.

45. *Tsirk*, dir. Grigorii V. Aleksandrov (1936).

46. See, for example, *Rabotnitsa i krest'ianka*, 1936, no. 10, 9.

47. GARF, f. 5446, op. 18a, d. 2753, l. 26. See also Petrone, *Life Has Become More Joyous*, 108.

48. Sarah Davies, *Popular Opinion in Stalin's Russia: Terror, Propaganda, and Dissent* (New York, 1997), 26–27.

49. Hessler, "Cultured Trade," 198.

50. Davies, *Popular Opinion*, 35–39.
51. Andrei Arzhilovskii, "Dnevnik 36–37-ogo godov," *Ural*, 1992, no. 3, 142–43. Arzhilovskii expressed the same cynicism toward the celebration of Soviet pilots' polar expeditions; see 159–60.
52. Petrone, *Life Has Become More Joyous*, 19–20.
53. As cited in Rogovin, *Stalinskii Neonep*, 22.
54. See Amy E. Randall, "'Revolutionary Bolshevik Work': Stakhanovism in Retail Trade," *The Russian Review*, 2000, no. 3, 428.
55. Even before Soviet leaders abolished rationing, they took steps to reestablish the legitimacy of trade. See Amy E. Randall, "The Campaign for Soviet Trade: Creating Socialist Retail Trade in the 1930s" (dissertation, Princeton University, 2000).
56. Hessler, "Cultured Trade," 186–87; *Vecherniaia krasnaia gazeta*, December 21, 1933, 2. See also Rudolf Schlesinger, *The Spirit of Postwar Russia: Soviet Ideology, 1917–1946* (London, 1947), 19.
57. Hessler, "Cultured Trade," 188–99.
58. Ibid., 191–92.
59. *Za kul'turnyi univermag*, 1937, nos. 1–3.
60. Nicholas S. Timasheff, *The Great Retreat: The Growth and Decline of Communism in Russia* (New York, 1946), 140.
61. Randall, "'Revolutionary Bolshevik Work,'" 427.
62. Hessler, "Cultured Trade," 190.
63. Randall, "'Revolutionary Bolshevik Work,'" 432.
64. *Za kul'turnyi univermag*, 1937, no. 1, 10–11.
65. Randall, "'Revolutionary Bolshevik Work,'" 434.
66. *Rabochii deputat*, 1935, no. 2, 2.
67. As quoted in Randall, "'Revolutionary Bolshevik Work,'" 429.
68. Randall, "'Revolutionary Bolshevik Work,'" 430.
69. As quoted in Yuri Slezkine, *Arctic Mirrors: Russia and the Small Peoples of the North* (Ithaca, 1994), 318–19.
70. As quoted in Randall, "'Revolutionary Bolshevik Work,'" 433.
71. Hessler, "Cultured Trade," 197. See also Randi Barnes Cox, "The Creation of the Socialist Consumer: Advertising, Citizenship and NEP" (dissertation, Indiana University, 1999).
72. For further discussion of shock workers, see Hiroaki Kuromiya, *Stalin's Industrial Revolution: Politics and Workers, 1928–1932* (New York, 1988), 115–23.
73. *Labour in the Land of the Soviets: Stakhanovites in Conference* (Moscow, 1936), 210. See also *Profsoiuznyi rabotnik*, 1937, no. 1, 3.
74. RGASPI, f. 17, op. 120, d. 146, ll. 11, 43.
75. *Rabotnitsa i krest'ianka*, 1936, no. 6, 12–13; *Gigiena i zdorov'e*, 1936, no. 21, 7. See also Lewis H. Siegelbaum, *Stakhanovism and the Politics of Productivity in the USSR, 1935–1941* (New York, 1988), 231.
76. *Stakhanovets*, 1937, no. 2, 53–54.
77. *Rabotnitsa i krest'ianka*, 1936, no. 8, 10–11.
78. As cited in Siegelbaum, *Stakhanovism*, 188, 227–31. See also *Rabotnitsa i krest'ianka*, 1936, no. 6, 12–13.
79. Khlevniuk, "Izmenenie kul'turnogo oblika," 151–52, 173; Aleksandr Kh. Busygin, *Moia zhizn' i moia rabota* (Leningrad, 1935); Ivan Gudov, *Sud'ba rabochego* (Moscow, 1974).
80. GARF, f. 5451, op. 20, d. 21, l. 18.
81. *Kul'turnaia rabota profsoiuzov*, 1938, no. 5, 48.

82. *Rabotnitsa i krest'ianka*, 1936, no. 6, 11; see also RGASPI, f. 17, op. 120, d. 251, l. 238.
83. RGASPI, f. 17, op. 120, d. 139, l. 6.
84. RGASPI, f. 89, op. 9, d. 91, l. 8.
85. TsKhDMO, f. 1, op. 23, d. 1074, ll. 107–8.
86. Catriona Kelly, *Refining Russia: Advice Literature, Polite Culture, and Gender from Catherine to Yeltsin* (New York, 2001), 284–87, 290–91; C. Kelly, *"Kul'turnost'* in the Soviet Union: Ideal and Reality," in *Reinterpreting Russia*, ed. Geoffrey Hosking and Robert Service (London, 1999), 204.
87. Sheila Fitzpatrick, "'Middle-Class Values' and Social Life in the 1930s," in *Soviet Culture and Society*, ed. Richard Sheldon and Tony L. Thompson (Boulder, Colo., 1989), 36.
88. See *Biulleten' Narkomata kommunal'nogo khoziaistva*, 1935, no. 6, 96; *Ukhtomskii rabochii*, May 27, 1938, 3; Andrew Smith, *I Was a Soviet Worker* (New York, 1936), 47–48.
89. *Legkaia industriia*, November 10, 1935, 2. On violence against shock workers, see *Govoriat stroiteli sotsializma: Vospominaniia uchastnikov sotsialisticheskogo stroitel'stva v SSSR* (Moscow, 1959), 128–29; *Rabochaia gazeta*, January 5, 1930, 6.
90. Donald Filtzer, *Soviet Workers and Stalinist Industrialization: The Formation of Modern Soviet Production Relations, 1928–1941* (New York, 1986), 201. On resistance to rural Stakhanovism, see Mary Buckley, "Categorising Resistance to Rural Stakhanovism," in *Politics and Society under the Bolsheviks: Selected Papers from the Fifth World Congress of Central and East European Studies*, ed. Kevin McDermott and John Morison (New York, 1999).
91. F. Kulikov, "Za novogo cheloveka: Iz dnevnika kul'tarmeitsa," *Na rubezhe*, 1935, no. 10, 97–102.
92. GARF, f. A-353, op. 10, d. 76, l. 5.
93. Nataliia Lebina, "O pol'ze igry v biser: Mikroistoriia kak metod izucheniia norm i anomalii sovetskoi povsednevnosti 20–30-kh godov," in Vikhavainen, *Normy i tsennosti*, 18–25.
94. Elena Osokina, *Za fasadom "Stalinskogo izobiliia": Raspredelenie i rynok v snabzhenii naseleniia v gody industrializatsii, 1927–1941* (Moscow, 1998), 193–94.
95. See Pierre Bourdieu, *Distinction: A Social Critique of the Judgement of Taste*, trans. Richard Nice (Cambridge, Mass., 1984), 173.
96. Sheila Fitzpatrick, "Becoming Cultured: Socialist Realism and the Representation of Privilege and Taste," in Fitzpatrick, *The Cultural Front: Power and Culture in Revolutionary Russia* (Ithaca, 1992), 218. See also Boym, *Common Places*, 105.
97. Dunham, *In Stalin's Time*, 23.
98. Ia. Fridlianskii, "Za samogo kul'turnogo inzhenera samogo kul'turnogo gosudarstva v mire," *Voprosy profdvizheniia*, October 1935, 55.
99. See, for example, *Mody*, 1936, no. 3, 1; 1937, no. 3–4, 1.
100. M. Kitaev, in Nikolaevsky Collection, Hoover Institution Archives, box 274, folder 19, pp. 16, 38.
101. Victor Kravchenko, *I Chose Freedom* (New York, 1946), 83; *Vecherniaia Moskva*, May 17, 1939.
102. Kitaev, 4–5; RGASPI, f. 17, op. 3, d. 978, l. 44.
103. TsKhDMO, f. 1, op. 23, d. 1268, l. 12.
104. RGASPI f. 17, op. 3, d. 995, l. 21; op. 21, d. 754, l. 64; op. 120, d. 326, ll. 125–26; A. V. Kvashonkin et al., eds., *Bol'shevistskoe rukovodstvo: Perepiska* (Moscow, 1996), 191–94.
105. Hoffmann, *Peasant Metropolis*, 136–41, 146–52.
106. Davies, *Popular Opinion*, 138–41.

107. Sarah Davies, "'Us against Them': Social Identity in Soviet Russia, 1934–41," *The Russian Review,* 1997, no. 1, 185.

108. GARF, f. 3316, s. ch., op. 64, d. 1994, ll. 2–6.

109. Ibid., op. 40, d. 14, ll. 25, 44. Other such letters proposed that directors and officials have their salaries cut; see d. 18, l. 26.

110. Fitzpatrick, "Middle-Class Values," 30–31. See also RGASPI, f. 17, op. 21, d. 754, l. 23.

111. Osokina, *Za fasadom "Stalinskogo izobiliia,"* 206; Alec Nove, *An Economic History of the USSR* (New York, 1982), 257–61.

112. Osokina, *Za fasadom "Stalinskogo izobiliia,"* 206–10. See also E. A. Osokina, "Krizis snabzheniia 1939–1941 gg. v pis'makh sovetskikh liudei," *Voprosy istorii,* 1996, no. 1.

Chapter 5. Social and Cultural Unity under Soviet Socialism

1. Given Party leaders' claim that they had eliminated class enemies by 1934, Iagoda's reference to class struggle is slightly anachronistic. Apparently he continued to refer to political opposition as "class struggle" even after the purported elimination of antagonistic classes. My thanks to Paul Hagenloh for supplying me with this quotation from "Rech' NKVD SSSR tov. Iagoda na soveshchanii nachal'nikov oblastnykh i kraevykh upravlenii RKM 16-go aprelia 1935 g.," in GARF, f. 9401, op. 12, d. 135, document 119.

2. Paul Rabinow, *French Modern: Norms and Forms of the Social Environment* (Cambridge, Mass., 1989), 169–70, 185–86; Sanford Elwitt, *The Third Republic Defended: Bourgeois Reform in France, 1880–1914* (Baton Rouge, 1986), 23.

3. George L. Mosse, *The Nationalization of the Masses: Political Symbolism and Mass Movements in Germany from the Napoleonic Wars through the Third Reich* (New York, 1975), 21, 190–92.

4. RGASPI, f. 17, op. 120, d. 146, l. 54.

5. In practice, having dekulakized relatives could still be used to deny someone Party membership; see TsGAODM, f. 432, op. 1, d. 222, t. 3, ll. 144–45.

6. RGASPI, f. 78, op. 6, d. 87, ll. 13–15.

7. *Komsomol'skaia pravda,* May 28, 1936, 3, as cited in Robert W. Thurston, "The Soviet Family during the Great Terror, 1935–1941," *Soviet Studies,* 1991, no. 3, 558–59.

8. RGASPI, f. 17, op. 120, d. 179, ll. 54–69.

9. Victoria E. Bonnell, *Iconography of Power: Soviet Political Posters under Lenin and Stalin* (Berkeley, 1997), 29; James Van Geldern, "The Centre and the Periphery: Cultural and Social Geography in Mass Culture of the 1930s," in *New Directions in Soviet History,* ed. Stephen White (New York, 1992), 74–75.

10. RGASPI, f. 17, op. 3, d. 958, l. 38; Ellen Wimberg, "Socialism, Democratism, and Criticism: The Soviet Press and the National Discussion of the 1936 Draft Constitution," *Soviet Studies,* 1992, no. 2, 313.

11. *Pravda,* November 26, 1936, 1–2. See also Molotov's speech in *Pravda,* November 30, 1936, 1.

12. N. V. Krylenko, *Stalinskaia konstitutsiia v voprosakh i otvetakh,* 2d ed. (Moscow, 1937), 22; G. Amfiteatrov, "Proekt konstitutsii SSSR i grazhdanskii kodeks sotsialisticheskogo obshchestva," *Sovetskoe gosudarstvo,* 1936, no. 4, 84.

13. GARF, f. 3316, op. 40, d. 22, l. 4.

14. Peter H. Solomon Jr., *Soviet Criminal Justice under Stalin* (New York, 1996), 191–95. The fact that the Soviet embassy in Washington wrote detailed reports on how the

new Soviet constitution was being covered in the American press corroborates Solomon's argument that a primary motive for issuing it was to appear more democratic to foreign observers; GARF, f. 3316, op. 40, d. 23, l. 2.

15. *Istoriia sovetskoi konstitutsii: Sbornik dokumentov, 1917–1957* (Moscow, 1957), 85; Elise Kimerling, "Civil Rights and Social Policy in Soviet Russia, 1918–1936," *The Russian Review,* 1982, no. 1, 25–27; Golfo Alexopoulos, *Stalin's Outcasts: Aliens, Citizens, and the Soviet State, 1926–1936* (Ithaca, 2003). See also Ia. Berman, "Stalinskaia konstitutsiia i izbiratel'naia sistema," *Sovetskoe gosudarstvo,* 1936, no. 5, 11.

16. *Istoriia sovetskoi konstitutsii,* 356–58; *Sovetskaia iustitsiia,* 1936, no. 19, 6.

17. *Sovetskaia iustitsiia,* 1936, no. 20, 1–4; no. 21, 3.

18. *Pravda,* November 30, 1936, 2.

19. As quoted in *Uchitel'skaia gazeta,* October 17, 1937, 1.

20. RGASPI, f. 477, op. 1, d. 14, l. 9.

21. For further discussion, see David L. Hoffmann, "European Modernity and Soviet Socialism," in *Russian Modernity: Politics, Knowledge, Practices,* ed. Hoffmann and Yanni Kotsonis (New York, 2000), 247.

22. On the shift throughout Europe from royal processions at which people were observers to mass parades and rituals in which people became participants, see Eric Hobsbawm and Terence Ranger, eds., *The Invention of Tradition* (Cambridge, 1983), 305.

23. *Izvestiia,* June 4, 1936, 1. In a similar fashion, plans for important buildings and monuments began to be exhibited at this time, allowing the public to write comments and give their suggestions for changes: Van Geldern, "Centre and the Periphery," 71.

24. Wimberg, "Socialism, Democratism, and Criticism," 315–16.

25. *Pravda,* November 30, 1936, 3. For further discussion, see Sheila Fitzpatrick, *Everyday Stalinism: Ordinary Life in Extraordinary Times: Soviet Russia in the 1930s* (New York, 1999), 178.

26. RGASPI, f. 17, op. 120, d. 232, ll. 85–87; Sarah Davies, *Popular Opinion in Stalin's Russia: Terror, Propaganda, and Dissent* (New York, 1997), 104–5.

27. GARF, f. 3316, op. 40, d. 14, ll. 32–33, 56–58; d. 18, ll. 155–57; op. 41, d. 52, l. 59.

28. GARF, f. 3316 s. ch., op. 64, d. 2005, l. 5; RGASPI, f. 78, op. 1, d. 833, l. 23; TsKhDMO, f. 1, op. 23, d. 1264, l. 13.

29. Sheila Fitzpatrick, *Stalin's Peasants: Resistance and Survival in the Russian Village after Collectivization* (New York, 1994), 280–85. J. Arch Getty links Party leaders' fear of participation in elections with the Politburo's decision to undertake the mass operations against "anti-Soviet elements." See Getty, "'Excesses are not Permitted': Mass Terror and Stalinist Governance in the Late 1930s," *The Russian Review,* 2002, no. 1, 124–26.

30. Karen Petrone, *Life Has Become More Joyous, Comrades: Celebrations in the Time of Stalin* (Bloomington, 2000), 176–79.

31. *XVIII s'ezd Vsesoiuznoi kommunisticheskoi partii (b): 10–21 marta 1939 g.: Stenograficheskii otchet* (Moscow, 1939), 26–27.

32. Both quoted in Sarah Davies, "The Leader Cult: Propaganda and Its Reception in Stalin's Russia," in *Politics, Society, and Stalinism in the USSR,* ed. John Channon (New York, 1998), 117.

33. As quoted ibid.,120.

34. James Heizer, "The Cult of Stalin, 1929–39" (dissertation, University of Kentucky, 1977), 177; Davies, "Leader Cult," 117.

35. As quoted in Regine Robin, "Stalinism and Popular Culture," in *The Culture of the Stalin Period,* ed. Hans Gunther (New York, 1990), 29.

36. Jeffrey Brooks, *Thank You, Comrade Stalin: Soviet Public Culture from Revolution to Cold War* (Princeton, 2000), xv. See also Lewis H. Siegelbaum, "'Dear Comrade, You Ask

What We Need': Socialist Paternalism and Soviet Rural 'Notables' in the Mid-1930s," in *Stalinism: New Directions,* ed. Sheila Fitzpatrick (New York, 2000).

37. *Labour in the Land of the Soviets: Stakhanovites in Conference* (Moscow, 1936); Lewis H. Siegelbaum, *Stakhanovism and the Politics of Productivity in the USSR, 1935–1941* (New York, 1988), 179–81. See also Choi Chatterjee, *Celebrating Women: Gender, Festival Culture, and Bolshevik Ideology, 1910–1939* (Pittsburgh, 2002), 144, on Party leaders' attendance at the 1936 International Women's Day Celebration at the Bolshoi Theater.

38. RGASPI, f. 17, op. 120, d. 146, l. 34.

39. *Letchiki: Sbornik rasskazov* (Moscow, 1938), 567. Katerina Clark has pointed out that such meetings were a ritual acting out of a primary theme of socialist realist novels, in which the heroes have great spontaneous energy but gain consciousness only from a mentor-parental figure: *The Soviet Novel: History as Ritual,* 2d ed. (Chicago, 1985), 143–44.

40. Chatterjee, *Celebrating Women,* 157–58.

41. Heizer, "Cult of Stalin," 164–73; *Pravda,* August 15, 1936, 1.

42. Heizer, "Cult of Stalin," 174.

43. Mary McIntosh, "The Family, Regulation and the Public Sphere," in *State and Society in Contemporary Britain: A Critical Introduction,* ed. Gregor McLennon et al. (Cambridge, 1984), 237. On the use of romanticized family metaphors in twentieth-century Japan, see John Dower, *War without Mercy: Race and Power in the Pacific War* (New York, 1986), 280–82.

44. Brooks, *Thank You, Comrade Stalin,* 69.

45. See Jan Plamper, "The Stalin Cult in the Visual Arts, 1929–1953" (dissertation, University of California, Berkeley, 2001).

46. Vera Dunham, *In Stalin's Time: Middleclass Values in Soviet Fiction* (New York, 1976), 26.

47. Davies, "Leader Cult," 122.

48. GARF, f. 5446, op. 18a, d. 2753, l. 15.

49. Sarah Davies, "'Us against Them': Social Identity in Soviet Russia, 1934–41," *The Russian Review,* 1997, no. 1; Davies, *Popular Opinion,* 171–77; F. M. Selivanova, comp., *Chastushki* (Moscow, 1990), 153.

50. See Katerina Clark, *Petersburg, Crucible of Cultural Revolution* (Cambridge, Mass., 1995).

51. Jeffrey Brooks, *When Russia Learned to Read: Literacy and Popular Literature, 1861–1917* (Princeton, 1985), 295–96; Svetlana Boym, *Common Places: Mythologies of Everyday Life in Russia* (Cambridge, 1994), 104–5.

52. Vladimir Papernyi, *Kul'tura "dva"* (Ann Arbor, 1985), 17–18, 31–46.

53. Sheila Fitzpatrick, "The *Lady Macbeth* Affair: Shostakovich and the Soviet Puritans," in Fitzpatrick, *The Cultural Front: Power and Culture in Revolutionary Russia* (Ithaca, 1992), 207.

54. Clark, *Petersburg,* 66–67.

55. Ibid., 286.

56. See Boris Groys, *The Total Art of Stalinism: Avant-Garde, Aesthetic Dictatorship, and Beyond* (Princeton, 1992).

57. Abram Tertz, *On Socialist Realism,* trans. Max Hayward (New York, 1960).

58. As quoted in Brooks, *Thank You, Comrade Stalin,* 108.

59. GARF, f. A-305, op. 1, d. 1, ll. 53–56; d. 3, ll. 1–14; Petrone, *Life Has Become More Joyous,* 113; Angela Brintlinger, *Writing a Usable Past: Russian Literary Culture, 1917–1937* (Evanston, 2000), 4–5.

60. As quoted in Clark, *Petersburg,* 157; Maurice Friedberg, *Russian Classics in Soviet Jackets* (New York, 1962), 12.

61. *Sovetskoe iskusstvo,* December 23, 1935, 1; Brintlinger, *Writing a Usable Past,* 4–5; Petrone, *Life Has Become More Joyous,* 115, 131–32.

62. *Sovetskoe iskusstvo,* November 11, 1935, 3. See also RGASPI, f. 17, op. 120, d. 127, l. 46.

63. RGASPI, f. 17, op. 120, d. 326, ll. 46–47.

64. *Partrabotnik* (Stalingrad), 1937, no. 1, 37.

65. Clark, *Petersburg,* 289.

66. *Profsoiuznyi rabotnik,* 1937, no. 3, 12.

67. *Partrabotnik* (Stalingrad), 1937, no. 1, 33–34. For further discussion, see Petrone, *Life Has Become More Joyous,* 117.

68. Petrone, *Life Has Become More Joyous,* 129.

69. *Sovetskoe iskusstvo,* November 17, 1935, 2.

70. RGASPI, f. 17, op. 120, d. 301, l. 7.

71. *Kul'turnaia rabota profsoiuzov,* 1938, no. 9, 51–58.

72. See the following section and Terry Martin, *The Affirmative Action Empire: Nations and Nationalism in the Soviet Union, 1923–1939* (Ithaca, 2001), 441, for further discussion.

73. See David Brandenberger, "Who Killed Pokrovskii (the Second Time)? The Prelude to the Denunciation of the Father of Soviet Marxist Historiography, January 1936," *Revolutionary Russia,* 1998, no. 1, 67–73.

74. D. L. Brandenberger and A. M. Dubrovsky, "'The People Need a Tsar': The Emergence of National Bolshevism as Stalinist Ideology, 1931–1941," *Europe-Asia Studies,* 1998 no. 5, 874–76, 880.

75. RGASPI, f. 17, op. 3, d. 998, l. 73. For further discussion of the film *Peter I* see Petrone, *Life Has Become More Joyous,* 159.

76. As quoted in Brandenberger and Dubrovsky, "'The People Need a Tsar,'" 880.

77. TsMAM, f. 1934, op. 1, d. 105, l. 130.

78. TsKhDMO, f. 1, op. 23, d. 1360, l. 49. See also *Komsomol'skii rabotnik,* 1940, no. 8, 1.

79. RGASPI, f. 89, op. 9, d. 99, ll. 1–3. After the Nazi invasion, Soviet education was even further geared toward patriotic historical teaching and military preparation; see RGASPI, f. 17, op. 126, d. 2, ll. 165–69.

80. See *Komsomol'skaia pravda,* October 18, 1934, and other newspaper citations in Nicholas S. Timasheff, *The Great Retreat: The Growth and Decline of Communism in Russia* (New York, 1946), 166.

81. TsKhDMO, f. 1, op. 23, d. 1389, l. 27. On Kalinin's advocacy of "Spartan training" to prepare citizens to defend Soviet socialism, see RGASPI, f. 78, op. 1, d. 824, l. 47.

82. RGASPI, f. 89, op. 9, d. 95, ll. 30–32.

83. See Brandenberger and Dubrovsky, "'The People Need a Tsar,'" 879.

84. As quoted in Martin, "Modernization or Neo-traditionalism? Ascribed Nationality and Soviet Primordialism," in Hoffmann and Kotsonis, *Russian Modernity,* 162.

85. Francine Hirsch, "Toward an Empire of Nations: Border-Making and the Formation of Soviet National Identities," *The Russian Review,* 2000, no. 2, 203.

86. Yuri Slezkine, "The USSR as a Communal Apartment, or How a Socialist State Promoted Ethnic Particularism," *Slavic Review,* 1994, no. 2; Ronald Grigor Suny, *The Revenge of the Past: Nationalism, Revolution, and the Collapse of the Soviet Union* (Stanford, 1993); Martin, *Affirmative Action Empire.*

87. *Pravda,* December 6, 1935, 3.

88. Martin, *Affirmative Action Empire,* 438–40.

89. Ibid., 444–45.

90. Ibid., 408–10. For further discussion, see Francine Hirsch, "The Soviet Union as a Work in Progress: Ethnographers and the Category of Nationality in the 1926, 1937, and 1939 Censuses," *Slavic Review,* 1997, no. 2; Hirsch writes that the consolidation of nationalities "was not a Thermidorian turn in nationality policy dictated by a sudden ideological shift, but a development that enabled the realization of a fundamental revolutionary goal: the creation of what Soviet officials envisioned as a 'modern' socialist multinational federation." 257.

91. I. Isakov, "O natsional'noi konsolidatsii Kazakhskogo naroda," *Bol'shevik Kazakhstana,* 1937, no. 5, 70, as quoted in Martin, *Affirmative Action Empire,* 447.

92. Martin, *Affirmative Action Empire,* 447.

93. Serhy Yekelchyk, "Stalinist Patriotism as Imperial Discourse: Reconciling the Ukrainian and Russian 'Heroic Pasts,' 1939–1945," *Kritika* 3, no. 1 (2002): 58–61.

94. Ibid., 57. See also RGASPI, f. 17, op. 3, d. 1005, ll. 79–80, on plans for the film *Bohdan Khmel'nyts'kyi.*

95. As quoted in Brooks, *Thank You, Comrade Stalin,* 94, 114.

96. Heizer, "Cult of Stalin," 177–78.

97. Petrone, *Life Has Become More Joyous,* 54.

98. Ibid., 23–37.

99. RGASPI, f. 17, op. 3, d. 987, l. 91. See also GARF, f. 3316 s. ch., op. 64, d. 1651, ll. 5–7, for the detailed plans behind a 1935 physical culture parade.

100. *Fizkul'tura i sport,* 1937, no. 13, 4–5.

101. F. J. Oinas, "The Political Uses and Themes of Folklore in the Soviet Union," in *Folklore, Nationalism, and Politics,* ed. Oinas (Columbus, 1972), 77–82; Timasheff, *Great Retreat,* 270–71; Martin, "Modernization or Neo-traditionalism?" 171.

102. Hobsbawm and Ranger, *Invention of Tradition,* 1–5; Hoffmann, "European Modernity," 247.

103. Stephen Kotkin, "Modern Times: The Soviet Union and the Interwar Conjuncture," *Kritika* 2, no. 1 (2001), 156. See also Greg Castillo, "Peoples at an Exhibition: Soviet Architecture and the National Question," in *Socialist Realism without Shores,* ed. Thomas Lahusen and Evgeny Dobrenko (Durham, 1997).

104. David L. Hoffmann, *Peasant Metropolis: Social Identities in Moscow, 1929–1941* (Ithaca, 1994), 182–89.

105. Oinas, "Political Uses and Themes of Folklore," 80.

106. Frank J. Miller, *Folklore for Stalin: Russian Folklore and Pseudofolklore of the Stalin Era* (Armonk, N.Y., 1990).

107. Martin, "Modernization or Neo-traditionalism?" 171.

108. See ibid., 167–69; Slezkine, "USSR as a Communal Apartment."

109. Terry Martin, "The Origins of Soviet Ethnic Cleansing," *Journal of Modern History,* 70, no. 4 (1998), 838.

110. As quoted in Amir Weiner, "Nature, Nurture, and Memory in a Socialist Utopia: Delineating the Soviet Socio-Ethnic Body in the Age of Socialism," *American Historical Review,* 1999, no. 4, 1129

111. Martin, "Origins of Soviet Ethnic Cleansing," 848–49, 851–84.

112. Attempts to categorize the population were the culmination of long-term pan-European developments in social science and state practices; in Russia, as elsewhere, the colonial context had been a crucial arena for the implementation of such classificatory schemes. See David L. Hoffmann and Peter Holquist, *Cultivating the Masses: The Modern Social State in Russia, 1914–1939* (Ithaca, forthcoming), chap. 5.

113. Francine Hirsch, "Race without the Practice of Racial Politics," *Slavic Review* 61, no. 1 (2002): 38.

114. Weiner, "Nature, Nurture, and Memory," 1133.

115. Hiroaki Kuromiya, *Freedom and Terror in the Donbas: A Ukrainian-Russian Borderland, 1870s–1990s* (New York, 1998), 231–35.

116. Martin, "Origins of Soviet Ethnic Cleansing," 855.

117. O. V. Khlevniuk, "The Objectives of the Great Terror, 1937–1938," in *Soviet History, 1917–1953: Essays in Honour of R. W. Davies,* ed. Julian Cooper, Maureen Perrie, and E. A. Rees (New York, 1995).

118. Weiner, "Nature, Nurture, and Memory." For interpretations that stress the social and political tensions behind the terror, see Gábor Tamas Rittersporn, *Stalinist Simplifications and Soviet Complications: Social Tensions and Political Conflicts in the USSR* (Philadelphia, 1991); J. Arch Getty, *The Origins of the Great Purges* (New York, 1985).

119. I. V. Stalin, "Itogi pervoi piatiletki" (January 7, 1933), in his *Sochineniia* (Moscow, 1946–52), 13:211–12.

120. See Amir Weiner, *Making Sense of the War: The Second World War and the Fate of the Bolshevik Revolution* (Princeton, 2001).

121. As quoted in David R. Shearer, "Crime and Social Disorder in Stalin's Russia: A Reassessment of the Great Retreat and the Origins of Mass Repression," *Cahiers du monde russe,* 1998, no. 1–2, 137–38. Shearer emphasizes that it was no coincidence that less class-based, more universal repression began shortly after the victory of socialism was declared in 1934.

122. A. Gertsenzon, "Klassovaia bor'ba i perezhitiki starogo byto," *Sovetskaia iustitsiia,* 1934, no. 2, 16; RGASPI, f. 17, op. 21, d. 741, ll. 297–98.

123. Stalin, "Itogi pervoi piatiletki," 207. For further discussion, see Kuromiya, *Freedom and Terror,* 184–85.

124. As quoted in Weiner, "Nature, Nurture, and Memory," 1121.

125. Shearer, "Crime and Social Disorder," 139.

126. TsKhDMO, f. 1, op. 23, d. 1072, ll. 15–16.

127. As quoted in Paul Hagenloh, "'Socially Harmful Elements' and the Great Terror," in Fitzpatrick, *Stalinism,* 299.

128. GARF, f. A-353, op. 10, d. 50, l. 24; Peter Solomon, *Soviet Criminal Justice,* 225. See also British Foreign Office, 371/19469, 190–91.

129. GARF, f. 8131 s. ch., op. 37, d. 48, ll. 185–86, 225; British Foreign Office, 371/19469, 190–91.

130. N. B. Lebina, "'Len'ka Panteleev—syshchikov groza' . . . : Prestupnost' v sovetskom obshchestve 20–30-kh godov," *Rodina,* 1995, no. 1, 63.

131. Shearer, "Crime and Social Disorder," 129–30. On homeless children, see Alan Ball, *And Now My Soul Is Hardened: Abandoned Children in Soviet Russia, 1918–1930* (Berkeley, 1994).

132. *Sobranie zakonov,* 1935, no. 19, art. 155, as reprinted in *O rassledovanii i rassmotrenii del o nesovershennoletnikh* (Moscow, 1937), 25.

133. TsMAM, f. 528, op. 1, d. 465, ll. 24–25.

134. Shearer, "Crime and Social Disorder," 120.

135. Stalin, "Itogi pervoi piatiletki," 209.

136. See Hiroaki Kuromiya, *Stalin's Industrial Revolution: Politics and Workers, 1928–1932* (New York, 1988).

137. Peter Solomon, *Soviet Criminal Justice,* 242.

138. TsMAM, f. 819, op. 2, dd. 14, 21.

139. *Pravda,* November 7, 1937, as quoted in Weiner, "Nature, Nurture, and Memory," 1122.

140. Brooks, *Thank You, Comrade Stalin,* 136.

141. *History of the Communist Party of the Soviet Union (Bolsheviks): Short Course* (New York, 1939), 346–48, as cited in Weiner, "Nature, Nurture, and Memory," 1131.

142. Hagenloh, "'Socially Harmful Elements,'" 291.
143. Shearer, "Crisis and Social Disorder," 134–36.
144. Hagenloh, "'Socially Harmful Elements,'" 287, 297–301.
145. TsKhSD, f. 89, op. 73, d. 50, ll. 1–2; Hoffmann and Holquist, *Cultivating the Masses,* chap. 5.
146. J. Arch Getty and Oleg V. Naumov, eds., *The Road to Terror: Stalin and the Self-Destruction of the Bolsheviks, 1932–1939* (New Haven, 1999), 518.
147. For further discussion, see Shearer, "Crisis and Social Disorder," 140–43.
148. See Hoffmann and Holquist, *Cultivating the Masses,* chap. 5.
149. A full discussion of the origins of the Great Terror lies outside the scope of this study. For further discussion, see Robert Conquest, *The Great Terror: A Reassessment* (New York, 1990); Getty, *Origins of the Great Purges;* Rittersporn, *Stalinist Simplifications and Soviet Complications.*
150. On Politburo quotas for the mass operations, see Khlevniuk, "Objectives of the Great Terror."

Conclusion

1. See, respectively, Richard Pipes, *A Concise History of the Russian Revolution* (New York, 1995); Moshe Lewin, "The Social Background of Stalinism," in Lewin, *The Making of the Soviet System: Essays in the Social History of Interwar Russia* (New York, 1985); Martin Malia, *The Soviet Tragedy: A History of Socialism in Russia, 1917–1991* (New York, 1994).
2. Catriona Kelly notes that many Soviet values, including a demonstrative appreciation of high culture, continue to be held by Russians even in the post-Soviet era. See Kelly, *Refining Russia: Advice Literature, Polite Culture, and Gender from Catherine to Yeltsin* (New York, 2001), 392–93.
3. See, for example, Sheila Fitzpatrick, *Everyday Stalinism: Ordinary Life in Extraordinary Times: Soviet Russia in the 1930s* (New York, 1999); Lynne Viola, *Peasant Rebels under Stalin: Collectivization and the Culture of Peasant Resistance* (New York, 1996); David L. Hoffmann, *Peasant Metropolis: Social Identities in Moscow, 1929–1941* (Ithaca, 1994).
4. See Anson Rabinbach, *The Human Motor: Energy, Fatigue, and the Origins of Modernity* (New York, 1990).
5. See Stephen Kotkin, "Modern Times: The Soviet Union and the Interwar Conjuncture," *Kritika* 2, no. 1 (2001), 162–64.

Bibliography

PRIMARY SOURCES

ARCHIVES

British Foreign Office

Russia—Correspondence, 1930–1940

Gosudarstvennyi Arkhiv Rossiiskoi Federatsii (GARF)

f. 305 Vsesoiuznyi Pushkinskii komitet
f. 353 Narkomiust RSFSR
f. 413 Narkomsobes RSFSR
f. 482 Narkomzdrav RSFSR
f. 1795 Vserossiiskoe popechitel′stvo ob okhrane materinstva i mladenchestva
f. 2306 Narkompros RSFSR
f. 3316 Tsentral′nyi ispolnitel′nyi komitet SSSR
f. 3931 Tsentral′nyi ispolnitel′nyi komitet vserossiiskogo soiuza pomoshchi uvech-nym voinam
f. 4085 Narkom raboche-krest′ianskoi inspektsii RSFSR
f. 4100 Ministerstvo truda Vremennogo Pravitel′stva
f. 4265 Tsentral′nyi statisticheskii komitet pri narodnom komissariate vnutrennykh del.
f. 5446 Sovnarkom
f. 5451 Vsesoiuznyi tsentral′nyi sovet profsoiuzov
f. 5465 Tsentral′nyi komitet profsoiuzov meditsinskikh rabotnikov
f. 5528 Tsentral′noe upravlenie sotsial′nogo strakhovaniia pri Narkomtruda
f. 5515 Narkomtrud SSSR
f. 6787 Ministerstvo gosudarstvennogo prizreniia Vremennogo Pravitel′stva

f. 7062   Soiuznyi sovet sotsial'nogo strakhovaniia pri Narkomtrude
f. 7576   Komitet po fizkul'ture i sportu
f. 7709   Tsentral'nyi komitet profsoiuza rabotnikov gosudarstvennykh uchrezhdenii
f. 7710   Tsentral'noe biuro fizkul'tury VTsSPS
f. 7897   Tsentral'nyi komitet profsoiuza kino-fotorabotnikov
f. 8009   Narkomzdrav SSSR
f. 8131   Prokuratura SSSR
f. 9226   Glavnaia gosudarstvennaia sanitarnaia inspektsiia pri Narkomzdrava
f. 9492   Narkomiust SSSR
f. 9505   Tsentral'nyi komitet sotsial'no-politicheskogo prosveshcheniia Vremennogo Pravitel'stva

Hoover Institution Archives

Boris Nikolaevsky Papers: correspondence, articles, documents

Public Record Office (PRO), U.K.

CAB   Cabinet
ED   Board of Education
HLG   Local Government Board
HO   Home Office
Inter-Departmental Commission on Physical Deterioration
LAB   Ministry of Labour
MH   Ministry of Health
MUN   Ministry of Munitions
RG   Registrar General
Royal Commission on Physical Training
WO   War Office

Rossiiskii Gosudarstvennyi Arkhiv Ekonomiki (RGAE)

f. 399   Sovet po izucheniiu proizvoditel'nykh sil pri Gosplane
f. 1562   Tsentral'noe statisticheskoe upravlenie
f. 4372   Gosplan
f. 7733   Ministerstvo finansov
f. 7995   Narkomtiazhprom SSSR

Rossiiskii Gosudarstvennyi Arkhiv Sotsial'noi i Politicheskoi Istorii (RGASPI)

f. 17   Tsentral'nyi komitet VKP(b)
f. 77   Lichnyi fond Zhdanova
f. 78   Lichnyi fond Kalinina
f. 85   Lichnyi fond Ordzhonikidze
f. 88   Lichnyi fond Shcherbakova
f. 89   Lichnyi fond Iaroslavskogo
f. 112   Politupravlenie Narkomzema

f. 477   Vosemnadtsatyi s″ezd VKP(b)
f. 558   Lichnyi fond Stalina
f. 607   Biuro po delam RSFSR pri TsK
f. 613   Tsentral'naia kontrol'naia komissiia
f. 616   Vysshaia shkola partiinykh organizatorov pri TsK
f. 619   Vysshaia shkola propagandistov
f. 623   Izdatel'stvo politicheskoi literatury TsK

Smolensk Party Archive

Tsentr Khraneniia Dokumentov Molodezhnykh Organizatsii (TsKhDMO)

f. 1   Tsentral'nyi komitet Komsomola

Tsentr Khraneniia Sovremmenoi Dokumentatsii (TsKhSD)

f. 6   Komissiia partiinogo kontrol'ia
f. 89   Sud kommunisticheskoi partii sovetskogo soiuza

Tsentral'nyi Gosudarstvennyi Arkhiv Obshchestvennykh Dvizhenii Moskvy (TsGAODM)

f. 3   Moskovskii oblastnoi komitet VKP(b)
f. 4   Moskovskii gorodskoi komitet VKP(b)
f. 69   Krasnopresnenskii raionnyi komitet VKP(b)
f. 80   Proletarskii raionnyi komitet VKP(b)
f. 262   Partiinaia organizatsiia Pervoi sittsenabivnoi fabriki
f. 429   Partiinaia organizatsiia zavoda Serp i Molot
f. 432   Partiinaia organizatsiia zavoda Dinamo (im. Kirova)
f. 433   Partiinaia organizatsiia Pervogo gosudarstvennogo avtomobil'nogo zavoda (im. Stalina)
f. 459   Partorganizatsiia kommunisticheskogo universiteta im. Sverdlova
f. 468   Partiinaia organizatsiia Elektrozavoda (im. Kuibysheva)
f. 1934   Partorganizatsiia ministerstva prosveshcheniia RSFSR
f. 4083   Partorganizatsiia raionnogo otdela narodnogo obrazovaniia frunzenskogo raiona

Tsentral'nyi Munitsipal'nyi Arkhiv Moskvy (TsMAM)

f. 126   Moskovskoe gosudarstvennoe upravlenie narodnogo-khoziaistvennogo ucheta Gosplana
f. 214   Moskovskii gorodskoi komitet soiuza rabochikh mashinostroenia
f. 493   Prezidium Moskovskoi gorodskoi kollegii advokatov
f. 528   Glavnoe upravlenie narodnogo obrazovaniia Mosgorispolkoma
f. 552   Glavnoe upravlenie zdravookhraneniia Mosgorispolkoma
f. 819   Moskovskyi gorodskoi sud Verkhovnogo suda RSFSR
f. 901   Narodnyi sud Leninskogo raiona
f. 1289   Moskovskii komitet raboche-krest'ianskoi inspeksii

f. 2399	Rabochii fakul'tet im. Kirova Narkomtiazhproma
f. 2429	Upravlenie militsii goroda Moskvy

PERIODICALS (PUBLISHED IN MOSCOW UNLESS OTHERWISE NOTED)

Amostroika	Newspaper of the Stalin automobile plant
Aviamotor	Newspaper of the Frunze aviation engine plant
Bednota	Newspaper for peasants published by the Communist Party
Bol'shevik	Journal of the Central Committee of the Communist Party
Bor'ba klassov	Journal of the Institute of History of the Academy of Sciences
Fizkul'tura i sport	Journal of the All-Union Committee on Physical Culture
Gigiena i sotsialisticheskoe zdravookhranenie	Journal of the Commissariat of Health, RSFSR
Gigiena i zdorov'e (rabochei i krest'ianskoi sem'i)	Journal of the Leningrad Branch of the Biomedical Institute
Gigiena truda i tekhnika bezopasnosti	Journal of the Central Council of Trade Unions
Gimnastika	Journal of the All-Union Committee on Physical Culture
Iunyi kommunist	Journal of the Central Committee of the Komsomol
Klub i revoliutsiia	Journal of the mass-culture sector of the Commissariat of Education
Komsomol'skaia pravda	Newspaper of the Central Committee of the Komsomol
Komsomol'skii rabotnik	Journal of the Central Committee of the Komsomol
Krest'ianskaia gazeta	Newspaper published for peasants by the Central Committee of the Communist Party
Kul'turnaia revoliutsiia	Journal on cultural work published by the All-Union Council of Trade Unions
Mody	Journal of the department stores of the Commissariat of Trade
Molodaia gvardiia	Journal of the Central Committee of the Komsomol
Novyi proletarii	Newspaper for newly literate workers, published by the All-Union Council of Trade Unions
Obshchestvennitsa	Journal for socially active women published by the Commissariat of Heavy Industry
Obshchestvennoe pitanie	Journal of the Commissariat of Trade
Ogonek	Popular journal published by the journal-newspaper conglomerate
Organizatsiia truda	Journal of the Central Institute of Labor
Partiinoe stroitel'stvo	Journal of the Central Committee of the Communist Party
Partorganizator (Leningrad)	Journal of the Leningrad Party Committee
Partrabotnik (Gorky)	Journal of the Gorky Oblast Party Committee
Partrabotnik (Sverdlovsk)	Journal of the Sverdlovsk Oblast Party Committee
Pravda	Newspaper copublished by the Moscow Committee and the Central Committee of the Communist Party
Rabotnitsa	Journal for female workers published by the Communist Party
Sobranie zakonov i rasproiazhenii	Journal of the Council of People's Commissars
Sotsialisticheskaia zakonnost'	Journal of the Procuracy of the USSR
Sovetskaia iustitsiia	Journal of the Commissariat of Justice
Sovetskoe gosudarstvo i pravo	Journal of the Institute of State and Law of the Academy of Sciences
Sovetskoe iskusstvo	Newspaper of the administration of visual arts of the RSFSR

Sputnik kommunista Journal of the Moscow Oblast Committee of the Communist
  Party
Sudebnaia praktika RSFSR Journal of the Commissariat of Justice, RSFSR
Trud Newspaper of the All-Union Council of Trade Unions
Uchitel'skaia gazeta Newspaper of the Commissariat of Education
Voprosy profdvizheniia Journal of the All-Union Council of Trade Unions
Za kul'turnyi univermag Bulletin of the Commissariat of Trade
Za novyi byt Journal of the Moscow Oblast Department of Health

OTHER PRIMARY PUBLICATIONS

Aliakrinskii, A. I. *Brak, sem'ia i opeka: Prakticheskoe rukovodstvo dlia organov ZAGS*. Moscow,
  1930.
Amfiteatrov, G. "Proekt konstitutsii SSSR i grazhdanskii kodeks sotsialisticheskogo ob-
  shchestva." *Sovetskoe gosudarstvo*, 1936, no. 4.
Arkin, E. A. *Pis'ma o vospitanii detei*. Izd. 3, vyp. 1. Moscow, 1936.
Arzhilovskii, Andrei. "Dnevnik 36–37-ogo godov." *Ural*, 1992, no. 3.
Bachelis, I., and S. Tregub, eds. *Za liubov' i schast'e v nashei sem'e*. Moscow, 1936.
Balabanov, L. (L. Tol'm). "Zateriannaia tsennost'." In *Kakim dolzhen byt' kommunist:
  Sbornik*, ed. E. Iaroslavskii. Moscow/Leningrad, 1926.
Berman, Ia. "Stalinskaia konstitutsiia i izbiratel'naia sistema." *Sovetskoe gosudarstvo*, 1936,
  no. 5.
Bukharin, N. "Vospitanie smeny: Kak dolzhen vesti sebia komsomolets." In *Komsomol'skii
  byt: Sbornik*, ed. I. Razin. Moscow/Leningrad, 1927.
Busygin, Aleksandr Kh. *Moia zhizn' i moia rabota*. Leningrad, 1935.
Fridlianskii, Ia. "Za samogo kul'turnogo inzhenera samogo kul'turnogo gosudarstva v
  mire." *Voprosy profdvizheniia*, October 1935.
Garshtein, S. *Za zdorovyi kul'turnyi byt*. Moscow, 1932.
Gertsenzon, A. "Klassovaia bor'ba i perezhitki starogo byta." *Sovetskaia iustitsiia*, 1934,
  no. 2.
Gimnastika na predpriiatiak i proizvoditel'nost' truda. Moscow, 1936.
Gofshtein, A. S. "Ratsionalizatsiia materinstva." *Vrachebnoe delo*, 1927, no. 19.
*Gosudarstvennoe upravlenie: Kodifitsirovannyi sbornik zakonodatel'stva RSFSR na 1 ianvariia
  1935 goda*. Moscow, 1934.
Govoriat stroiteli sotsializma: Vospominaniia uchastnikov sotsialisticheskogo stroitel'stva v SSSR.
  Moscow, 1959.
Gudov, Ivan. *Sud'ba rabochego*. Moscow, 1974.
History of the Communist Party of the Soviet Union (Bolsheviks): Short Course. New York, 1939.
Iaroslavskii, E. *Moral i byt proletariata v perekhodnyi period*. Leningrad, 1926.
———. "O partetike." In *Partiinaia etika: Dokumenty i materialy diskussii 20-kh godov*. Ed.
  M. A. Makarevich. Moscow, 1989.
———, ed. *Kakim dolzhen byt' kommunist: Sbornik*. Moscow/Leningrad, 1926.
Industrializatsiia SSSR: Dokumenty i materialy, vol 3. Moscow, 1971.
Istoriia sovetskoi konstitutsii: Sbornik dokumentov, 1917–1957. Moscow, 1957.
Kanevskii, A. E. *Sud nad Annoi Gorbovoi, po obvineniiu v proizvodstve sebe vykidysha (aborta)*.
  Odessa, 1925.

Kaplun, S. I. *Obshchaia gigiena truda*. Moscow/Leningrad, 1940.

Kareva, M. P. *Sotsialisticheskoe pravo i sotsialisticheskaia nravstvennost'*. Moscow, 1940.

Kataev, Valentin. *Time, Forward*. Trans. Charles Malamuth. Bloomington, 1976.

Kats, Ia. "Tekuchest' rabochei sily v krupnoi promyshlennosti." *Plan*, 1937, no. 9.

Kingsbury, Susan M., and Mildred Fairchild. *Factory, Family, and Woman in the Soviet Union*. New York, 1935.

Kollontai, Alexandra. *Alexandra Kollontai: Selected Articles and Speeches*. Ed. I. M. Dazhina et al. Trans. Cynthia Carlile. Moscow, 1984.

——. *Sem'ia i kommunisticheskoe gosudarstvo*. Moscow, 1918.

——. *Trud zhenshchiny v evoliutsii khoziaistva*. Moscow/Petrograd, 1923.

Kornakovskii, I. L., ed. *Iz istorii razvitiia metallurgicheskoi promyshlennosti Moskvy, 1883–1932 gg: Dokumenty i materialy*. Moscow, 1981.

Kosarev, A. *Otchet TsK VLKSM desiatomy vsesoiuznomy s"ezdu Leninskogo Komsomola*. Moscow, 1936.

——, ed. *Istoriia metro Moskvy: Rasskazy stroitelei metro*. Moscow, 1935.

Kovalev, K. N. *Voprosy pola, polovogo vospitaniia, braka i sem'i*. Moscow, 1931.

Kravchenko, Victor. *I Chose Freedom*. New York, 1946.

Krupskaia, N. *Kakim dolzhen byt' kommunist*. Moscow, 1933.

Krylenko, N. V. "Ob izmeneniiakh i dopolneniiakh kodeksov RSFSR." *Sovetskaia iustitsiia*, 1936, no. 7.

——. *Stalinskaia konstitutsiia v voprosakh i otvetakh*. 2d ed. Moscow, 1937.

Kulikov, F. "Za novogo cheloveka: Iz dnevnika kul'tarmeitsa." *Na rubezhe*, 1935, no. 10.

Kvashonkin, A. V., et al., eds. *Bol'shevistskoe rukovodstvo: Perepiska*. Moscow, 1996.

Labour in the Land of the Soviets: Stakhanovites in Conference. Moscow, 1936.

Lapitskaia, S. *Byt rabochikh Trekhgornoi manufaktury*. Moscow, 1935.

Lekarenko, D., and V. A. Nevskii. "Chitatel'skii spros rabochei molodezhi." *Krasnyi bibliotekar'*, 1935, no. 6.

Lenin, V. I. "Zadachi Soiuzov Molodezhi." In *O kommunisticheskoi nravstvennosti*. Moscow, 1961.

Letchiki: Sbornik rasskazov. Moscow, 1938.

Liadov, M. N. *Voprosy byta*. Moscow, 1925.

Ludendorff, General. *The General Staff and Its Problems: The History of the Relations between the High Command and the German Imperial Government as Revealed by Official Documents*. Trans. F. A. Holt. New York, 1920.

Makarenko, A. *A Book for Parents*. Trans. Robert Daglish. Moscow, n.d.

——. *Problems of Soviet School Education*. Trans. O. Shartse. Moscow, 1965.

Makarevich, M. A., ed. *Partiinaia etika: Dokumenty i materialy diskussii 20-kh godov*. Moscow, 1989.

Malinovskii, M. S., and E. M. Shvartzman. *Gigiena zhenshchiny*. 3d ed. Moscow/Leningrad, 1935.

Meierhold, Vsevolod. "The Actor of the Future and Biomechanics." In *Meierhold on Theater*, ed. Edward Brown. New York, 1969.

Mol'kov, A. V., ed. *Shkol'naia gigiena*. Moscow/Leningrad, 1937.

Mol'kov, A. V., and N. A. Semashko, eds. *Sotsial'naia gigiena: Rukovodstvo dlia studentov-medikov*. Moscow/Leningrad, 1927.

Neznamov, M. "O zateriannoi tsennosti." *Kakim dolzhen byt' kommunist: Sbornik.* Ed. E. Iaroslavskii. Moscow/Leningrad, 1926.

O rassledovanii i rassmotrenii del o nesovershennoletnikh. Moscow, 1937.

Panforov, F. *The Village Bruski.* Moscow, 1937.

Piil'man, Gans. *Byt v kolkhozakh.* Moscow/Leningrad, 1923.

Pindiur, Iv. "Kak my rastim i vospityvaem partiinye kadry." *Partrabotnik* (Gorky), 1936, no. 5/6.

Pramnek, E. K. *Kak rabotat' i rukovodit' (iz opyta partraboty).* Gorky, 1933.

Resoliutsii III Vsesoiuznogo soveshchaniia po okhane materinstva i mladenchestva. Moscow, 1926.

Razin, I., ed. *Komsomol'skii byt: Sbornik.* Moscow/Leningrad, 1927.

Sbornik deistvuiushchikh uzakonenii i rasporiazhenii pravitel'stva soiuza SSSR i pravitel'stva RS-FSR, postanovlenii detkomissii pri VTsIK i vedomstvennykh rasporiazhenii. Moscow, 1929.

Sbornik vazhneishikh postanovlenii po trudu. Moscow, 1935.

Selivanova, F. M., comp. *Chastushki.* Moscow, 1990.

Semashko, N. A. *Iskusstvo odevat'sia.* Moscow/Leningrad, 1927.

——. *Novyi byt i polovoi vopros.* Moscow/Leningrad, 1926.

——. "Zamechatel'nyi zakon (o zapreshchenii aborta)." *Front nauki i tekhniki,* 1936, no. 7.

XVII s'ezd VKP(b), 26 ianvar'–10 fevral' 1934 g.: Stenograficheskii otchet. Moscow, 1934.

Shtakov, E. "O vospitanii kommunista." *Partrabotnik* (Gorky), 1936, no. 1.

Shveitser, V., and A. Ul'rikh. *Zheny komandirov tiazheloi promyshlennosti.* Moscow, 1936.

Smith, Andrew. *I Was a Soviet Worker.* New York, 1936.

Sol'ts, A. A. "Iz otcheta tsentral'noi kontrol'noi komissii na XI s''ezde RKP(b)." In *Partiinaia etika: Dokumenty i materialy diskussii 20–kh godov,* ed. M. A. Makarevich. Moscow, 1989.

Stalin, I. V. *O Lenine.* Moscow, 1937.

——. *Sochineniia.* 13 vols. Moscow, 1946–52.

——. *Sochineniia.* Vol. 1. Stanford, 1967.

Stratonitskii, A. *Voprosy byta v Komsomole.* Moscow/Leningrad, 1926.

Strumilin, S. G. "K probleme rozhdaemosti v rabochei srede." In *Problemy ekonomiki truda.* Moscow, 1957.

Temperley, H. W. V., ed. *A History of the Peace Conference of Paris,* vol. 3. London, 1920.

Toporkov, A. K. *Kak stat' kul'turnym.* Moscow, 1929.

Trotskii, L. *Voprosy byta: Epokha "kul'turnichestva" i ee zadachi.* 3d ed. Moscow, 1925.

Trotsky, Leon. *The Revolution Betrayed: What Is the Soviet Union and Where Is It Going?* Trans. Max Eastman. 5th ed. New York, 1972 [1937].

Trud v SSSR: Ekonomiko-statisticheskii spravochnik. Moscow, 1932.

Tsetkin, K. "Lenin o morale i voprosakh pola." In *Komsomol'skii byt: Sbornik,* ed. O. Razin. Moscow/Leningrad, 1927.

Vasilevskaia, V. "Kak chitaiut knigu malogramotnye." *Krasnyi bibliotekar',* 1931, no.5/6.

Vol'fson, S. Ia. *Sotsiologiia braka i sem'i.* Minsk, 1929.

XVIII S''ezd Vsesoiuznoi kommunisticheskoi partii (b): 10–21 marta 1939 g.: Stenograficheskii otchet. Moscow, 1939.

Vsesoiuznoe soveshchanie zhen khoziaistvennikov i inzhenerno-tekhnicheskikh rabotnikov tiazheloi promyshlennosti: Stenograficheskii otchet. Moscow, 1936.

Za bol'shevistskii stil'. Moscow, 1937.

Zak, L. M., and S. S. Zimina, eds. *Gor'kii i sozdanie istorii fabrik i zavodov: Sbornik doku-mentov.* Moscow, 1959.

Za kommunicheskie kadry. Leningrad, 1931.

Zalkind, A. B., "Etika, byt i molodezh." In *Komsomol'skii byt: Sbornik,* ed. I. Razin. Moscow/Leningrad, 1927.

——, ed. *Polovoi vopros v usloviiakh sovetskoi obshchestvennosti: Sbornik statei.* Leningrad, 1926.

——, ed. *Psikhonevrologicheskie nauki v SSSR: Materialy I Vsesoiuznogo s"ezda po izucheniiu povedeniia cheloveka.* Moscow, 1930.

Za zdorovyi kul'turnyi byt: Sbornik statei. Moscow/Leningrad, 1931.

Zenzinov, V. *Vstrecha s Rossiei: Kak i chem zhivut v sovetskom soiuze: pis'ma v Krasnuiu armiiu 1939–1940.* New York, 1944.

Zheny inzhenerov i tekhnikov. Moscow, 1936.

FILMS

East Side Story. Dir. Dana Ranga. Germany, 1997.

Traktoristy. Dir. Gleb Aleinikov and Igor' Aleinikov. USSR, 1939.

Tsirk. Dir. Grigorii V. Aleksandrov. USSR, 1936.

Veselye rebiata. Dir. Grigorii V. Aleksandrov. USSR, 1934.

SECONDARY SOURCES

Alexopoulos, Golfo. *Stalin's Outcasts: Aliens, Citizens, and the Soviet State, 1926–1936.* Ithaca, 2003.

Anderson, Barbara, Ansley Coale, and Erna Harm. *Human Fertility in Russia since the Nineteenth Century.* Princeton, 1979.

Attwood, Lynne. *Creating the New Soviet Woman: Women's Magazines as Engineers of Female Identity, 1922–1953.* New York, 1999.

Bailes, Kendall E. *Technology and Society under Lenin and Stalin.* Princeton, 1978.

Ball, Alan M. *And Now My Soul Is Hardened: Abandoned Children in Soviet Russia, 1918–1930.* Berkeley, 1994.

Barnes, David S. *The Making of a Social Disease: Tuberculosis in Nineteenth-Century France.* Berkeley, 1995.

Bauman, Zygmunt. *Modernity and the Holocaust.* Ithaca, 1991.

Bernstein, Frances Lee. "What Everyone Should Know about Sex: Gender, Sexual Enlightenment, and the Politics of Health in Revolutionary Russia, 1918–1931." Dissertation, Columbia University, 1997.

Bock, Gisela. "Antinatalism, Maternity, and Paternity in National Socialist Racism." In *Maternity and Gender Policies: Women and the Rise of the European Welfare State, 1880s–1950s,* ed. Gisela Bock and Pat Thane. New York, 1991.

Bock, Gisela, and Pat Thane, eds. *Maternity and Gender Policies: Women and the Rise of the European Welfare State, 1880s-1950s.* New York, 1991.

Bonnell, Victoria E. *Iconography of Power: Soviet Political Posters under Lenin and Stalin.* Berkeley, 1997.

Bourdieu, Pierre. *Distinction: A Social Critique of the Judgment of Taste.* Trans. Richard Nice. Cambridge, 1984.
——. *Outline of a Theory of Practice.* New York, 1977.
Boym, Svetlana. *Common Places: Mythologies of Everyday Life in Russia.* Cambridge, 1994.
Brandenberger, D. L., and A. M. Dubrovsky. "'The People Need a Tsar': The Emergence of National Bolshevism as Stalinist Ideology, 1931–1941." *Europe-Asia Studies,* 1998, no. 5.
Brandenberger, David. "Who Killed Pokrovskii (the Second Time)? The Prelude to the Denunciation of the Father of Soviet Marxist Historiography, January 1936." *Revolutionary Russia,* 1998, no. 1.
Brintlinger, Angela. *Writing a Usable Past: Russian Literary Culture, 1917–1937.* Evanston, 2000.
Brooks, Jeffrey. "Public Identities in *Pravda* during the 1920s." In *New Directions in Soviet History,* ed. Stephen White. New York, 1992.
——. *Thank You, Comrade Stalin: Soviet Public Culture from Revolution to Cold War.* Princeton, 2000.
——. *When Russia Learned to Read: Literacy and Popular Literature, 1861–1917.* Princeton, 1985.
Brovkin, Vladimir. *Russia after Lenin: Politics, Culture, and Society, 1921–1929.* New York, 1998.
Brower, Daniel R. *Training the Nihilists: Education and Radicalism in Tsarist Russia.* Ithaca, 1975.
Buckley, Mary. "Categorising Resistance to Rural Stakhanovism." In *Politics and Society under the Bolsheviks: Selected Papers from the Fifth World Congress of Central and Eastern European Studies,* ed. Kevin McDermott and John Morison. New York, 1999.
——. "The Untold Story of *Obshchestvennitsa* in the 1930's: A Research Note." Paper presented at the World Slavic Congress, 1995.
Cassidy, Julie A. *The Enemy on Trial: Early Soviet Courts on Stage and Screen.* De Kalb, Ill., 2000.
Chatterjee, Choi. *Celebrating Women: Gender, Festival Culture, and Bolshevik Ideology, 1910–1939.* Pittsburgh, 2002.
Chernyshevsky, Nikolai. *What Is to Be Done?* Trans. Michael R. Katz. Ithaca, 1989.
Chevalier, Louis. *Laboring Classes and Dangerous Classes in Paris during the First Half of the Nineteenth Century.* Trans. Frank Jellinek. New York, 1973.
Clark, Katerina. *Petersburg, Crucible of Cultural Revolution.* Cambridge, Mass., 1995.
——. *The Soviet Novel: History as Ritual.* 2d ed. Chicago, 1985.
Clark, Toby. "The 'New Man's' Body: A Motif in Early Soviet Culture." In *Art of the Soviets: Painting, Sculpture, and Architecture in a One-Party State, 1917–1992,* ed. Matthew Cullerne Bown and Brandon Taylor. New York, 1993.
Clements, Barbara Evans. *Bolshevik Feminist: The Life of Aleksandra Kollontai.* Bloomington, 1979.
——. "The Effects of the Civil War on Women and Family Relations." In *Party, State, and Society in the Russian Civil War: Exploration in Social History,* ed. Diane P. Koenker et al. Bloomington, 1989.
Conquest, Robert. *The Great Terror: A Reassessment.* Philadelphia, 1991.
David-Fox, Michael. *Revolution of the Mind: Higher Learning among the Bolsheviks.* Ithaca, 1997.

——. "What Is Cultural Revolution?" *The Russian Review,* 1999, no. 2.

Davies, R. W. *Crisis and Progress in the Soviet Economy, 1931–1933.* London, 1996.

——. *The Soviet Economy in Turmoil.* Cambridge, 1989.

Davies, Sarah. "The Leader Cult: Propaganda and Its Reception in Stalin's Russia." In *Politics, Society, and Stalinism in the USSR,* ed. John Channon. New York, 1998.

——. *Popular Opinion in Stalin's Russia: Terror, Propaganda, and Dissent.* New York, 1997.

——. "'Us against Them': Social Identity in Soviet Russia, 1934–41." *The Russian Review,* 1997, no. 1.

De George, Richard T. *Soviet Ethics and Morality.* Ann Arbor, 1969.

de Grazia, Victoria. *How Fascism Ruled Women: Italy, 1922–1945.* Berkeley, 1992.

——. "Nationalizing Women: The Competition between Fascist and Commercial Cultural Models in Mussolini's Italy." In *The Sex of Things: Gender and Consumption in Historical Perspective,* ed. Victoria de Grazia and Ellen Furlough. Berkeley, 1996.

Domansky, Elisabeth. "Militarization and Reproduction in World War I Germany." In *Society, Culture, and the State in Germany, 1870–1930,* ed. Geoff Eley. Ann Arbor, 1996.

Donzelot, Jacques. *The Policing of Families.* Trans. Robert Hurley. New York, 1979.

Dower, John. *War without Mercy: Race and Power in the Pacific War.* New York, 1986.

Drobizhev, V. Z. *V istokov sovetskoi demografii.* Moscow, 1987.

Dunham, Vera S. *In Stalin's Time: Middleclass Values in Soviet Fiction.* New York, 1976.

Elias, Norbert. *The Civilizing Process: Sociogenetic and Psychogenetic Investigations.* Trans. Edmund Jephcott. Rev. ed. Malden, Mass., 2000.

Engelstein, Laura. *The Keys to Happiness: Sex and the Search for Modernity in Fin-de-Siècle Russia.* Ithaca, 1992.

——. "Soviet Policy toward Male Homosexuality: Its Origins and Historical Roots." *Journal of Homosexuality* 25, no. 3/4 (1994).

Ewing, E. Thomas. "Stalinism at Work: Teacher Certification (1936–39) and Soviet Power." *The Russian Review* 57, no. 2 (April 1998).

——. *The Teachers of Stalinism: Policy, Practices, and Power in Soviet Schools of the 1930s.* New York, 2002.

Filtzer, Donald. *Soviet Workers and Stalinist Industrialization: The Formation of Modern Soviet Industrial Relations, 1928–1941.* New York, 1986.

Fitzpatrick, Sheila. *The Cultural Front: Power and Culture in Revolutionary Russia.* Ithaca, 1992.

——. *Everyday Stalinism: Ordinary Life in Extraordinary Times: Soviet Russia in the 1930s.* New York, 1999.

——. "'Middle-Class Values' and Social Life in the 1930s." In *Soviet Culture and Society,* ed. Richard Sheldon and Tony L. Thompson. Boulder, Colo., 1989.

——. *Stalin's Peasants: Resistance and Survival in the Russian Village after Collectivization.* New York, 1994.

——, ed. *Stalinism: New Directions.* New York, 2000.

Foucault, Michel. *The History of Sexuality.* Trans. Robert Hurley. New York, 1980.

Friedberg, Maurice. *Russian Classics in Soviet Jackets.* New York, 1962.

Garon, Sheldon G. *Molding Japanese Minds: The State in Everyday Life.* Princeton, 1997.

Gasiorowska, Xenia. *Women in Soviet Fiction.* Madison, Wis., 1968.

Getty, J. Arch. "'Excesses Are Not Permitted': Mass Terror and Stalinist Governance in the Late 1930s." *The Russian Review,* 2002, no. 1.

——. *The Origins of the Great Purges*. New York, 1985.

Getty, J. Arch, and Oleg V. Naumov, eds. *The Road to Terror: Stalin and the Self-Destruction of the Bolsheviks, 1932–1939*. New Haven, 1999.

Giddens, Anthony. *The Consequences of Modernity*. Stanford, 1990.

Ginzburg, Eugenia Semyonovna. *Journey into the Whirlwind*. Trans. Paul Stevenson and Max Hayward. New York, 1967.

Goldman, Wendy Z. "Babas at the Bench: Gender Conflict in Soviet Industry in the 1930s." In *Women in the Stalin Era*, ed. Melanie Ilic. New York, 2001.

——. *Women, the State, and Revolution: Soviet Family Policy and Social Life, 1917–1936*. New York, 1993.

Gordon, L. A., and E. V. Klopov. *Chto eto bylo? Razmyshleniia o predposylkakh i itogakh togo, chto sluchilos' s nami v 30–40e gody*. Moscow, 1989.

Gorsuch, Anne E. *Youth in Revolutionary Russia: Enthusiasts, Bohemians, Delinquents*. Bloomington, 2000.

Green, Harvey. *Fit for America: Health, Fitness, Sport, and American Society*. New York, 1986.

Grossmann, Atina. "The New Woman and the Rationalization of Sexuality in Weimar Germany." In *Powers of Desire: The Politics of Sexuality*, ed. Ann Snitow, Christine Stansell, and Sharon Thompson. New York, 1983.

Groys, Boris. *The Total Art of Stalinism: Avant-Garde, Aesthetic Dictatorship, and Beyond*. Princeton, 1992.

Gunther, Hans, ed. *The Culture of the Stalin Period*. New York, 1990.

Hagenloh, Paul M. "'Socially Harmful Elements' and the Great Terror." In *Stalinism: New Directions*, ed. Sheila Fitzpatrick. New York, 2000.

Halfin, Igal. *From Darkness to Light: Class, Consciousness, and Salvation in Revolutionary Russia*. Pittsburgh, 2000.

Hanson, Stephen E. *Time and Revolution: Marxism and the Design of Soviet Institutions*. Chapel Hill, 1997.

Harris, James R. "The Growth of the Gulag: Forced Labor in the Urals Region, 1929–1931." *The Russian Review*, 1997, no. 2.

——. "The Purging of Local Cliques in the Urals Region, 1936–1937." In *Stalinism: New Directions*, ed. Sheila Fitzpatrick. New York, 2000.

Healey, Dan. *Homosexual Desire in Revolutionary Russia: The Regulation of Sexual and Gender Dissent*. Chicago, 2001.

Heizer, James. "The Cult of Stalin, 1929–1939." Dissertation, University of Kentucky, 1977.

Hellbeck, Jochen. "Self-Realization in the Stalinist System: Two Soviet Diaries of the 1930s." In *Russian Modernity: Politics, Knowledge, Practices*, ed. David L. Hoffmann and Yanni Kotsonis. New York, 2000.

——. "Working, Struggling, Becoming: Stalin-Era Autobiographical Texts." *The Russian Review* 60, no. 3 (2001).

Hessler, Julie. "Cultured Trade: The Stalinist Turn toward Consumerism." In *Stalinism: New Directions*, ed. Sheila Fitzpatrick. New York, 2000.

Hirsch, Francine. "Race without the Practice of Racial Politics." *Slavic Review* 61, no. 1 (2002).

——. "The Soviet Union as a Work in Progress: Ethnographers and the Category of Nationality in the 1926, 1937, and 1939 Censuses." *Slavic Review* 1997, no. 2.

——. "Toward an Empire of Nations: Border-Making and the Formation Of Soviet National Identities." *The Russian Review* 61, no. 2 (2000).

Hirschfield, Magnus. *The Sexual History of the World War.* New York, 1941.

Hobsbawm, Eric. *The Age of Extremes: A History of the World, 1914–1991.* New York, 1996.

Hobsbawm, Eric, and Terence Ranger, eds. *The Invention of Tradition.* Cambridge, 1983.

Hoffmann, David L. "European Modernity and Soviet Socialism." In *Russian Modernity: Politics, Knowledge, Practices,* ed. David L. Hoffmann and Yanni Kotsonis. New York, 2000.

——. *Peasant Metropolis: Social Identities in Moscow, 1929–1941.* Ithaca, 1994.

Hoffmann, David L., and Peter Holquist. *Cultivating the Masses: The Modern Social State in Russia, 1914–1939.* Ithaca, forthcoming.

Hoffmann, David L., and Yanni Kotsonis, eds. *Russian Modernity: Politics, Knowledge, Practices.* New York, 2000.

Holmes, Larry E. *The Schoolhouse and the Kremlin: Reforming Education in Soviet Russia, 1917–1931.* Bloomington, 1991.

Horn, David G. *Social Bodies: Science, Reproduction, and Italian Modernity.* Princeton, 1994.

Hull, Isabel V. *Sexuality, State, and Civil Society in Germany, 1700–1815.* Ithaca, 1996.

Husband, William. *"Godless Communists": Atheism and Society in Soviet Russia, 1917–1932.* De Kalb, Ill., 2000.

Hyer, Janet. "Managing the Female Organism: Doctors and the Medicalization of Women's Paid Work in Soviet Russia during the 1920s." In *Women in Russia and Ukraine,* ed. Rosalind Marsh. New York, 1996.

Ilic, Melanie. *Women Workers in the Soviet Interwar Economy: From "Protection" to "Equality."* New York, 1999.

——, ed. *Women in the Stalin Era.* New York, 2001.

Ipsen, Carl. *Dictating Demography: The Problem of Population in Fascist Italy.* New York, 1996.

Izmeneniia sotsial'noi struktury sovetskogo obshchestva, 1921–seredina '30-kh godov. Moscow, 1979.

Kelly, Catriona. *"Kul'turnost'* in the Soviet Union: Ideal and Reality." In *Reinterpreting Russia,* ed. Geoffrey Hosking and Robert Service. London, 1999.

——. *Refining Russia: Advice Literature, Polite Culture, and Gender from Catherine to Yeltsin.* New York, 2001.

Kharkhordin, Oleg. *The Collective and the Individual in Russia: A Study of Practices.* Berkeley, 1999.

Khillig, Getts. "Kak A. S. Makarenko otkryl sem'iu: K istorii sozdaniia i vozdeistviia *Kniga dlia roditelei* 1936–1939 gg." *Cahiers du monde russe et soviétique* 33 (1992), no. 1.

Khlevniuk, O. V. "26 iiulia 1940 goda: Illiuzii i real'nosti administrirovaniia." *Kommunist,* 1989, no. 9.

——. "1937 god: Protivodeistvie repressiam." *Kommunist,* 1989, no. 18.

——. *1937-i: Stalin, NKVD, i sovetskoe obshchestvo.* Moscow, 1992.

——. "Izmenenie kul'turnogo oblika gorodskikh rabochikh SSSR, 1926–1939." Dissertation, Institute of History, USSR, 1986.

——. "The Objectives of the Great Terror, 1937–1938." In *Soviet History, 1917–1953: Essays in Honour of R. W. Davies,* ed. Julian Cooper, Maureen Perrie, and E. A. Rees. New York, 1995.

——. *Udarniki pervoi piatiletki.* Moscow, 1989.

Kimerling, Elise. "Civil Rights and Social Policy in Soviet Russia, 1918–1936." *The Russian Review,* 1982, no. 1.

Kon, Igor. "Sexual Minorities." In *Sex and Russian Society,* ed. Igor Kon and James Riordan. Bloomington, 1993.

Koonz, Claudia. *Mothers in the Fatherland: Women, the Family, and Nazi Politics.* New York, 1987.

Kopp, Anatole. *Town and Revolution: Soviet Architecture and City Planning, 1917–1935.* Trans. Thomas E. Burton. New York, 1970.

Kotkin, Stephen. *Magnetic Mountain: Stalinism as a Civilization.* Berkeley, 1995.

——. "Modern Times: The Soviet Union and the Interwar Conjuncture." *Kritika* 2, no. 1 (2001).

Kozlova, Nataliia. "Krest'ianskii syn." *Sotsiologischeskie issledovaniia,* 1994, no. 6.

——. "Zalozhniki slova." *Sotsiologischeskie issledovaniia,* 1995, no. 9/10.

Kuromiya, Hiroaki. *Freedom and Terror in the Donbas: A Ukrainian-Russian Borderland, 1870s–1990s.* New York, 1998.

——. *Stalin's Industrial Revolution: Politics and Workers, 1928–1932.* New York, 1988.

Lampert, Nick, and Gábor Tamas Rittersporn, eds. *Stalinism: Its Nature and Aftermath: Essays in Honour of Moshe Lewin.* Armonk, N.Y., 1991.

Lane, Christel. *The Rites of Rulers.* New York, 1981.

Lapidus, Gail Warshofsky. *Women in Soviet Society.* Berkeley, 1978.

Lebina, N. B. "'Len'ka Panteleev—syshchikov groza' . . . : Prestupnost' v sovetskom obshchestve 20–30-kh godov." *Rodina,* 1995, no. 1.

——. "O pol'ze igry v biser: Mikroistoriia kak metod izucheniia norm i anomalii sovetskoi povsednevnosti 20–30-kh godov." In *Normy i tsennosti povsednevnoi zhizni: Stanovlenie sotsialisticheskogo obraza zhizni v Rossii 1920–30-e gody,* ed. Timo Vikhavainen. St. Petersburg, 2000.

——. *Povsednevnaia zhizn' sovetskogo goroda: Normy i anomalii, 1920–1930 gody.* St. Petersburg, 1999.

Lebina, N. B., and M. V. Shkarovskii. *Prostitutsiia v Peterburge (40-e gg. XIX v.–40-e gg. XX v.).* Moscow, 1994.

Lewin, Moshe. *The Making of the Soviet System: Essays in the Social History of Interwar Russia.* New York, 1985.

Lorimer, Frank. *The Population of the Soviet Union.* Geneva, 1946.

Maier, Robert. "Die Hausfrau als Kulturtreger im Sozialismus: Zur Geschichte der Ehefrauen-Bewegung in den 30er Jahrer." In *Kultur im Stalinismus,* ed. Gabriele Gorzka. Bremen, 1994.

Malia, Martin. *The Soviet Tragedy: A History of Socialism in Russia, 1917–1991.* New York, 1992.

Mally, Lynn. *Culture of the Future: The Proletkult Movement in Revolutionary Russia.* Berkeley, 1990.

——. *Revolutionary Acts: Amateur Theater and the Soviet State, 1917–1938.* Ithaca, 2000.

Marsh, Rosalind, ed. *Women in Russia and Ukraine.* New York, 1996.

Martin, Terry. *The Affirmative Action Empire: Nations and Nationalism in the Soviet Union, 1923–1939.* Ithaca, 2001.

——. "Modernization or Neo-traditionalism? Ascribed Nationality and Soviet Primordialism." In *Russian Modernity: Politics, Knowledge, Practices,* ed. David L. Hoffmann and Yanni Kotsonis. New York, 2000.

——. "The Origins of Soviet Ethnic Cleansing." *Journal of Modern History,* 1998, no. 4.

McIntosh, Mary. "The Family, Regulation and the Public Sphere." In *State and Society in Contemporary Britain: A Critical Introduction,* ed. Gregor McLennon et al. Cambridge, 1984.

Michaels, Paula. "Medical Propaganda and Cultural Revolution in Soviet Kazakhstan, 1928–41." *The Russian Review,* 2000, no. 2.

Miller, Frank J. *Folklore for Stalin: Russian Folklore and Pseudofolklore of the Stalin Era.* Armonk, N.Y., 1990.

The Modern Encyclopedia of Russian and Soviet History. Ed. Joseph L. Wieczynski. 60 vols. Gulf Breeze, Fla., 1976–2000. Vol. 20.

Mosse, George L. *The Nationalization of the Masses: Political Symbolism and Mass Movements in Germany from the Napoleonic Wars through the Third Reich.* New York, 1975.

Naiman, Eric. *Sex in Public: The Incarnation of Early Soviet Ideology.* Princeton, 1997.

Nash, Mary. "Pronatalism and Motherhood in Franco's Spain." In *Maternity and Gender Policies: Women and the Rise of the European Welfare State, 1880s–1950s,* ed. Gisela Bock and Pat Thane. New York, 1991.

Neary, Rebecca Balmas. "Mothering Socialist Society: The Wife-Activists' Movement and the Soviet Culture of Daily Life, 1934–1941." *The Russian Review,* 1999, no. 3.

Neuberger, Joan. *Hooliganism: Crime, Culture, and Power in St. Petersburg.* Berkeley, 1993.

Northrop, Douglas. "Subaltern Dialogues: Subversion and Resistance in Soviet Uzbek Family Law." In *Contending with Stalinism: Soviet Power and Resistance in the 1930s,* ed. Lynne Viola (Ithaca, 2002).

Nove, Alec. *An Economic History of the USSR.* New York, 1982.

Obertreis, Iulia. "'Byvshee' i 'izlishnee': Izmenenie sotsial'nykh norm v zhilishchnoi sfere v 1920–1930-e gg. Na materialakh Leningrada." In *Normy i tsennosti povsednevnoi zhizni: Stanovlenie sotsialisticheskogo obraza zhizni v Rossii 1920–30-e gody,* ed. Timo Vikhavainen. St. Petersburg, 2000.

Offen, Karen. "Body Politics: Women, Work, and the Politics of Motherhood in France, 1900–1950." In *Maternity and Gender Policies: Women and the Rise of the European Welfare State, 1880s–1950s,* ed. Gisela Bock and Pat Thane. New York, 1991.

Oinas, F. J. "The Political Uses and Themes of Folklore in the Soviet Union." In *Folklore, Nationalism, and Politics,* ed. F. J. Oinas. Columbus, Ohio, 1972.

Osokina, Elena A. *Ierarkhiia potrebleniia: O zhizni liudei v usloviiakh Stalinskogo snabzheniia, 1928–1935 gg.* Moscow, 1993.

——. "Krizis snabzheniia 1939–1941 gg. v pis'makh sovetskikh liudei." *Voprosy istorii,* 1996, no. 1.

——. *Za fasadom "Stalinskogo izobiliia": Raspredelenie i rynok v snabzhenii naseleniia v gody industrializatsii, 1927–1941.* Moscow, 1998.

Papernyi, Vladimir. *Kul'tura "dva."* Ann Arbor, 1985.

Pederson, Susan. *Family, Dependence and the Origins of the Welfare State: Britain and France, 1914–1945.* Cambridge, 1993.

Peris, Daniel. *Storming the Heavens: The Soviet League of the Militant Godless.* Ithaca, 1998.

Petrone, Karen. *Life Has Become More Joyous, Comrades: Celebrations in the Time of Stalin.* Bloomington, 2000.

Phillips, Laura L. *Bolsheviks and the Bottle: Drink and Worker Culture in St. Petersburg, 1900–1929.* De Kalb, Ill., 2000.

Pipes, Richard. *A Concise History of the Russian Revolution.* New York, 1995.

Pine, Lisa. *Nazi Family Policy, 1933–1945.* New York, 1997.

Plaggenborg, Stefan. *Revolutionskultur: Menschenbilder und kulturelle Praxis in Sowjetrussland zwischen Oktoberrevolution und Stalinismus.* Cologne, 1996.

Plamper, Jan. "The Stalin Cult in the Visual Arts, 1929–1953." Dissertation, University of California, Berkeley, 2001.

Quine, Maria Sophia. *Population Politics in Twentieth-Century Europe: Fascist Dictatorships and Liberal Democracies.* New York, 1996.

Rabinbach, Anson. *The Human Motor: Energy, Fatigue, and the Origins of Modernity.* New York, 1990.

Rabinow, Paul. *French Modern: Norms and Forms of the Social Environment.* Cambridge, Mass., 1989.

Randall, Amy E. "The Campaign for Soviet Trade: Creating Socialist Retail Trade in the 1930s." Dissertation, Princeton University, 2000.

——. "'Revolutionary Bolshevik Work': Stakhanovism in Retail Trade." *The Russian Review,* 2000, no. 3.

Ransel, David L. *Village Mothers: Three Generations of Change in Russia and Tataria.* Bloomington, 2000.

Reisdorfer, Kathryn Helen. "Seeing through the Screen: An Examination of Women in Soviet and German Popular Cinema in the Inter-War Years." Dissertation, University of Minnesota, 1993.

Rigby, T. H. *Communist Party Membership in the USSR, 1917–1967.* Princeton, 1968.

Riordan, James. "Sexual Minorities: The Status of Gays and Lesbians in Russian–Soviet–Russian Society." In *Women in Russia and Ukraine,* ed. Rosalind Marsh. New York, 1996.

——. *Sport in Soviet Society.* New York, 1977.

Ritterspoon, Gábor Tamas. "The Omnipresent Conspiracy: On Soviet Imagery of Politics and Social Relations in the 1930s." In *Stalinism: Its Nature and Aftermath: Essays in Honour of Moshe Lewin,* ed. Nick Lampert and Gábor T. Rittersporn. Armonk, N.Y., 1991.

——. *Stalinist Simplifications and Soviet Complications: Social Tensions and Political Conflicts in the USSR.* Philadelphia, 1991.

Robin, Regine. *Socialist Realism: An Impossible Aesthetic.* Stanford, 1992.

——. "Stalinism and Popular Culture." In *The Culture of the Stalin Period,* ed. Hans Gunther. New York, 1990.

Rogovin, Vadim. *Stalinskii Neonep.* Moscow, 1992.

Rosenberg, William G., ed. *Bolshevik Visions: First Phase of the Cultural Revolution in Soviet Russia.* Ann Arbor, 1984.

Rossman, Jeffrey J. "The Teikovo Cotton Workers' Strike of April 1932: Class, Gender, and Identity Politics in Stalin's Russia." *The Russian Review,* 1997, no. 1.

Sadvokasova, E. A. *Sotsial'no-gigienicheskie aspekty regulirovaniia razmerov sem'i.* Moscow, 1969.

Sartorti, Rosalinde. "Stalinism and Carnival: Organization and Aesthetics of Political Holidays." In *The Culture of the Stalin Period,* ed. Hans Gunther. New York, 1990.

Schapiro, Leonard. *The Communist Party of the Soviet Union.* 2d ed. New York, 1971.

Schlesinger, Rudolf. *The Spirit of Postwar Russia: Soviet Ideology, 1917–1946*. London, 1947.

——, ed. *Changing Attitudes in Soviet Russia: The Family in the USSR*. London, 1949.

Schneider, William H. *Quality and Quantity: The Quest for Biological Regeneration in Twentieth-Century France*. New York, 1990.

Schrand, Thomas. "Industrialization and the Stalinist Gender System: Women Workers in the Soviet Economy, 1928–1941." Dissertation, University of Michigan, 1994.

Schröder, Han-Henning. "Upward Social Mobility and Mass Repression: The Communist Party and Soviet Society in the Thirties." In *Stalinism: Its Nature and Aftermath*, ed. Nick Lampert and Gábor T. Rittersporn. Armonk, N.Y., 1992.

Scott, James C. *Seeing Like a State: How Certain Schemes to Improve the Human Condition Have Failed*. New Haven, 1998.

Shearer, David R. "Crisis and Social Disorder in Stalin's Russia: A Reassessment of the Great Retreat and the Origins of Mass Repression." *Cahiers du monde russe*, 1998, no. 1–2.

Siegelbaum, Lewis H. "'Dear Comrade, You Ask What We Need': Socialist Paternalism and Soviet Rural 'Notables' in the Mid-1930s." In *Stalinism: New Directions*, ed. Sheila Fitzpatrick. London, 2000.

——. "*Okhrana truda.*" In *Health and Society in Revolutionary Russia*, ed. Susan Gross Solomon and John F. Hutchinson. Bloomington, 1990.

——. "The Shaping of Soviet Workers' Leisure: Workers' Clubs and Palaces of Culture in the 1930s." *International Labor and Working Class History*, Fall 1999.

——. *Stakhanovism and the Politics of Productivity in the USSR, 1935–1941*. New York, 1988.

Siegelbaum, Lewis H., and Andrei Sokolov. *Stalinism as a Way of Life: A Narrative in Documents*. New Haven, 2000.

Slezkine, Yuri. *Arctic Mirrors: Russia and the Small Peoples of the North*. Ithaca, 1994.

——. "The USSR as a Communal Apartment, or How a Socialist State Promoted Ethnic Particularism." *Slavic Review*, 1994, no. 2.

Smith, Steve. "The Soviet Meaning of Swearing: Workers and Bad Language in Early Soviet Russia." *Past and Present*, August 1998.

Solomon, Peter H., Jr. *Soviet Criminal Justice under Stalin*. New York, 1996.

Solomon, Susan Gross. "The Demographic Argument in Soviet Debates over the Legalization of Abortion in the 1920s." *Cahiers du monde russe et soviétique* 33 (1992), no. 1.

—— "Innocence and Sexuality in Soviet Medical Discourse." In *Women in Russia and Ukraine*, ed. Rosalind Marsh. New York, 1996.

Starks, Tricia Ann. "The Body Soviet: Health, Hygiene, and the Path to a New Life in the Soviet Union in the 1920s." Dissertation, Ohio State University, 2000.

Starr, S. Frederick. "Visionary Town Planning during the Cultural Revolution." In *Cultural Revolution in Russia*, ed. Sheila Fitzpatrick. Bloomington, 1978.

Stites, Richard. *Revolutionary Dreams: Utopian Vision and Experimental Life in the Russian Revolution*. New York, 1989.

——. *Russian Popular Culture: Entertainment and Society since 1900*. New York, 1997.

——. *The Women's Liberation Movement in Russia: Feminism, Nihilism, and Bolshevism, 1860–1930*. Princeton, 1977.

Suny, Ronald Grigor. *The Revenge of the Past: Nationalism, Revolution, and the Collapse of the Soviet Union.* Stanford, 1993.

Tertz, Abram. *On Socialist Realism.* Trans. Max Hayward. New York, 1960.

Thompson, E. P. "Time, Work-Discipline, and Industrial Capitalism." *Past and Present,* 1967, no. 38.

Thurston, Robert W. "The Soviet Family during the Great Terror, 1935–1941." *Soviet Studies,* 1991, no. 3.

Timasheff, Nicholas S. *The Great Retreat: The Growth and Decline of Communism in Russia.* New York, 1946.

Todes, Daniel P. *Darwin without Malthus: The Struggle for Existence in Russian Evolutionary Thought.* Oxford, 1990.

Transchel, Kathy. "Under the Influence: Drinking, Temperance, and Cultural Revolution in Russia, 1900–1932." Dissertation, University of North Carolina, Chapel Hill, 1996.

Tucker, Robert C. "Stalinism as Revolution from Above." In *Stalinism: Essays in Historical Interpretation,* ed. Tucker. New York, 1977.

Tverdokhleb, A. A. "Material'noe blagosostoianie rabochego klassa Moskvy v 1917–1937 gg." Dissertation, Moscow State University, 1970.

Usborne, Cornelia. *The Politics of the Body in Weimar Germany: Women's Reproductive Rights and Duties.* London, 1992.

van Geldern, James. "The Centre and the Periphery: Cultural and Social Geography in Mass Culture of the 1930s." In *New Directions in Soviet History,* ed. Stephen White. New York, 1992.

Vikhavainen, Timo, ed. *Normy i tsennosti povsednevnoi zhizni: Stanovlenie sotsialisticheskogo obraza zhizni v Rossii 1920–40-e gody.* St. Petersburg, 2000.

Viola, Lynne. *Peasant Rebels under Stalin: Collectivization and the Culture of Peasant Resistance.* New York, 1996.

——, ed. *Contending with Stalinism.* Ithaca, 2002.

Volkov, Vadim. "The Concept of *Kul'turnost'*: Notes on the Stalinist Civilizing Process." In *Stalinism: New Directions,* ed. Sheila Fitzpatrick. New York, 2000.

Wagner, William G. *Marriage, Property, and Law in Late Imperial Russia.* New York, 1994.

Waters, Elizabeth. "The Modernization of Russian Motherhood, 1917–37." *Soviet Studies,* 1992, no. 1.

Weindling, Paul. "German-Soviet Cooperation in Science: The Case of the Laboratory for Racial Research." *Nuncius,* 1986, no. 1.

——. *Health, Race, and German Politics between National Unification and Nazism, 1870–1945.* New York, 1989.

Weiner, Amir. *Making Sense of War: The Second World War and the Fate of the Bolshevik Revolution.* Princeton, 2001.

——. "Nature, Nurture, and Memory in a Socialist Utopia: Delineating the Soviet Socio-Ethnic Body in the Age of Socialism." *American Historical Review,* 1999, no. 4.

Werth, Nicolas. "Alphabetisation et idéologie en Russe Soviétique." *Vingtième siècle: Revue d'histoire,* 1986, no. 10.

——, ed. *Etre Communist en URSS sous Staline.* Paris, 1981.

Wimberg, Ellen. "Socialism, Democratism, and Criticism: The Soviet Press and the National Discussion of the 1936 Draft Constitution." *Soviet Studies,* 1992, no. 2.

Wood, Elizabeth. *The Baba and the Comrade: Gender and Politics in Revolutionary Russia.* Bloomington, 1997.

——. "The Trial of Lenin: Legitimating the Revolution through Political Theater, 1920–1923." *The Russian Review,* 2002, no. 2.

Yekelchyk, Serhy. "*Diktat* and Dialogue in Stalinist Culture: Staging Patriotic Historical Opera in Soviet Ukraine, 1936–1954." *Slavic Review,* 2000, no. 3.

——. "Stalinist Patriotism as Imperial Discourse: Reconciling the Ukrainian and Russian 'Heroic Pasts,' 1939–1955." *Kritika* 3, no. 1 (2002).

Index